Programs
and
Machines

WILEY SERIES IN COMPUTING

Consulting Editor
Professor D. W. Barron, *Department of Mathematics, Southampton University*

Numerical Control—Mathematics and Applications

P. Bézier
Professeur au Conservatoire National des Arts et Métiers
and
Technological Development Manager, Renault, France

Communication Networks for Computers

D. W. Davies
and
D. L. A. Barber
National Physical Laboratory,
Teddington

Macro Processors
and Techniques for Portable Software

P. J. Brown
University of Kent at Canterbury

A Practical Guide to Algol 68

Frank G. Pagan
The University of Aston in Birmingham

Programs and Machines

Richard Bird
University of Reading

Programs
and
Machines

An Introduction to the Theory of Computation

Richard Bird
Department of Computer Science,
University of Reading

A Wiley–Interscience Publication

JOHN WILEY & SONS
London · New York · Sydney · Toronto

Library of Congress Cataloging in Publication Data:

Bird, Richard, fl. 1969–
  Programs and machines.

  (Wiley series in computing)
  'A Wiley–Interscience publication.'
  Bibliography: p.
  Includes index.
  1. Electronic digital computers—Programming.
I. Title.
QA76.6.B57   001.6'42   75-38893

ISBN 0 471 01650 0

Photoset in Great Britain by
Tecnical Filmsetters Europe Limited,
76 Great Bridgewater Street, Manchester M1 5JY
and printed by The Pitman Press, Bath

To my wife Norma

and my parents, Kay and Jack

Preface

This book is intended primarily for programmers and computer science students, either at the undergraduate or first-year graduate level, who desire a self-contained introduction to the theory of computation. Throughout, I have attempted to develop the subject from programming concepts, and not as an abstract mathematical theory. I have assumed that the reader possesses a basic knowledge of computers and programming languages (hopefully, but not essentially, including at least one of the Algol variety) and have built upon this knowledge in the selection and discussion of topics. Naturally there are results of a mathematical nature, but I have tried to present the proofs as simply as possible, often resorting to proof by example when a rigorous argument would involve too many tedious details. Mathematically, the book requires no formal background apart from some elementary algebra and a familiarity with modern mathematical notation.

The theory of computation has undergone many shifts of emphasis in the last fifteen years. Generally speaking, the trend has been away from the study of formal computing devices, and towards a basic understanding of program structures. This trend is reflected in the present material. Starting off with a discussion of three basic types of program (Chapter 1), the book covers the equivalence of programs (Chapter 2), the limitations of programming (Chapters 3 and 4), the correctness of programs (Chapter 5), and the theory and use of recursion (Chapters 6, 7, and 8). In particular, as the experienced reader will notice, no mention is made of the theory of automata, finite or otherwise. One simple reason for this apparently major omission is that automata theory has already received comprehensive treatment in several excellent existing texts. A second reason is that I have followed the recommendations of Dana Scott* and drawn a fundamental distinction between the concepts of program and machine, a distinction which underlies the whole book. Given this approach, it is inappropriate to include material from automata theory in which this distinction is not drawn. In any case, many automata-theoretic results can be reformulated as results about programs; for instance, Chapter 2 deals essentially with the state equivalence of finite automata in a different guise.

---

*Scott, D. (1967) Some definitional suggestions for automata theory. *Journal of Computer and System Sciences* 1 (2), 187–212.

Rather than over-burden the text with extensive attributions, I have included bibliographic comments and references at the end of the book. Above all, I have profited from the papers of John McCarthy and Dana Scott on the foundations of the subject.

This book developed from the courses I have given at the University of London Institute of Computer Science, the University of British Columbia, and the University of Reading. It is a pleasure to record my gratitude to Michael Bell, David Cooper, Peter Landin, Ray Reiter, Richard Rosenberg and David Till whose comments and suggestions have helped me greatly. Finally, special thanks go to the ever patient Margaret Lambden who typed the manuscript.

University of Reading   RICHARD BIRD
March 1975

Contents

Chapter 1
Programs and Machines

We must begin our investigation into the nature of computation by defining exactly what we mean by a program and a machine. Rather than attempt to describe any existing programming language or computing machine, of which there is a great abundance and variety, we shall characterize their essential features in simple mathematical models. Throughout, we shall treat programs and machines as distinct but complementary entities, which come together, on an equal footing, to define computations. As well as being natural, this division enables us to consider particular aspects of computation, such as the properties of a certain type of program structure or the capabilities of a certain machine, in isolation from the rest of the computational process, and so avoid unnecessary detail.

1.1 Programs

Speaking generally, a program can be regarded as a structured set of instructions which enables a machine—human or mechanical—to successively apply certain basic operations and tests in a strictly deterministic fashion to given initial data, until the data has been transformed into some desirable form. For the moment we do not wish to be too concerned with the precise nature of the operations and tests which constitute instructions, so we shall just give them names. We suppose the existence of two sets of *identifiers*

$$\begin{aligned} &\text{operation identifiers} \quad F,G,H,\ldots \\ &\text{test identifiers} \quad\quad\; T,U,V,\ldots \end{aligned}$$

Thus F denotes an operation of some sort, and T denotes a test. A test is just an operation which produces one of two possible truth-values, *true* or *false*.

In order that these operations and tests can be carried out in a prescribed manner, the program has to provide a control structure for its constituent instructions. This structure determines the flow of the computation. Among the many examples of such structures in present day programming languages, we select three representative types for study. These structures lead directly to the definition of three types of program: flowcharts, **while** programs, and procedure definitions. We consider the most important one first.

(a) Flowchart programs

Informally, a flowchart program is a geometric diagram made up, according to certain rules, of the following types of components:

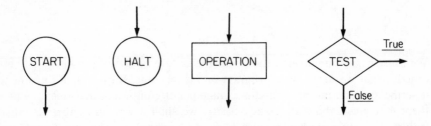

A simple example of a flowchart program is given in Figure 1.

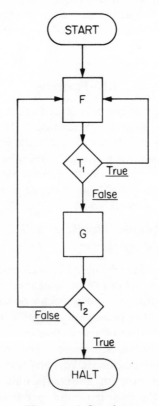

Figure 1. A flowchart

With the judicious use of labels and jumps, flowchart programs can also be specified by sets of labelled instructions. Thus Figure 1 can be equally well described by the following set of instructions:

> *1*: **do** *F* **then goto** *2*
>
> *2*: **if** T_1 **then goto** *1* **else goto** *3*
>
> *3*: **do** *G* **then goto** *4*
>
> *4*: **if** T_2 **then goto** *5* **else goto** *1*.

Two assumptions have been made in translating the flowchart into the above form. Firstly, the computation must begin at label 1, and secondly, the computation should terminate successfully when an attempt is made to jump to a non-existent instruction. This indeed will be the case when we come to define computations with sets of labelled instructions.

The formal definition of the class of flowchart programs is best given by using this idea of a labelled instruction. We suppose that *L* is some standard set of *label identifiers* (usually, the set of arabic numerals).

A *labelled instruction i* is a string of symbols of one of the two forms:

> *l*: **do** *F* **then goto** *l'*
>
> *l*: **if** *T* **then goto** *l'* **else goto** *l''*,

where *F* is an operator identifier, *T* is a test identifier, and *l*, *l'*, and *l''* are label identifiers in *L*. The label $\lambda(i)$ of instruction *i* is the label identifier to the left of the colon sign in *i*.

A *flowchart program* (or more shortly, a *flowchart*) *P* is a finite set of labelled instructions with the property:

> for all *i*, *j* in *P*, if $\lambda(i) = \lambda(j)$, then $i = j$.

In other words, *P* is a set of instructions no two of which can have the same label. In addition, *P* also specifies a particular label identifier in *L*. This label is referred to as the *initial label* of *P*.

A *terminal label* of *P* is a label *l* appearing in some instruction of *P* such that for no *i* in *P* do we have $l = \lambda(i)$. Thus, in the flowchart of Figure 1 represented as a set of labelled instructions, label 1 is the initial label, and label 5 is the unique terminal label. By introducing these special labels we can avoid having to specify explicit start and halt instructions for each program. Notice that the definition of a flowchart does not absolutely require either the presence of terminal labels, or the presence of an instruction with the initial label. Indeed, it is possible that *P* contains no instructions whatsoever. The sort of computations such programs carry out will be described in the appropriate place.

Arguably, the sequencing mechanism given by labelled instructions is the most fundamental type of control structure. It is the basic structure utilized by most assembly and machine languages, and is incorporated in some way or other in most 'high-level' programming languages. On the other hand, the next control structure has made its appearance in programming languages only comparatively recently.

(b) While programs

While programs are based on three sequencing mechanisms which can be found in a number of present day high-level languages (e.g. ALGOL 68, PASCAL). They are described as follows:

(i) *composition.*   Suppose that P and Q are two programs. Their composition, which we write as P ; Q, denotes a further program whose effect is to execute P and Q in the order: P followed by Q. More generally, since composition is clearly associative, we can write P_1 ; P_2 ; ...; P_n for the program which executes $P_1, P_2, \ldots, P_n$ from left to right.

(ii) *conditional statements.*   Suppose that P and Q are two programs. The statement

(if T then P else Q)

denotes the program which executes P if T is *true*, or executes Q if T is *false.*

(iii) **while** *statements.*   Suppose P is a program. The statement

while T do P

denotes the program which repeatedly tests T and performs P until the result of testing T yields the value *false* (if it ever does), in which case the iteration terminates. The same sequence of operations is carried out by the following flowchart.

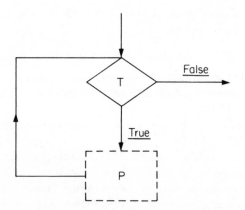

Since termination can only be caused by returning a value *false* for the test identifier, it is convenient to introduce the further statement

until T do P,

whose effect is to repeatedly test T and perform P until the value of T is *true*. The statement **until T do P** is therefore equivalent to **while** *not-T* **do** P; we prefer, however, not to introduce negations of basic test identifiers.

In order to define the class of **while** programs formally, we introduce the idea of the null program I, which corresponds to the dummy operation 'do nothing'. It is clear that I acts as an identity element under composition, i.e. $I; P = P; I = P$ for any program P. The class of **while** programs is defined recursively according to the following rules:

1. Each operation identifier standing by itself is a **while** program; so, conventionally, is the null program I.

2. If W and V are **while** programs, then so are each of the following:

   (2a) $V; W$,
   (2b) (**if** T **then** V **else** W),
   (2c) **while** T **do** (V)
   (2d) **until** T **do** (V)

   where in (2b)–(2d), T is an arbitrary test identifier.

Notice that the pairs of brackets which appear in the constructions (2b)–(2d) are necessary if we wish to be able to unambiguously analyse a **while** program into its constituent parts. Otherwise, for example, the program

$$\textbf{while } T \textbf{ do } V; W$$

would admit two distinct interpretations, corresponding to

$$\textbf{while } T \textbf{ do } (V); W \quad \text{and} \quad \textbf{while } T \textbf{ do } (V; W).^*$$

It may appear that nothing much has been gained by considering **while** programs. It is easy to see, in an intuitive way, that **while** programs can be translated into flowcharts without any loss of information. This remark will be made more precise later. There are two basic reasons why **while** programs are still worth considering. Firstly, the converse of the above remark is false, so that the class of computations that can be carried out by **while** programs is a proper

---

* Occasionally, especially in Chapter 5 onwards, we shall use the Algol symbols **begin** and **end** instead of parentheses to delimit the extent of the **while** statement. Thus

$$\textbf{while } T \textbf{ do begin } V; W \textbf{ end}$$

is regarded as an alternative way of writing

$$\textbf{while } T \textbf{ do } (V; W).$$

When V consists of a single operation identifier F we shall sometimes omit parentheses, i.e. we write

$$\textbf{while } T \textbf{ do } F$$

instead of **while** T **do** (F). Furthermore, we shall sometimes employ the Algol syntax

$$\textbf{if } T \textbf{ then } F$$
and
$$\textbf{if } T \textbf{ then begin } V; W \textbf{ end}$$

as alternatives for

$$(\textbf{if } T \textbf{ then } F \textbf{ else } I)$$
and
$$(\textbf{if } T \textbf{ then } V; W \textbf{ else } I)$$

respectively.

subclass of the computations defined by flowcharts. Secondly, writing **while** programs is often easier and leads to a more compact and elegant program than writing down sets of labelled instructions or drawing flowcharts.

(c) Procedure programs

The final type of control mechanism is found, in one form or another, in every high-level programming language which allows recursive subroutines to be defined. First, we need another set of identifiers, called *procedure identifiers*, which are denoted by $R_1, R_2, \ldots$ etc.

A *procedure program* has the form

$$E \text{ where } R_1 \text{ is } E_1, \ R_2 \text{ is } E_2, \ldots, R_n \text{ is } E_n,$$

where $R_1, R_2, \ldots R_n$ are procedure identifiers, and $E, E_1, \ldots E_n$ are *expressions*. E is referred to as the *initial* expression, and E_j as the *defining* expression for R_j. Expressions are defined recursively according to the following rules:

1. Each procedure identifier (from the set $\{R_1, R_2, \ldots R_n\}$), and each operation identifier, standing by itself, is an expression. So, by convention, is the special null expression, denoted by I.

2 If D and E are expressions, then so are each of the following:

   (2a) $D; E$,

   (2b) (**if** T **then** D **else** E),

   where T is an arbitrary test identifier.

Thus, for example, the following is a procedure program:

$$R_1; R_2 \text{ where}$$
$$R_1 \text{ is } F; (\text{if } T \text{ then } R_1 \text{ else } G; R_2),$$
$$R_2 \text{ is } (\text{if } T \text{ then } I \text{ else } F; R_1).$$

Notice the important condition that the procedure identifiers which occur in the expressions $E, E_1, \ldots, E_n$ must be among the set $\{R_1, R_2, \ldots R_n\}$, i.e. every procedure identifier appearing in the program must have an associated definition.

The computation of a procedure program consists in evaluating the expression E using the given definitions. Every procedure identifier appearing in E is replaced at the appropriate time by its defining expression, and the evaluation continues until E has been transformed into the null expression I. The formal definition of this process is given later.

So far we have defined three types of program which model some of the features of real programming languages in a simple and straightforward manner. However, by themselves, these programs are quite unable to describe computations. Programs need to be supplemented with the *meaning* of the various test and operation identifiers occurring in them. This is exactly what the concept of a machine accomplishes, and this we turn to next.

1.2 Machines

The task of a machine is to supply all the information that is missing from a program in order that computations can be described. First, a machine has to supply the meanings of the operation and test identifiers. Logically, each operation identifier must denote a transformation on the memory structure of the machine, and each test identifier must denote some truth function. In addition, a machine has to describe how to get information into and out of this memory structure, which amounts to providing input and output functions.

Formally, a *machine* M consists of the specification of the following sets and functions:

(a) an *input* set X,

(b) a *memory* set V,

(c) an *output* set Y,

(d) an *input* function $I_M: X \to V$

(e) an *output* function $O_M: V \to Y$,

(f) for each operation identifier F, a function $F_M: V \to V$

(g) for each test identifier T, a function $T_M: V \to \{true, false\}$.

By a function in (d)–(g), we mean a *total* function, i.e. a function that is defined for every element in its domain.

As a simple example, consider the machine M defined by taking

(a) $X = Z$ (the set of all integers, positive and negative).

(b) $V = Z \times Z$,

(c) $Y = Z$

(d) $I_M: Z \to Z \times Z$, defined by $I_M(x) = (x, 0)$

(e) $O_M: Z \times Z \to Z$, defined by $O_M(x, y) = y$,

(f) $F_M: Z \times Z \to Z \times Z$, defined by $F_M(x, y) = (x - 1, y)$
    $G_M: Z \times Z \to Z \times Z$, defined by $G_M(x, y) = (x, y + 1)$

(g) $T_M: Z \times Z \to \{true, false\}$ defined by $T_M(x, y) = true$, if $x = 0$
    $= false$, otherwise.

When defining machines, we shall be free to choose the operation and test identifiers in such a way as to suggest the nature of their associated functions. For the above example, we can regard the memory set as consisting of two *registers* A and B. Each operation and test acts on one or other of these registers. Moreover, the nature of these operations is captured by the following alternative names for F, G and T:

$$\text{for } F, \quad A: = A - 1$$
$$\text{for } G, \quad B: = B + 1$$
$$\text{for } T, \quad A = 0.$$

To avoid having to specify functions for every possible operation and test identifier that may arise in programs, we shall say that P is a *program for M* if every test and operation identifier appearing in P is specified by M. Thus, for example, the program

$$\textbf{until } A = 0 \textbf{ do } (A := A - 1 ; B := B + 1)$$

is a **while** program for the register machine M.

As a mathematical model of real computing machines, the above definition may appear hopelessly inadequate. No attempt is apparently made to characterize the important hardware features of computers, such as the structure of the memory or the presence of a control unit. More important, there is apparently no way of representing the fact that programs are *stored* inside the memory of a machine, and may themselves be subject to modification during the course of a computation. However, we shall show in Sections 1.5 and 1.6 that the objections are illusory, since these features can be incorporated into the above framework.

1.3   Computations

We now show how the definitions of program and machine come together to define computations. Having defined computations, we can then specify the nature of the function computed by a given program on a given machine. We first deal with the computations associated with flowchart programs.

Suppose that P is an arbitrary flowchart program represented as a set of labelled instructions with label identifiers in the set L.

A *terminating computation* of P on a machine M is a finite sequence

$$(l_1, v_1), (l_2, v_2), \ldots, (l_n, v_n)$$

of elements of $L \times V$ such that:

(i) l_1 is the designated initial label of P, and l_n is some terminal label of P,

(ii) for each j, where $1 \leqslant j < n$, either l_j: **do** F **then goto** l is an instruction in P, for some F and l, in which case

$$l_{j+1} = l \quad \text{and} \quad v_{j+1} = F_M(v_j),$$

or l_j: **if** T **then goto** l' **else goto** l'' is an instruction in P for some T, l', and l'', in which case

$$l_{j+1} = l' \quad \text{if} \quad T_M(v_j) = true$$

$$= l'', \text{ otherwise}$$

and $v_{j+1} = v_j$.

Clearly, there is at most one terminating computation associated with a given value v_1 of V since the rest of the sequence is then uniquely determined. On the other hand, the computation associated with a given v_1 may be infinite in length, because we never reach an element (l_n, v_n) for which l_n is a terminal label of P. In such a case we say that the computation is *non-terminating*.

Notice one important fact implied by the above definition, namely that the execution of a test does not change the current value of the memory set of the machine.

Having defined the concept of a terminating computation, we can now specify the function computed by a given program on a given machine.

The *function mP*: $X \to Y$ *computed by a program P on a machine M* is defined for a value x in X only if the computation

$$(l_1, v_1), (l_2, v_2), \ldots, (l_n, v_n),$$

where $v_1 = I_M(x)$, is terminating, in which case

$$mP(x) = O_M(v_n).$$

We choose the notation mP rather than P_M to describe the function computed by P on M simply to avoid subscripts. We shall often identify machines by proper names, e.g. NORMA, TURING, etc., and it is more convenient to write *normaP*, *turingP*, etc., rather than P_{NORMA} or P_{TURING}.

The definition of the function computed by a given program on a given machine is just what one would naturally expect. The computation begins at the initial label on the initial memory contents as prescribed by the input data, and proceeds step by step, applying the tests and operations in the order determined by the program, until a terminal label and value is reached, if it ever is, in which case the terminal value is output. Unlike the basic operations and tests, the function computed by a program may be *partial*, i.e. not necessarily defined for each value in its domain.

In a similar spirit, we can define the computations associated with procedure programs. The description of the computations associated with **while** programs is left as an exercise for the reader.

Suppose P is a procedure program

$$E \text{ where } R_1 \text{ is } E_1, R_2 \text{ is } E_2, \ldots, R_m \text{ is } E_m.$$

A terminating computation of P on a machine M is a finite sequence

$$(X_1, v_1), (X_2, v_2), \ldots (X_n, v_n)$$

of expressions X_j and elements v_j in V, such that

(i) $X_1 = E$ and $X_n = I$,

(ii) for each j, where $1 \leqslant j < n$, either

    (a) X_j is of the form F; X' for some operation identifier F, in which case

$$X_{j+1} = X' \quad \text{and} \quad v_{j+1} = F_M(v_j),$$

or   (b) X_j is of the form (**if** T **then** X' **else** X''); X''' in which case

$$X_{j+1} = X'; X''', \text{ if } T_M(v_j) = \ true$$
$$= X''; X''', \text{ otherwise}$$

    and $v_{j+1} = v_j$

or   (c) X_j is of the form $R_k; X'$ for some k, $1 \leqslant k \leqslant m$, in which case

$$X_{j+1} = E_k; X' \quad \text{and} \quad v_{j+1} = v_j.$$

Provided we always replace $I; X$ by X whenever it occurs, the three cases under (ii) enumerate all the possible types of expression.

The definition of the function $mP: X \to Y$ computed by P on M is now defined in exactly the same way as for flowcharts. In Chapter 2, where we consider procedure programs in more detail, we use the alternative notation $m[E]: X \to Y$ to describe the function evaluated by the expression E, relative to a specified set of definitions, on a machine M.

As an example of a procedure program that has no terminating computations, consider the program

$$R_1 \textbf{ where } R_1 \textbf{ is } R_1.$$

For any machine M and v in V, the computation of this program associated with v, is

$$(R_1, v), (R_1, v), \dots$$

and clearly is non-terminating.

1.4   Equivalence

In this section, we describe some of the ways in which two programs or two machines can be regarded as equivalent.

Definition 1.   Let P and Q be two arbitrary programs, not necessarily of the same type. P is said to be *strongly equivalent* to Q, and we write $P \equiv Q$, if $mP = mQ$ for every machine M.

It is important to emphasize what the assertion $f = g$ means when f and g are partial functions:

$f = g$ *if and only if for each* x, *either both* $f(x)$ *and* $g(x)$ *are undefined, or both* $f(x)$ *and* $g(x)$ *are defined and* $f(x) = g(x)$.

Thus $P \equiv Q$ if and only if for every machine M the function computed by P on M is identical with the function computed by Q on M. Consider, for example, the four programs of Figure 2.

Although these programs are distinct from each other, each pair is strongly equivalent. This is fairly obvious, but as practice in using the definitions of the previous section, we shall prove, for example, that $P \equiv S$. The other equivalences can be proved by very similar reasoning.

As a first step, we write P as the following set of instructions:

1: **if** T **then goto** *2* **else goto** *3*

2: **do** F **then goto** *1*.

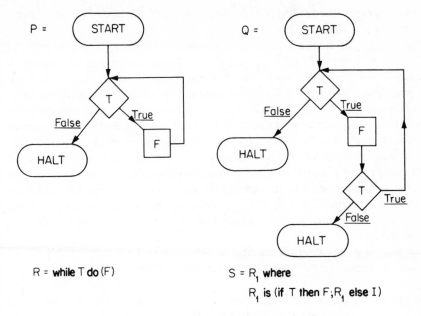

R = **while** T **do** (F)   S = R₁ **where**

R₁ is (**if** T **then** F;R₁ **else** I)

Figure 2. Four strongly equivalent programs

Let M be an arbitrary machine, x any element of X, and suppose $I_M(x) = v$. The computation of P on M with input x begins as follows:

$$(1, v), (2, v), (1, F_M(v)), (2, F_M(v)), (1, F_M^2(v)), \ldots$$

where $F_M^n(v) = F_M(\ldots F_M(v) \ldots)$ (n times). Supposing that $n \geqslant 0$ is the first integer, if it exists, such that $T_M(F_M^n(v)) = \textit{false}$, the computation terminates with the final value $(3, F_M^n(v))$, and we have

$$mP(x) = O_M(F_M^n(v)).$$

On the other hand, if no such integer exists, then $mP(x)$ is undefined.

The corresponding computation sequence for S begins

$$(R_1, v), (\textbf{if } T \textbf{ then } F; R_1 \textbf{ else } I, v), (F; R_1, v), (R_1, F_M(v)), \ldots$$

and these three terms are repeated, with $F_M(v)$ in place of v, until an n is reached for which $T_M(F_M^n(v)) = \textit{false}$, in which case the computation terminates with the final value $(I, F_M^n(v))$, and we have

$$mS(x) = O_M(F_M^n(v)).$$

If no such n exists, then $mS(x)$ is undefined. Thus $mP(x) = mS(x)$. Since M and x were arbitrary, it follows that $P \equiv S$.

The concept of strong equivalence is worth considering for a number of reasons. It is a natural and fundamental definition in terms of the theory of programs and machines, and one that has many interesting and difficult problems associated with it. Its importance lies in the fact that it allows us to identify programs which, though different in form, have in a certain sense 'isomorphic' computations. The computations on strongly equivalent programs have the property that the same tests and operations are carried out in the same order, independently of the actual meaning of these tests and operations. Furthermore, the concept of strong equivalence enables us to make certain judgements concerning the structural complexity of programs. For example, program Q of Figure 2 is a 'bad' flowchart program because it contains three instructions, while the strongly equivalent flowchart P contains only two instructions.

The idea of strong equivalence also allows us to make statements about the translations between one type of program and another.

Theorem 1.   (i) Given any **while** program P, we can construct a flowchart program Q such that $P \equiv Q$.

   (ii) Given any flowchart program P, we can construct a procedure program Q such that $P \equiv Q$.

Proof. (i) Given a **while** program P, we can build up a strongly equivalent flowchart Q according to the following translation rules:

(1) translate F as

(2) translate I as

(3) translate **(if** *T* **then** *U* **else** *V***)** as

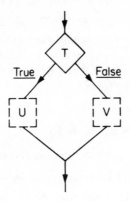

(4) translate *U*; *V* as

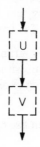

(5) translate **while** *T* **do** (*U*) as

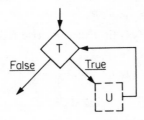

(6) translate **until** *T* **do** (*U*) as

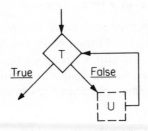

It is left to the reader to formally verify that the resulting flowchart Q, when provided with START and HALT boxes at the appropriate positions, is strongly equivalent to P.

(ii) Suppose P is a flowchart written as a set of labelled instructions, with label identifiers in the set $\{l_1, l_2, \ldots, l_n\}$, where without loss of generality we can suppose that l_1 is the initial label of P and l_n is the unique terminal label of P. The procedure program Q has the form

$$R_1 \textbf{ where}$$

$$R_1 \textbf{ is } E_1, \ R_2 \textbf{ is } E_2, \ldots R_n \textbf{ is } E_n,$$

where $E_n = I$ and $E_1, \ldots E_{n-1}$ are defined by the rules:

(a) $E_i = F; R_j$ if P contains the instruction l_i: **do** F **then goto** l_j,

(b) $E_i = (\textbf{if } T \textbf{ then } R_j \textbf{ else } R_k)$ if P contains the instruction l_i: **if** T **then goto** l_j **else goto** l_k.

It is again left as an exercise to verify that $P \equiv Q$.

Another simple result, whose proof is left to the reader, is the following.

Theorem 2. For each procedure program P let $S(P)$ denote the procedure program that results from P by substituting, for any procedure identifier occurring in an expression, the defining expression for that procedure identifier. Then $S(P) \equiv P$.

As an example of Theorem 2, we can use repeated substitutions to simplify the procedure program

$$R_1 \textbf{ where}$$

$$R_1 \textbf{ is } (\textbf{if } T \textbf{ then } R_2 \textbf{ else } R_5),$$

$$R_2 \textbf{ is } F; R_3,$$

$$R_3 \textbf{ is } (\textbf{if } T \textbf{ then } R_2 \textbf{ else } R_4),$$

$$R_4 \textbf{ is } G; R_1,$$

$$R_5 \textbf{ is } I,$$

to obtain the strongly equivalent program

$$R_1 \textbf{ where}$$

$$R_1 \textbf{ is } (\textbf{if } T \textbf{ then } F; R_3 \textbf{ else } I),$$

$$R_3 \textbf{ is } (\textbf{if } T \textbf{ then } F; R_3 \textbf{ else } G; R_1)$$

It is natural to ask whether the converse of Theorem 1 is also true, i.e. can every procedure program be translated into a strongly equivalent flowchart, and can every flowchart be translated into a strongly equivalent **while** program? The answer in each case is no, and we can see this by examining appropriate examples.

First, consider the procedure program P given by

$$R \textbf{ where}$$

$$R \textbf{ is } (\textbf{if } T \textbf{ then } I \textbf{ else } F; R; G; G).$$

We claim that there is no flowchart program strongly equivalent to P. The proof is very instructive: we define a machine M and show that for no flowchart Q is it possible that $mP = mQ$. The machine M is constructed as follows:

(a) $X_M = V_M = Y_M = N$ (the set of non-negative integers)

(b) $I_M(x) = O_M(x) = x$ for all x in N

(c) $T_M(x) = true$ if and only if $x = 0$

(d) $F_M(x) = x - 1$ and $G_M(x) = x + 1$ for all x in N.

It is easy to see that program P computes the function $mP(x) = 2x$ on M. Now assume, by way of contradiction, that there is some flowchart program Q for which $mQ(x) = 2x$. Suppose Q possesses k G-operations (i.e. instructions involving the identifier G) and consider the computation of Q on M with any input x greater than k. In order to deliver the final value $2x$, this computation must contain at least x G-operations, each of which is associated with successively greater values of the memory set. It follows that at least one instruction involving G must occur twice in the computation. But this means the computation must enter an infinite loop and fail to terminate. Hence Q does not exist.

The proof that not every flowchart can be translated into a strongly equivalent **while** program proceeds along similar lines. Consider the flowchart P given by

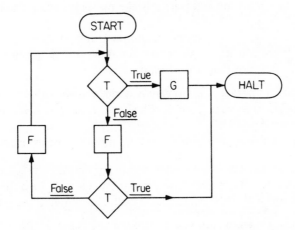

The function computed by this program on the given machine M is

$$mP(x) = 1 \quad \text{if } x \text{ is even}$$
$$= 0 \quad \text{if } x \text{ is odd.}$$

Again, assume that there is some **while** program Q equivalent to P on M. Suppose Q contains k distinct F-operations, and consider the computation of Q on M with any input x greater than k. This computation must contain at least x F-operations each of which is associated with successively smaller values of the memory set. It follows that at least one of these operations must occur within the body of some loop **until** T **do** .... However, this loop terminates in exactly the same way for both even and odd x, and consequently the computation is unable to distinguish between the two cases. Hence Q cannot exist.

We shall take up the subject of strong equivalence in more detail in Chapter 2. The following final facts about strong equivalence are worth noting, however.

Facts 1. There is an algorithm to effectively determine, given two flowcharts P and Q, whether or not $P \equiv Q$. (Proved in Chapter 2.)

2. There is an algorithm to determine, given two **while** programs P and Q, whether or not $P \equiv Q$. (Follows from Fact 1 and Theorem 1(i).)

3. At the time of writing, no-one knows whether or not a similar algorithm exists for two arbitrary procedure programs. (However, an algorithm for a restricted class of procedure programs is given in Chapter 2.)

Definition 2. Two programs P and Q are said to be *equivalent on a machine M*, or *M*-equivalent, if $mP = mQ$.

Undoubtedly, it is this definition of equivalence which is the more practically important one. Clearly, it would be very useful to possess, for a given machine M, an algorithm to effectively determine when two given programs are M-equivalent. The following fact puts a brake on such wishful thinking, however.

Fact. There are many very simple machines M for which we can actually prove that there can be no algorithm for determining, given two programs, whether or not they are M-equivalent

How one proves this fact, and how, in general, one goes about showing that no algorithm exists to solve a given problem, is a topic which we shall take up in Chapters 3 and 4.

It is also possible and profitable to talk about the equivalence of machines.

Definition 3. A machine M_2 is said to be able to *simulate* a machine M_1 if, given any program P for M_1, we can find a program Q for M_2 such that $m_2 Q = m_1 P$. M_1 and M_2 are said to be *equivalent* if each can simulate the other.

Of course, by introducing restrictions on the types of the programs, many variants of the above definition could be considered. For example, we could define the idea of a procedure-to-flowchart simulation of M_1 by M_2, in which procedure programs for M_1 are translated into equivalent flowchart programs for M_2. There is another direction in which we can usefully generalize the definition of simulation of one machine by another. One restriction of Definition 3 is that one machine can simulate another only if their corresponding input and output sets are identical. It is sometimes a nuisance to have machines, which specify different input and output sets, but are otherwise closely related, incomparable in this way. We can avoid this difficulty by taking a more general definition of simulation.

Definition 4.   A machine M_2 can *simulate* a machine M_1 if one can find coding and decoding functions

$$c: X_1 \to X_2 \quad \text{and} \quad d: Y_2 \to Y_1,$$

where X_j and Y_j are the input and output sets of M_j, such that given any program P for M_1, we can find a program Q for M_2 such that

$$d \cdot m_2 Q \cdot c = m_1 P.$$

The more general definition will be used when necessary.

1.5   Register machines

We have mentioned previously that one of the apparent shortcomings of our machines is that no structure has been imposed on the memory set. Actual computing machines, on the other hand, have at least one structural property in common, namely that the (main) memory can be regarded as being divided up into a large number of registers, each of which is capable of containing an arbitrary value from some basic set of possible values. In most computers, this basic set consists of the distinct binary patterns of some fixed length, called the word length of the computer. An important consequence of this structure is that real computers define tests and operations which act only on the contents of specified registers, rather than on the memory set as a whole.

Now our definition of a machine is a very general one, and there is no reason why this extra structure cannot be incorporated into the definition as a new feature.

A machine M is said to possess *n registers* if its memory set V has the structure

$$V = A \times A \times \cdots \times A \quad (n \text{ times}),$$

or more briefly, $V = A^n$, for some set A. In such a case M is said to be a *register machine*. We also allow the possibility that n is infinite, in which case M is referred to as an *infinite* register machine.

We shall suppose that the operation identifiers and test identifiers over which register machines are defined have the forms

$$\text{operation identifiers} \quad R_j: = f(R_j)$$
$$\text{test identifiers} \quad t(R_j),$$

where f and t are members of two further sets of identifiers, and j is some positive integer. (For a generalization of these new operation and test identifiers, see Exercise 12 at the end of the chapter).

The operations and tests defined by register machines can be uniquely determined once the meanings of the subsidiary identifiers f and t are determined. Thus, suppose that a n register machine M defines, in addition to the sets X, A, and Y, where $V = A^n$, an input and output function, and functions

$$f_M: A \to A \quad \text{and} \quad t_M: A \to \{true, false\}$$

for each subsidiary operation f and test t. Define, for $1 \leqslant j \leqslant n$, the *projection function* $u_j^n: A^n \to A$, by the equation

$$u_j^n(a_1, a_2, \ldots, a_n) = a_j.$$

If we denote the operation $R_j: = f(R_j)$ by F for brevity, and similarly denote $t(R_j)$ by T, then

$$F_M: A^n \to A^n \quad \text{and} \quad T_M: A^n \to \{true, false\}$$

are uniquely specified by the conditions

$$u_j^n(F_M(v)) = f_M(u_j^n(v))$$

$$u_k^n(F_M(v)) = u_k^n(v) \quad \text{for } k \neq j,$$

and
$$T_M(v) = t_M(u_j^n(v)),$$

where $v = (a_1, a_2, \ldots, a_n)$ is an arbitrary element of V. These conditions assert that the operation $R_j: = f(R_j)$ changes only the jth component of V (i.e. the jth *register*), and the test $t(R_j)$ depends only on the contents of the jth register.

We say that P is a program *for* a n register machine if the operations and tests occurring in P have the form $R_j: = f(R_j)$ and $t(R_j)$ for some f and t, where $1 \leqslant j \leqslant n$.

For register machines it is possible to consider a third type of equivalence relation on programs.

Definition 5. Let P and Q be two register machine programs. We say that P is *RM-equivalent* to Q if $mP = mQ$ for all register machines M.

Consider, for example, the two **while** programs:

$$P = \textbf{while } t(R_1) \textbf{ do } (R_1: = f(R_1));$$
$$\textbf{while } t(R_2) \textbf{ do } (R_2: = f(R_2)),$$

and
$$Q = \textbf{while } t(R_2) \textbf{ do } (R_2: = f(R_2));$$
$$\textbf{while } t(R_1) \textbf{ do } (R_1: = f(R_1)).$$

It is easy to see that P is *RM*-equivalent to Q since each loop operates independently of the other and so can be executed in either order. Note that P is *not* strongly equivalent to Q, that is equivalent under *any* interpretation of the identifiers $R_1: = f(R_1)$ etc. Both P and Q are *RM*-equivalent to S where

$$S = \textbf{while } t(R_1) \textbf{ do } (R_1: = f(R_1); (\textbf{if } t(R_2) \textbf{ then } R_2: = f(R_2) \textbf{ else } I));$$
$$\textbf{while } t(R_2) \textbf{ do } (R_2: = f(R_2)),$$

as the reader may verify. The following result is immediate.

Theorem 3. Let P and Q be two register machine programs, and let M be a register machine. Then each of the following three statements implies the one below it:

(i) P is strongly equivalent to Q,

(ii) P is RM-equivalent to Q,

(iii) P is M-equivalent to Q.

We note the following facts about RM-equivalence.

Facts 1. There is an algorithm for deciding, given two flowchart programs for
a 2-register machine, whether or not they are RM-equivalent. (See
Bird [1973]).

2. At the time of writing, no-one knows whether or not there exists an
algorithm to decide RM-equivalence for flowchart programs for an n-register machine, where $n > 2$.

3. Supposing programs were allowed to contain the more general
operation identifiers

$$R_j: = f(R_k)$$

where j and k may be different integers, then the problem corresponding to Fact (1) above is *not* effectively decidable. (Proved in Chapter 4).

1.6   The control machine of a machine

Another objection raised in Section 2 concerns the inability of our machines to
reflect the fact that, in real computers, the program is actually stored in the
memory structure of the machine, and may itself be modified during the course of
a computation. In this section we show how the idea of a stored program machine
can be modelled within our framework. For simplicity, we consider only
flowchart programs.

Suppose M is a fixed arbitrary machine with input set X, memory set V, and
output set Y. Let S denote the collection of all flowchart programs for M,
represented as sets of labelled instructions with label identifiers in L.

The *control machine* $C(M)$ of M is constructed as follows:

input set $= S \times X$,

memory set $= S \times L \times V$,

output set $= Y$,

input function I (omitting the qualifying subscript),
defined by

$$I(P, x) = (P, l_1, I_M(x)),$$

where l_1 is the designated initial label of P,

output function O, defined by

$$O(P, l, v) = O_M(v).$$

In addition, $C(M)$ defines a single operation NEXTSTEP and a single test
TERMINAL as follows:

$$\text{NEXTSTEP}(P, l, v) = (P, k, u)$$

where

$$k = l' \quad \text{and} \quad u = F_M(v) \qquad \text{if } l: \textbf{do } F \textbf{ then goto } l' \text{ is in } P, \text{ or}$$

$$k = l' \quad \text{and} \quad u = v \qquad \text{if } l: \textbf{if } T \textbf{ then goto } l' \textbf{ else goto } l''$$
$$\text{is in } P \text{ with } T_M(v) = true, \text{ or}$$

$$k = l'' \quad \text{and} \quad u = v \qquad \text{if as above, but with } T_M(v) = false, \text{ or}$$

$$k = l \quad \text{and} \quad u = v \qquad \text{if } l \text{ is a terminal label of } P.$$

and

$$\text{TERMINAL}(P, l, v) = true, \text{ if } l \text{ is a terminal label of } P$$
$$= false, \text{ otherwise.}$$

The program we are interested in executing on $C(M)$ is

$$\textbf{until TERMINAL do NEXTSTEP.}$$

Suppose that COMPUTE denotes the function computed by this program on $C(M)$. It is straightforward to show that

$$\text{COMPUTE}(P, x) = mP(x),$$

for any flowchart program P and $x \in X$.

It is clear that $C(M)$ represents the essential features of a stored program computer. The program we run on $C(M)$ defines the sequence of operations carried out by the control unit in such a computer. Although we do not pursue the possibility, we can easily define further operations for $C(M)$ which change the stored program P in an appropriate fashion, and so incorporate the idea of program modification in the model.

Exercises

1. Translate the flowchart of Figure 1.1 into a strongly equivalent **while** program.
2. Give a formal definition of the function mW computed by a **while** program W on a machine M.
3. Write down a **while** program which has no terminating computations.
4. Draw a distinction between: (i) the flowchart of no instructions; and (ii) a flowchart with no terminal labels.
5. Give a definition of the class of **while** programs which minimizes the number of parentheses needed to resolve ambiguities.
6. Suppose we write $M_1 \subseteq M_2$ if machine M_2 is compatible with machine M_1 but possibly defines further tests and operations. What is the relationship between $m_1 P$ and $m_2 P$ if $M_1 \subseteq M_2$?
7. Suppose, in the definition of a machine, we allow partial functions to be specified for the operation and test identifiers. Give the appropriate definition of the function computed by a program on a machine in such a case.

8. Call a machine M *I/O-free* if $X_M = V_M = Y_M$ and $I_M(v) = O_M(v) = v$ for all v in V. Prove that two programs are strongly equivalent if and only if they are equivalent on all *I/O*-free machines.

9. Prove Theorem 1.2.

10. Which of the following pairs of **while** programs are strongly equivalent?

   (i) (**if** T **then while** T **do** (F) **else** I)
        and **while** T **do** (F),
   (ii) **while** T **do** (**if** T **then** I **else** F) and
        while T **do** $(F;$ **until** T **do** $(G))$,
   (iii) **while** T **do** $(F;$ (**if** T **then** I **else** G)) and
        while T **do** $(F;$ **while** T **do** $(F);$ $G)$.

11. Write down a list of simplifying substitutions involving conditional expressions which preserve strong equivalence.

12. Generalize the definition of a register machine to allow for operation identifiers of the form

$$R_j: = f(R_{j_1}, R_{j_2}, \ldots, R_{j_n})$$

and test identifiers of the form

$$t(R_{j_1}, R_{j_2}, \ldots, R_{j_n}).$$

Chapter 2

The Equivalence of Programs

In this chapter we take up the study of strong equivalence in more detail. Our attention will be directed to providing a partial answer to the following question: how can we determine whether or not two given programs are strongly equivalent? Since both **while** programs and flowchart programs can be translated into strongly equivalent procedure programs (Theorem 1.1), a completely satisfactory answer to the question would be to provide some general method, applicable to any pair of procedure programs P and Q, which will decide in a finite number of steps whether or not $P \equiv Q$. However, up to now, the search for such a general method, or in other words an *algorithm*, has proved unsuccessful. Indeed it may turn out that no algorithm can be found. We shall see in Chapter 4 that similar decision problems do not possess algorithmic solutions; such problems are said to be *unsolvable*. Now, the phenomena of unsolvability arises surprisingly often, and it may turn out that the strong equivalence problem for procedure problems is one of these unsolvable problems. To establish unsolvability one needs a very precise idea of exactly what constitutes an algorithm. The job of formally characterizing algorithms is undertaken in Chapter 3.

In the absence of a general algorithm for procedure programs, we shall see what can be done for simpler classes of programs. It turns out that an algorithm can be given to decide strong equivalence for any pair of flowchart programs, and this is presented in Section 2. Better still, the algorithm can be generalized to deal with pairs of procedure programs, provided only that the programs do not contain the null expression I in their defining expressions. Section 3 is devoted to this generalization, but is considerably more difficult than Section 2. Since the material is not used in the rest of the book, the reader may prefer to omit Section 3 on a first reading.

The following section contains some useful background notation, and an important characterization of strong equivalence in terms of a very simple class of machines.

2.1 Trace machines

In this section we introduce a special type of machine, called a trace machine, which turns out to be very useful in the study of strong equivalence. Since these machines carry out computations on strings of operation identifiers, we first introduce some simple notation and terminology regarding strings of symbols.

We denote by $\{F, G, \ldots\}^*$ the set of finite strings of operation identifiers F, $G, \ldots$, each of which will henceforth be regarded as single symbols. Included in this set is the special string of zero length, called the *null string*, which we shall always denote by λ. The *length* $|\phi|$ of a string ϕ is just the number of symbols in ϕ. Thus, for example, $|\lambda| = 0$ and $|FGFF| = 4$.

More generally, we denote by A^* the set of finite strings made up of symbols from a set A of symbols. For example, if $A = \{a, b\}$, then

$$A^* = \{\lambda, a, b, aa, ab, ba, bb, \ldots\}.$$

As an aid to comprehension strings of symbols will usually be denoted by greek letters.

Concatenation of strings will be represented, as already has been assumed, by juxtaposition. Thus, if $\alpha = a_1 a_2 \ldots a_j$ and $\beta = b_1 b_2 \ldots b_k$, then $\alpha\beta$ denotes the string $a_1 a_2 \ldots a_j b_1 \ldots b_k$.

Concatenation of strings should always be carefully distinguished from the composition of functions and programs.
Thus,

$\alpha\beta$ denotes the concatenation of strings α and β.

$f \cdot g$ denotes the composition of functions f and g,
    defined by $(f \cdot g)(x) = f(g(x))$ for all x.

and $P; Q$ denotes the composition of programs P and Q.

We now proceed with the definition of a trace machine.

Definition 1.   A machine M is a *trace machine* if

$$X_M = V_M = Y_M = \{F, G, \ldots\}^*, \quad \text{and} \quad F_M(\phi) = \phi F$$

and $$I_M(\phi) = O_M(\phi) = \phi$$

for every $\phi \in \{F, G, \ldots\}^*$.

Thus the effect of each operation defined by a trace machine is simply to append its name to the right hand end of the current value of the memory set. The output value of a computation will therefore consist of a record, or *trace*, of the operations performed during the computation. In order to define a trace machine, one only needs to specify the truth functions associated with the test identifiers, since all the other functions are predetermined.

The reason we introduce trace machines is contained in the following theorem.

Theorem 1.   Two programs are strongly equivalent if and only if they are equivalent on all trace machines. Symbolically,

$$P \equiv Q \text{ if and only if } mP = mQ \text{ for every trace machine } M.$$

Proof.   It is immediate from the definition of strong equivalence that $P \equiv Q$ implies $mP = mQ$ for every trace machine M. We prove the converse in the case that P and Q are both flowchart programs, the proof for other types of programs being very similar.

Suppose that $P \not\equiv Q$ and that N is some machine, and x some element of its input set, such that $nP(x) \neq nQ(x)$. For any string $\phi = FG \ldots H$ in $\{F, G, \ldots\}^*$ let

$$[\phi]_N = H_N \cdot \cdots \cdot G_N \cdot F_N \cdot I_N(x),$$

so that $[\phi]_N$ is an element of V_N.

Let M be the trace machine defined by taking

$$T_M(\phi) = T_N([\phi]_N)$$

for each ϕ and test identifier T. We shall show, by induction on the computation sequences, that

$$(*) \qquad nR(x) = O_N([mR(\lambda)]_N),$$

for any (flowchart) program R. The theorem then follows, since by $(*)$ $nP(x) \neq nQ(x)$ implies $mP(\lambda) \neq mQ(\lambda)$ and so $mP \neq mQ$ on the trace machine M.

Let the computation sequence of R on N with input x be

$$(l_0, v_0), (l_1, v_1), \ldots, \text{where } v_0 = I_N(x),$$

and let the computation sequence of R on M with input λ be

$$(m_0, \phi_0), (m_1, \phi_1), \ldots, \quad \text{where } \phi_0 = \lambda.$$

We show by induction that $l_k = m_k$ and $v_k = [\phi_k]_N$ for each $k \geq 0$, and this proves the assertion $(*)$.

For $k = 0$, we have $l_0 = m_0 \doteq$ initial label of R, and $v_0 = I_N(x) = [\lambda]_N = [\phi_0]_N$. Assume, by way of induction, that $l_k = m_k$ and $v_k = [\phi_k]_N$, and suppose $l_k = l$. Two cases arise:

(a)   either l: **do F then goto** l' is in R, in which case

$$l_{k+1} = m_{k+1} = l'$$

and

$$v_{k+1} = F_N(v_k) = F_N([\phi_k]_N) = [\phi_k F]_N = [\phi_{k+1}]_N,$$

or (b) l: **if T then goto** l' **else goto** l'' is in R, in which case

$$v_{k+1} = v_k = [\phi_k]_N = [\phi_{k+1}]_N$$

and

$$l_{k+1} = m_{k+1}, \quad \text{since} \quad T_M(\phi_k) = T_N([\phi_k]_N) = T_N(v_k).$$

Hence the induction is established.

The proof of the theorem actually establishes a stronger result.

Corollary. $P \equiv Q$ if and only if $mP(\lambda) = mQ(\lambda)$ for every trace machine M.

This last characterization of strong equivalence turns out to be the most helpful one in subsequent proofs, and will be used without explicit quotation.

2.2   Strong equivalence of flowcharts

We now consider the problem of determining whether two given flowchart programs are strongly equivalent. The first job is to represent the information given by a flowchart in a more compact and manageable form. Consider, for example, the flowchart P of Figure 3.

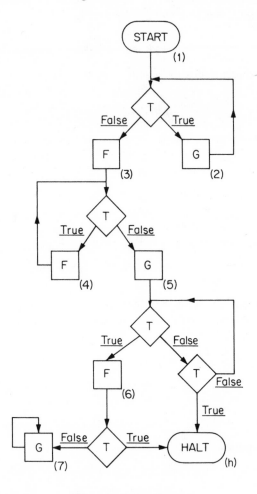

Figure 3. A flowchart

We are going to represent P as a finite set of labelled *compound instructions*. A compound instruction combines both tests and operations, and has the form

$$i: \textbf{if } T \textbf{ then do } F \textbf{ and goto } i_1 \textbf{ else do } G \textbf{ and goto } i_2,$$

where T is the (only) test identifier appearing in P. More generally, if the flowchart contains n distinct test identifiers $T_1, T_2, \ldots, T_n$, then each compound instruction will have 2^n branches, one for each possible combination of the outcomes of the tests $T_1, T_2,..., T_n$. However, to simplify the treatment as much as possible, we shall only consider the problem of deciding strong equivalence for pairs of flowcharts defined over a single test identifier T. The results of this section are easily extended to the more general case. Bearing this assumption in mind, we can denote a compound instruction more briefly by

$$i: (F, i_1) \text{ or } (G, i_2).$$

To translate P into a set of compound instructions, we label each node of the flowchart that is associated either with an operation identifier, or with the START and HALT boxes. We can suppose, without loss of generality, that there is a unique HALT box, and we choose the special label h for its label. As we shall see in a moment, these labels will be regarded as being attached to the exit of the appropriate box, rather than the beginning.

Next, for each label $i \neq h$, we construct a compound instruction

$$i: (F_1, i_1) \text{ or } (F_2, i_2),$$

by taking i_1 (alternatively, i_2) to be the label of the node we arrive at if we start at the node labelled i and follow the path determined by selecting the value *true* (alternatively, *false*) for the outcome of the single test identifier T. Both i_1 and i_2 are referred to as *successors* of i. The operation identifiers F_1 and F_2 are those contained in the boxes associated with labels i_1 and i_2 respectively. To avoid exceptions to the general form, we must also specify an operation identifier for the HALT box; this will be the special identifier H, supposed different from all other operation identifiers. To emphasize the association with i, we shall sometimes write $F_1(i)$ and $F_2(i)$ for F_1 and F_2 respectively.

It may happen, and indeed does in our example, that the two successors of a node cannot always be defined. This happens when the flowchart contains a closed path passing only through test instructions. Attempting to follow this path, we get caught in an infinite loop without ever reaching a new labelled node. When such cases are detected, we define the successor label to be the special looping label ω, and associate the special identifier L, distinct from H and any other operation identifier, with ω. In addition, we include in the set of compound instructions the special instruction

$$\omega: (L, \omega) \text{ or } (L, \omega)$$

to signify the occurrence of an infinite loop.

Applying this translation to the flowchart in Figure 3, we obtain the following set of compound instructions:

1: $(G, 2)$ **or** $(F, 3)$	5: $(F, 6)$ **or** (L, ω)
2: $(G, 2)$ **or** $(F, 3)$	6: (H, h) **or** $(G, 7)$
3: $(F, 4)$ **or** $(G, 5)$	7: $(G, 7)$ **or** $(G, 7)$
4: $(F, 4)$ **or** $(G, 5)$	ω: (L, ω) **or** (L, ω).

Henceforth, we shall consider computations with sets of compound instructions rather than with flowcharts. For terminating computations, the only difference lies in the presence of the identifier H. More precisely,

Lemma 1. Suppose P is a flowchart, and P_1 is the program formed from P by constructing the set of compound instructions, and taking label 1, the label associated with the START box of P, as the initial label. Then, for any trace machine M, we have

$$mP_1(\lambda) = mP(\lambda)H.$$

Proof. Straightforward. Notice that the other special identifier L only arises in non-terminating computations of P_1, so the conclusion remains true in the case that either side is undefined.

If P is a set of compound instructions, then we define P_j to be the program formed from P by selecting label j as the initial label. We write $i \equiv j$ as shorthand for the assertion $P_i \equiv P_j$. This is the relationship in which we are interested, since the problem of deciding, given a set P of compound instructions and labels i and j, whether or not $i \equiv j$, solves the problem of strong equivalence for flowcharts. Given two flowcharts Q and R, we merely take P as the union of the sets of compound instructions corresponding to Q and R (ensuring that distinct sets of labels are chosen), and test whether $q \equiv r$, where q and r are the original initial labels of Q and R respectively. Lemma 1 guarantees that this method works, since $P_q \equiv P_r$ if and only if $Q \equiv R$.

Before dealing with the general equivalence $i \equiv j$, it simplifies matters to first treat equivalences of the form $i \equiv \omega$. This is the problem of deciding whether a given flowchart has any terminating computations.

Definition 2. Suppose P is a set of compound instructions. For any label j in P, we define the *thickness* $\theta(j)$ of j by

$$\theta(j) = \min_M |mP_j(\lambda)|,$$

where the minimum is taken over all trace machines M. We suppose that $|mP_j(\lambda)| = \infty$ if the computation of P_j on M with input λ is non-terminating.

Informally, $\theta(j)$ is a measure of the shortest terminating computation of P beginning with label j. It follows from the definition of θ that $\theta(j) = 0$ if and only if $j = h$, and $\theta(j) = \infty$ if and only if $j \equiv \omega$. It is left as an exercise to verify that

$$\theta(j) = 1 + \min \{\theta(j_1), \theta(j_2)\},$$

where j_1 and j_2 are the successors of j. These facts are used in the next lemma. Before stating it, we need a simple mathematical idea.

A sequence of sets $H_0, H_1, \ldots$ is a *finite chain* if the following conditions hold:

(i) $H_k \subseteq H_{k+1}$ for $k \geqslant 0$,

(ii) for some n, $H_n = H_{n+k}$ for all $k \geqslant 0$.

If $H_0, H_1, \ldots$ is a finite chain, we define $\lim H_k$ to be H_n where n is the (least) integer such that (ii) holds.

Lemma 2. Suppose P is a finite set of n compound instructions. Define the sequence of sets $H_0, H_1, \ldots$ as follows:

$$H_0 = \{h\},$$
$$H_{k+1} = H_k \cup \{j : j_1 \in H_k \text{ or } j_2 \in H_k\} \quad \text{for} \quad k \geqslant 0,$$

where j_1 and j_2 are the successors of j. Then $H_0, H_1, \ldots$ is a finite chain of sets, and for all labels j in P we have

$$j \not\equiv \omega \text{ if and only if } j \in \lim H_k.$$

Proof. It is clear by construction that $H_0, H_1, \ldots$ is a finite chain of sets, since $size(H_k) \leqslant n + 1$ for each k. We show, by induction on k, that

$$j \in H_k \text{ if and only if } \theta(j) \leqslant k,$$

which establishes the lemma. Since $\theta(j) \leqslant 0$ if and only if $j = h$, the assertion is true for $k = 0$. Suppose, by way of induction, that $j \in H_{k+1}$, so that at least one of j_1, j_2 is in H_k. It follows that

$$\theta(j) = 1 + \min\{\theta(j_1), \theta(j_2)\} \leqslant 1 + k,$$

by the induction hypothesis. Conversely, if $\theta(j) \leqslant k + 1$, then at least one of $\theta(j_1), \theta(j_2)$ is no greater than k, and so at least one of j_1, j_2 is in H_k. Hence $j \in H_{k+1}$.

Lemma 2 provides an easy way of determining whether $j \equiv \omega$. Simply compute $\lim H_k$ and see if it contains j. As an example, consider the instructions corresponding to Figure 3. We have

$$H_0 = \{h\} \qquad H_3 = \{3, 4, 5, 6, h\}$$
$$H_1 = \{6, h\} \qquad H_4 = \{1, 2, 3, 4, 5, 6, h\}$$
$$H_2 = \{5, 6, h\} \qquad H_5 = \{1, 2, 3, 4, 5, 6, h\},$$

from which it follows that $7 \equiv \omega$.

We can now simplify a given set of compound instructions by eliminating all those instructions with labels $j \neq \omega$ for which $j \equiv \omega$. Every reference to label j is replaced with a reference to ω, and every associated operation identifier is replaced by L. That is, an instruction

$$i : (F_1, j) \text{ or } (F_2, k) \quad \text{where } j \equiv \omega,$$

is replaced by $i : (L, \omega) \text{ or } (F_2, k)$.

Thus, for example, the simplified set of compound instructions corresponding to the flowchart of Figure 3 is

$$1 : (G, 2) \text{ or } (F, 3) \qquad 5 : (F, 6) \text{ or } (L, \omega)$$
$$2 : (G, 2) \text{ or } (F, 3) \qquad 6 : (H, h) \text{ or } (L, \omega)$$
$$3 : (F, 4) \text{ or } (G, 5) \qquad \omega : (L, \omega) \text{ or } (L, \omega).$$
$$4 : (F, 4) \text{ or } (G, 5)$$

This simplification enables the next lemma to be stated in a cleaner form.

Lemma 3. Let P be a simplified set of compound instructions, as described above. Then for any two labels i, j of P both distinct from h, we have

$$i \equiv j \text{ if and only if } F_k(i) = F_k(j) \quad \text{and} \quad i_k \equiv j_k \quad \text{for } k = 1, 2,$$

where i_1 and i_2 are the successors of i, and $F_1(i)$ and $F_2(i)$ are the operation identifiers associated with i. Similarly for j.

Proof. First note that for any trace machine M and label $i (\neq h)$ of P we have

$$mP_i(\lambda) = mP_{i_1}(F_1(i)) \text{ if } T_M(\lambda) = \textit{true},$$
$$= mP_{i_2}(F_2(i)) \text{ otherwise.}$$

This means that if $F_k(i) = F_k(j)$ and $i_k \equiv j_k$ for $k = 1, 2$, then $i \equiv j$.

To prove the converse, let M be an arbitrary trace machine and define the trace machine N by taking $T_N(\lambda) = \textit{true}$ and $T_N(F\phi) = T_M(\phi)$ for all strings ϕ and operation identifiers F. Since $nP(F\phi) = FmP(\phi)$ for any program P, we have

$$nP_i(\lambda) = nP_{i_1}(F_1(i)) = F_1(i) mP_{i_1}(\lambda)$$

and

$$nP_j(\lambda) = nP_{j_1}(F_1(j)) = F_1(j) mP_{j_1}(\lambda).$$

Now suppose $i \equiv j$ in which case the above shows that

$$F_1(i) mP_{i_1}(\lambda) = F_1(j) mP_{j_1}(\lambda) \qquad (*)$$

for any trace machine M. From this fact we can deduce that $F_1(i) = F_1(j)$ and $i_1 \equiv j_1$. Firstly, if $F_1(i) = F_1(j)$, then $mP_{i_1}(\lambda) = mP_{j_1}(\lambda)$, and so $i_1 \equiv j_1$. On the other hand, suppose by way of contradiction that $F_1(i) \neq F_1(j)$. Since at least one of these identifiers must be different from L, and P is simplified, at least one of i_1, j_1 must be non-equivalent to ω. Hence we can pick an M so that both sides of $(*)$ are defined, which means that $F_1(i) = F_1(j)$.

By choosing $T_N(\lambda) = \textit{false}$, we can show in a similar manner that $F_2(i) = F_2(j)$ and $i_2 \equiv j_2$.

For the purpose of the following theorem we shall say that a set W of pairs of labels is *consistent* if for each (i, j) in W, either $(i, j) = (h, h)$, or i and j are both different from h and $F_k(i) = F_k(j)$ for $k = 1, 2$.

Theorem 2. Suppose P is a simplified set of n compound instructions, and i and j are labels in P. Define the sequence of sets $W_0, W_1, \ldots$ as follows:

$$W_0 = \{(i, j)\}$$
$$W_{r+1} = W_r \cup \{(s_k, t_k) : (s, t) \in W_r, s, t \neq h, k = 1, 2\}$$

for $r \geqslant 0$. Then $W_0, W_1, \ldots$ is a finite chain of sets and

$$i \equiv j \text{ if and only if } \lim W_r \text{ is consistent.}$$

Proof. Since $size(W_r) \leqslant (n + 1)^2$, it is clear by the construction that $W_0, W_1, \ldots$ is a finite chain. Suppose $i \equiv j$. It follows from Lemma 3 that $s \equiv t$ for each $(s, t) \in W_r$, so that W_r is consistent for each r. Hence $\lim W_r$ is consistent.

Conversely, suppose $i \not\equiv j$, and let M be a trace machine such that $mP_i(\lambda) \neq mP_j(\lambda)$. Without loss of generality we may suppose that $mP_i(\lambda)$ is defined and $|mP_i(\lambda)| \leqslant |mP_j(\lambda)|$. Let the computation of P_i on M with input λ be

$$(i_0, \phi_0), (i_1, \phi_1), \ldots, (i_d, \phi_d),$$

where $\phi_0 = \lambda$, $i_0 = i$ and $i_d = h$. Similarly, let the computation of P_j on M with input λ begin

$$(j_0, \psi_0), (j_1, \psi_1), \ldots, (j_d, \psi_d), \ldots$$

where $j_0 = j$ and $\psi_0 = \lambda$. Since $mP_i(\lambda) \neq mP_j(\lambda)$, one of the following two cases must arise:

(a) either there exists a (least) $t < d$ such that $\phi_{t+1} \neq \psi_{t+1}$,

   or

(b) if no such t exists, then $j_d \neq h$.

In the first case, $\lim W_r$ is inconsistent because it contains (i_t, j_t), and in the second case, $\lim W_r$ is inconsistent because it contains (i_d, j_d).

Theorem 2 provides an effective method for testing whether $i \equiv j$. A more efficient way to arrange the calculations is given in the following algorithm:

step 1: Set $U_0 = \{(i, j)\}$, and $r = 0$.

step 2: Check that U_r is consistent. If U_r is not consistent, terminate the algorithm with NOT EQUIVALENT.

step 3: Form U_{r+1} by generating for each $(s, t) \in U_r$, where $s \neq t$, and $s, t \neq h$, the successors (s_k, t_k) of (s, t). U_{r+1} consists of all the generated pairs that are not already in $U_1, U_2, \ldots U_r$. If U_{r+1} is not empty, then set $r = r + 1$ and return to step 2, else terminate the algorithm with EQUIVALENT.

Since $W_r = U_0 \cup U_1 \cup \cdots \cup U_r$, the algorithm terminates and is correct.

As an illustration of the algorithm, we prove that program P of Figure 3 is strongly equivalent to the program Q of Figure 4.

The simplified set S_1 of compound instructions corresponding to P is

1: $(G, 2)$ **or** $(F, 3)$	5: $(F, 6)$ **or** (L, ω)
2: $(G, 2)$ **or** $(F, 3)$	6: (H, h) **or** (L, ω)
3: $(F, 4)$ **or** $(G, 5)$	ω: (L, ω) **or** (L, ω)
4: $(F, 4)$ **or** $(G, 5)$	

since we know $7 \equiv \omega$.

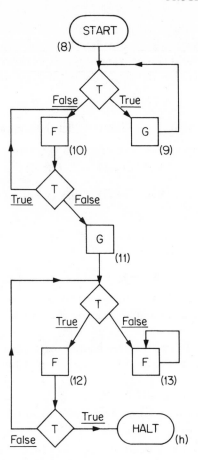

Figure 4. Another flowchart

The set of compound instructions corresponding to Q is the following:

8: $(G, 9)$ **or** $(F, 10)$ 11: $(F, 12)$ **or** $(F, 13)$
9: $(G, 9)$ **or** $(F, 10)$ 12: (H, h) **or** $(F, 13)$
10: $(F, 10)$ **or** $(G, 11)$ 13: $(F, 13)$ **or** $(F, 13)$

In order to simplify this set, we employ Lemma 2 and construct

$H_0 = \{h\}$ $H_3 = \{10, 11, 12, h\}$
$H_1 = \{12, h\}$ $H_4 = \{8, 9, 10, 11, 12, h\}$
$H_2 = \{11, 12, h\}$ $H_5 = \{8, 9, 10, 11, 12, h\}$.

We therefore have $13 \equiv \omega$. The simplified set S_2 is

$$8: (G, 9) \text{ or } (F, 10) \qquad 11: (F, 12) \text{ or } (L, \omega)$$
$$9: (G, 9) \text{ or } (F, 10) \qquad 12: (H, h) \text{ or } (L, \omega)$$
$$10: (F, 10) \text{ or } (G, 11)$$

To decide whether $P \equiv Q$, we have to determine whether $1 \equiv 8$ in the set $S_1 \cup S_2$. So we compute

$$U_0 = \{(1, 8)\}; U_0 \text{ is consistent,}$$
$$U_1 = \{(2, 9), (3, 10)\}; U_1 \text{ is consistent,}$$
$$U_2 = \{(4, 10), (5, 11)\}; U_2 \text{ is consistent,}$$
$$U_3 = \{(6, 12), (\omega, \omega)\}; U_3 \text{ is consistent,}$$
$$U_4 = \{(h, h)\}; U_4 \text{ is consistent,}$$
$$U_5 = \text{empty.}$$

Thus $1 \equiv 8$, and so $P \equiv Q$.

2.3 Strong equivalence of restricted procedures

We now generalize the results of the foregoing section in order to obtain a similar algorithm for deciding the strong equivalence of pairs of procedure programs. Not every procedure program yields to this treatment however, and we consider only a restricted class of programs in which no defining expression of a procedure identifier contains the null expression I as a subexpression. Computationally speaking, such programs have the property that, in every procedure call, at least one operation must be applied before returning to the calling expression. A list of procedure definitions satisfying this condition will be referred to as a list of *restricted* definitions. Once again, for reasons of convenience and simplicity, we suppose that our procedures are defined using only a single test identifier T. The discussion that follows can be extended in a straightforward fashion to meet the more general case.

By introducing new procedure identifiers and using the substitution operation (see Theorem 1.2), it is possible to render a list R of restricted definitions in a *standard form* in which the procedure identifiers, $R_1, R_2, \ldots, R_n$ say, have definitions of the form

$$R_j \text{ is (if } T \text{ then } F_1; A_j \text{ else } F_2; B_j),$$

where F_1 and F_2 are operation identifiers (not necessarily the same for each j), and A_j and B_j are sequences of procedure identifiers only. These latter expressions will be called *terms over* $R_1, R_2, \ldots R_n$, or more briefly, terms over R. The *null term*, i.e. the empty sequence of procedure identifiers, will again be denoted by I.

Rather than give a formal description of the translation to standard form, we illustrate the general method by considering, as an example, the following list of restricted definitions:

$$R_1 \text{ is } F; (\text{if } T \text{ then } R_1; F \text{ else } G; R_2)$$
$$R_2 \text{ is (if } T \text{ then } G \text{ else } R_2; R_1).$$

In order to remove the interior conditional from the defining expression for R_1, we introduce a new procedure identifier S_1, and redefine R_1 as

$$R_1 \text{ is } F; S_1,$$

where S_1 has the definition

$$S_1 \text{ is (if } T \text{ then } R_1; F \text{ else } G; R_2).$$

Next, we modify the definition of R_1 to read

$$R_1 \text{ is (if } T \text{ then } F; S_1 \text{ else } F; S_1)$$

in order to put it into standard form. To do the same for S_1, we must rewrite the expression $R_1; F$ in the form of an operation identifier followed by a term. This can be done in two steps. First, we replace $R_1; F$ by $R_1; S_2$, where S_2 has the definition

$$S_2 \text{ is (if } T \text{ then } F \text{ else } F).$$

Next, we substitute the defining expression of R_1 for R_1 in $R_1; S_2$, to obtain the following defining expression for S_1:

$$\text{if } T \text{ then (if } T \text{ then } F; S_1 \text{ else } F; S_1); S_2 \text{ else } G; R_2.$$

This can be simplified to read

$$\text{if } T \text{ then } F; S_1; S_2 \text{ else } G; R_2$$

and is now in standard form.

If we carry out a similar process of substituting the definition of R_2 for R_2 in the defining expression of R_2 and simplifying the resulting conditional expressions, we discover that the process does not terminate. The situation is analogous to the closed paths of test instructions that may arise in flowcharts. We can overcome the difficulty in a similar fashion by introducing an infinite loop Ω and defining

$$R_2 \text{ is (if } T \text{ then } G \text{ else } L; \Omega)$$

$$\Omega \text{ is (if } T \text{ then } L; \Omega \text{ else } L; \Omega),$$

where L is a new special operation identifier associated only with Ω. It is important to verify that such infinite loops of substitutions can be detected when they arise; this is left as an exercise. With renaming, the final list of definitions in standard form is

$$R_1 \text{ is (if } T \text{ then } F; R_3 \text{ else } F; R_3)$$

$$R_2 \text{ is (if } T \text{ then } G \text{ else } L; \Omega)$$

$$R_3 \text{ is (if } T \text{ then } F; R_3; R_4 \text{ else } G; R_2)$$

$$R_4 \text{ is (if } T \text{ then } F \text{ else } F)$$

$$\Omega \text{ is (if } T \text{ then } L; \Omega \text{ else } L; \Omega).$$

Note the similarity between lists of definitions in standard form and sets of compound instructions for flowcharts. In fact, it is a simple matter to translate sets of compound instructions into strongly equivalent lists of restricted definitions in standard form, so that the algorithm to be described in this section generalizes the previous algorithm.

The relationship in which we are interested in this section is the strong equivalence of terms. If A and B are two terms over R, we write

$$A \equiv B \text{ to mean that } m[A] = m[B] \text{ for every machine } M.$$

Equivalently, from Section 1, $A \equiv B$ if and only if $m[A](\lambda) = m[B](\lambda)$ for every trace machine M. It is easy to see, using the same sort of reasoning as in the last section, that an algorithm for deciding the strong equivalence of terms can immediately be applied to the problem of determining whether two given restricted procedure programs are strongly equivalent.

We shall say that a term A is *proper* if it is not strongly equivalent to either the null term I or the infinite loop Ω, i.e. $A \not\equiv I$ and $A \not\equiv \Omega$. Notice that $A \equiv I$ if and only if $A = I$, and $A \equiv \Omega$ signifies that A has no terminating computations on any machine. Just as in the last section it was useful to first identify proper labels for sets of compound instructions, it is convenient to first construct an algorithm for determining whether a given term A is proper. Sets of procedure definitions can then be simplified by eliminating all the improper non-null terms, except possibly Ω itself.

In order to ease the exposition, and retain the analogy with the algorithm for flowchart programs for as long as possible, we shall defer the proofs of some of the following results until after the generalized algorithm has been described. The first result says that improper terms must contain improper sub-terms.

Lemma 4.   Suppose X and Y are terms over R. Then

$$X; Y \equiv \Omega \text{ if and only if } X \equiv \Omega \text{ or } Y \equiv \Omega.$$

Definition.   Suppose X is a term over R. We define the *thickness* $\theta(X)$ of X by

$$\theta(X) = \min_{M} |m[X](\lambda)|$$

where the minimum is taken over all trace machines M. We suppose $|m[X](\lambda)| = \infty$ if the computation of X on M with input λ is non-terminating.

It is easy to verify that $\theta(X) = 0$ if and only if $X = I$, and $\theta(X) = \infty$ if and only if $X \equiv \Omega$. We also have the following result.

Lemma 5.   Suppose X and Y are two terms over R. Then

$$\theta(X; Y) = \theta(X) + \theta(Y).$$

Now let us consider the problem of identifying proper terms.

Lemma 6.   Suppose R is a finite set of n procedure definitions in standard form. Define the sequence of sets $H_0, H_1, \ldots$ as follows:

$$H_0 = \{I\}$$
$$H_{k+1} = H_k \cup \{R_j: A_j \text{ or } B_j \text{ is a term over } H_k\} \quad \text{for } k \geqslant 0.$$

Then $H_0, H_1, \ldots$ is a finite chain of sets, and for every procedure identifier R_j we have

$$R_j \not\equiv \Omega \text{ if and only if } R_j \in \lim H_k$$

Furthermore, a term X over R is proper if and only if each procedure identifier appearing in X is in $\lim H_k$.

Proof. It is clear that $H_0, H_1, \ldots$ is a finite chain of sets since $size(H_k) \leqslant n + 1$ for each k. We first show, by induction on k, that

$$R_j \in H_k \text{ implies } \theta(R_j) < \infty \quad \text{for } k \geqslant 0.$$

The assertion is trivially true for $k = 0$ since $\theta(I) = 0$. Suppose the assertion holds for k and let $R_j \in H_{k+1}$, where R_j has the definition

$$R_j \text{ is (if } T \text{ then } F_1; A_j \text{ else } F_2; B_j).$$

Without loss of generality, we may further suppose that $A_j = R_{j_1}; R_{j_2}; \ldots; R_{j_t}$, where $R_{j_r} \in H_k$ for $1 \leqslant r \leqslant t$. It follows from the definition of thickness and Lemma 5 that

$$\theta(R_j) \leqslant 1 + \theta(A_j) = 1 + \theta(R_{j_1}) + \cdots + \theta(R_{j_t}).$$

Since the right hand side of this inequality is finite by assumption, the induction is established.

Conversely, we show by a similar induction that

$$\theta(R_j) \leqslant k \text{ implies } R_j \in H_k \text{ for } k \geqslant 0.$$

Once again the assertion is immediate for $k = 0$. Suppose it holds for k, and let $\theta(R_j) \leqslant k + 1$. From the definition of R_j it follows that at least one of $\theta(A_j)$ or $\theta(B_j)$ is no greater than k. If $\theta(A_j) \leqslant k$ and $A_j = R_{j_1}; R_{j_2}; \cdots; R_{j_t}$, then $\theta(R_{j_r}) \leqslant k$ for $1 \leqslant r \leqslant t$. By the induction hypothesis, we therefore have $R_{j_r} \in H_k$ for $1 \leqslant r \leqslant t$, and so A_j is a term over H_k. Hence $R_j \in H_{k+1}$.

The final assertion follows at once from Lemma 4.

To illustrate Lemma 6, let us consider the following example:

$$R_1 \text{ is (if } T \text{ then } F; R_3; R_4 \text{ else } G; R_7)$$
$$R_2 \text{ is (if } T \text{ then } F; R_5; R_6 \text{ else } F; R_8)$$
$$R_3 \text{ is (if } T \text{ then } G; R_4 \text{ else } G; R_3; R_4; R_4)$$
$$R_4 \text{ is (if } T \text{ then } F \text{ else } F)$$
$$R_5 \text{ is (if } T \text{ then } G \text{ else } G; R_5; R_6)$$
$$R_6 \text{ is (if } T \text{ then } F; R_4 \text{ else } F; R_4)$$
$$R_7 \text{ is (if } T \text{ then } F; R_7 \text{ else } G; R_8; R_7)$$
$$R_8 \text{ is (if } T \text{ then } F; R_8 \text{ else } F; R_7).$$

We have

$$H_0 = \{I\},$$
$$H_1 = \{I, R_4, R_5\},$$

$$H_2 = \{I, R_4, R_5, R_3, R_6\},$$
$$H_3 = \{I, R_4, R_5, R_3, R_6, R_1, R_2\},$$

and

$$H_4 = H_3.$$

Thus we have shown $R_7 \equiv R_8 \equiv \Omega$.

Using the algorithm implicit in Lemma 6, we can simplify a given set of procedure definitions in standard form by eliminating all the improper non-null terms except Ω itself. That is, if the definition

$$R_j \text{ is (if } T \text{ then } F_1; A_j \text{ else } F_2; B_j)$$

is such that $A_j \equiv \Omega$ but $A_j \neq \Omega$, then we can redefine R_j to be

$$R_j \text{ is (if } T \text{ then } L; \Omega \text{ else } F_2; B_j).$$

Systematic replacement in this manner will eliminate every improper term from the definitions, except I and Ω themselves. Moreover, a term over a simplified set of definitions R is proper if and only if it is non-null and does not contain Ω. For the above example then, we arrive at the following list of simplified definitions:

$$R_1 \text{ is (if } T \text{ then } F; R_3; R_4 \text{ else } L; \Omega)$$
$$R_2 \text{ is (if } T \text{ then } F; R_5; R_6 \text{ else } L; \Omega)$$
$$R_3 \text{ is (if } T \text{ then } G; R_4 \text{ else } G; R_3; R_4; R_4)$$
$$R_4 \text{ is (if } T \text{ then } F \text{ else } F)$$
$$R_5 \text{ is (if } T \text{ then } G \text{ else } G; R_5; R_6)$$
$$R_6 \text{ is (if } T \text{ then } F; R_4 \text{ else } F; R_4)$$
$$\Omega \text{ is (if } T \text{ then } L; \Omega \text{ else } L; \Omega).$$

In order to state the next result, which is analogous to Lemma 3, we need to define the *successors* of a proper term X. If X is a proper term which begins with the identifier R_j, so that $X = R_j; X'$ for some X', and R_j has the definition

$$R_j \text{ is (if } T \text{ then } F_1; A_j \text{ else } F_2; B_j),$$

then we define the successors $\sigma_1(X)$ and $\sigma_2(X)$ of X by

$$\sigma_1(X) = A_j; X' \quad \text{and} \quad \sigma_2(X) = B_j; X'.$$

We also define

$$F_1(X) = F_1 \quad \text{and} \quad F_2(X) = F_2.$$

Lemma 7. Suppose X and Y are two proper terms over a simplified set of definitions R, as described above. Then

$$X \equiv Y \text{ if and only if } F_k(X) = F_k(Y) \quad \text{and} \quad \sigma_k(X) \equiv \sigma_k(Y) \quad \text{for } k = 1, 2.$$

At this point we can see where the analogy with flowchart programs breaks down, and how this difficulty can be resolved.

Suppose, in a similar spirit to Theorem 2, we test whether $A \equiv B$, where A and B are proper terms over a simplified set of definitions R, by constructing the sequence of sets $W_0, W_1, \ldots$ as follows:

$$W_0 = \{(A, B)\}$$
$$W_{r+1} = W_r \cup \{(\sigma_k X, \sigma_k Y): (X, Y) \in W_r, X, Y \text{ proper}, k = 1, 2\}.$$

Using Lemma 7 it is possible to show that $A \equiv B$ if and only if each set W_r is *consistent*, i.e. for each $(X, Y) \in W_r$: either X and Y are both null, or both non-null and $F_k(X) = F_k(Y)$ for $k = 1, 2$. The trouble is, that although the sequence $W_0, W_1, \ldots$ forms a chain, it will not in general be a *finite* chain, since there exist infinitely many terms over R. Unless we can guarantee a finite chain, the associated algorithm may not terminate. The solution to this problem is to split the pairs of terms in W_r into shorter pairs of terms, where each term in a pair is bounded in length below a fixed finite size. The splitting operation makes use of the following lemma.

Lemma 8. Suppose $A = A_1; A_2; \ldots; A_n$ (abbreviated: $A_{1,n}$) and $B = B_1; B_2; \ldots; B_m$ (abbreviated $B_{1,m}$) are two proper terms such that $\theta(A) = \theta(B)$. Then for each j, where $1 \leqslant j \leqslant n$, we can effectively determine an integer t, where $1 \leqslant t \leqslant m$, and a term C such that

(i) $\theta(B_{1,(t-1)}) < \theta(A_{1,j}) \leqslant \theta(B_{1,t})$ and

(ii) $A_{1,n} \equiv B_{1,m}$ if and only if $A_{1,j}; C \equiv B_{1,t}$ and $A_{(j+1),n} \equiv C; B_{(t+1),m}$.

In particular, if $\theta(A_{1,j}) = \theta(B_{1,t})$, then C is the null term I.

Using Lemma 8 and a slightly stronger definition of consistency, we can split pairs of terms into further pairs which have thicknesses no greater than 2μ, where

$$\mu = \max \{\theta(R_j): 1 \leqslant j \leqslant n\},$$

$R_1, R_2, \ldots, R_n$ being the proper procedure identifiers in R. The stronger definition of consistency is to say that a set W of pairs of terms is *consistent* if for each $(X, Y) \in W$

(i) $\theta(X) = \theta(Y)$ and

(ii) $F_k(X) = F_k(Y)$ for $k = 1, 2$, whenever X and Y are non-null.

As we shall see, there is no problem in calculating the thicknesses of terms, so that the test for consistency can be carried out. With this definition, Lemma 8 is used in conjunction with the construction of $W_0, W_1, \ldots$ given above, as follows. Suppose $(X, Y) = (A_{1,n}, B_{1,m}) \in W_r$ is the pair of proper terms we wish to split. If $\theta(X) \neq \theta(Y)$, then W_r is inconsistent and we have already demonstrated that $A \not\equiv B$. Otherwise, apply Lemma 8 with $j = 1$, and let $X_1 = A_1; C, Y_1 = B_{1,t}, X' = A_{2,n}$ and $Y' = C; B_{t+1,m}$. Now, either $\theta(X_1) \neq \theta(Y_1)$ in which case we again have $A \not\equiv B$, or

$$\theta(X_1) = \theta(Y_1) = \theta(B_{1,t-1}) + \theta(B_t) < \theta(A_1) + \theta(B_t) \leqslant 2\mu$$

by the definition of t and μ. In this latter case, we can repeat the process by splitting (X', Y') and so on. Thus, the splitting operation will either result in generating a finite set of new equivalence pairs $(X_1, Y_1), (X_2, Y_2), \ldots$ of thickness bounded by 2μ, or will terminate by proving that $A \not\equiv B$. Since there are only a finite number of terms X with $\theta(X) < 2\mu$, termination of the algorithm is guaranteed. Rather than formulate the precise analogy of Theorem 2, we proceed directly to the algorithm, which clarifies exactly what is going on.

In order to test whether $A \equiv B$, where A and B are proper terms over a simplified set of definitions R, we execute the following steps.

step 1: Set $U_0 = \{(A, B)\}$ and $r = 0$.

step 2: Check that U_r is consistent. If U_r is inconsistent, terminate the algorithm with NOT EQUIVALENT.

step 3: Form U_{r+1} by identifying the pairs (X, Y) of proper terms of U_r (for which $X \neq Y$), and generating their successors $(\sigma_k X, \sigma_k Y)$ for $k = 1, 2$, splitting these if necessary in the manner described above. Either the splitting operation will result in generating a pair (Z, W) for which $\theta(Z) \not\equiv \theta(W)$ in which case terminate the algorithm with NOT EQUIVALENT, or in generating a new set of pairs, no member of which exceeds 2μ in thickness. In the latter case, U_{r+1} consists of all these pairs not already in $U_1, U_2, \ldots U_r$. If U_{r+1} is not empty, then set $r = r + 1$ and return to step 2. If U_{r+1} is empty, then terminate the algorithm with EQUIVALENT.

To see that the algorithm always terminates, let $H_r = U_0 \cup U_1 \cup \cdots \cup U_r$. Since $H_r \subseteq H_{r+1}$, and H_r consists of pairs with thicknesses $< 2\mu$ (except possibly for (A, B)), it follows that $H_0, H_1, \ldots$ is a finite chain of sets. Hence we must eventually reach some N such that U_N is empty.

In order to show that each step of the algorithm can actually be carried out, we must prove that the test for consistency is effective. This involves computing the thicknesses of proper terms, which can be done using the following lemma in conjunction with Lemma 5:

Lemma 9. Suppose R is a list of definitions

$$R_j \text{ is (if } T \text{ then } F_1; A_j \text{ else } F_2; B_j)$$

in simplified form. For $k \geqslant 0$, define $\theta_k(\mathbf{R}) = (\theta_k(R_1), \theta_k(R_2), \ldots, \theta_k(R_n))$ by taking

$$\theta_0(R_j) = 1 \quad \text{and} \quad \theta_{k+1}(R_j) = 1 + \min \{\theta_k(A_j), \theta_k(B_j)\}$$

for each j, where $\theta_k(R_a; R_b; \ldots) = \theta_k(R_a) + \theta_k(R_b) + \ldots$, and $\theta_k(A) = \infty$ if $A \equiv \Omega$. Then the sequence of vectors

$$\theta_0(\mathbf{R}), \theta_1(\mathbf{R}), \ldots$$

is a finite chain under the relation $\leqslant$ defined by

$$(a_1, a_2, \ldots, a_n) \leqslant (b_1, b_2, \ldots, b_n) \quad \text{if } a_j \leqslant b_j \text{ for } 1 \leqslant j \leqslant n,$$

and $\theta(\mathbf{R}) = \lim \theta_k(\mathbf{R})$.

Proof. We first show by induction on k that

$$\theta_k(\mathbf{R}) \leqslant \theta_{k+1}(\mathbf{R}), \quad \text{for } k \geqslant 0.$$

The assertion is clearly true for $k = 0$, so assume it holds for k. We have

$$\theta_{k+1}(R_j) = 1 + \min\{\theta_k(A_j), \theta_k(B_j)\}$$
$$\leqslant 1 + \min\{\theta_{k+1}(A_j), \theta_{k+1}(B_j)\}$$
$$\leqslant \theta_{k+2}(R_j)$$

using the induction hypothesis, and this gives the desired result. A similar induction shows that $\theta_k(\mathbf{R}) \leqslant \theta(\mathbf{R})$, so that $\lim \theta_k(\mathbf{R})$ defined. Since

$$\lim \theta_k(R_j) = 1 + \min\{\lim \theta_k(A_j), \lim \theta_k(B_j)\}$$

it follows that $\theta(\mathbf{R}) = \lim \theta_k(\mathbf{R})$.

As an example, let us compute the thicknesses of $R_1, R_2, \ldots, R_6$ in the following list of definitions:

$$R_1 \text{ is (if } T \text{ then } F; R_3; R_4 \text{ else } L; \Omega)$$
$$R_2 \text{ is (if } T \text{ then } F; R_5; R_6 \text{ else } L; \Omega)$$
$$R_3 \text{ is (if } T \text{ then } G; R_4 \text{ else } G; R_3; R_4; R_4)$$
$$R_4 \text{ is (if } T \text{ then } F \text{ else } F)$$
$$R_5 \text{ is (if } T \text{ then } G \text{ else } G; R_5; R_6)$$
$$R_6 \text{ is (if } T \text{ then } F; R_4 \text{ else } F; R_4)$$

We can arrange the calculations as a table, the final column giving the values of $\theta(R_1), \theta(R_2), \ldots, \theta(R_6)$.

	θ_0	θ_1	θ_2	θ_3
R_1	1	3	4	4
R_2	1	3	4	4
R_3	1	2	2	2
R_4	1	1	1	1
R_5	1	1	1	1
R_6	1	2	2	2

Continuing with this example, let us prove that $R_1 \equiv R_2$. We have

(i) $U_0 = \{(R_1, R_2)\}$. U_0 is consistent as $\theta(R_1) = \theta(R_2) = 4$ and $F_1(R_1) = F_1(R_2) = F$, and $F_2(R_1) = F_2(R_2) = L$.

(ii) $U_1 = \{(R_3; R_4, R_5; R_6), (\Omega, \Omega)\}$. No splitting is necessary. U_1 is consistent as $\theta(R_3; R_4) = \theta(R_5; R_6) = 3$ and $F_k(R_3; R_4) = F_k(R_5; R_6) = G$ for $k = 1, 2$.

(iii) $U_2 = \{(R_4; R_4, R_6)\}$, since the successors of $(R_3; R_4, R_5; R_6)$ are $(R_4; R_4, R_6)$ and $(R_3; R_4; R_4; R_4, R_5; R_6; R_6)$, and if we split this last pair using Lemma 8 with $j = 2$, we obtain the two pairs $(R_3; R_4, R_5; R_6)$ and $(R_4; R_4, R_6)$ since $\theta(R_3; R_4) = \theta(R_5; R_6)$. U_2 is consistent.

(iv) $U_3 = \{(R_4; R_4)\}$. Clearly U_3 is consistent and U_4 is empty.

Hence $R_1 \equiv R_2$.

We turn now to the proofs of Lemmas 4, 5 and 8. (Lemma 7 is similar to Lemma 3 and is left as an exercise). To this end, we need some further results concerning trace machines.

Lemma 10. For any trace machine M and terms X and Y, we have

$$m[X; Y](\lambda) = m[Y] \cdot m[X](\lambda).$$

Proof. Immediate from the definition of a trace machine.

Lemma 11. Let X be a term over a restricted set of definitions R, and let M and N be any two trace machines. Then there exists a trace machine K, which we shall refer to as the *composition of M and N with respect to X*, such that

$$k[X; Y](\lambda) = m[X](\lambda)n[Y](\lambda)$$

for any term Y.

Proof. There are three cases to be considered. First, if $X = I$ then take $K = N$. In this case the lemma follows at once. Second, if $m[X](\lambda)$ is undefined, then take $K = M$. Since $m[X; Y](\lambda) = m[Y] \cdot m[X](\lambda)$, the lemma follows also in this case as both sides are undefined. Finally, if $m[X](\lambda) = \phi$, where $|\phi| < \infty$, then define K by taking

$$T_K(\phi\alpha) = T_N(\alpha) \text{ for all } \alpha$$

and $\quad T_K(\alpha) = T_M(\alpha) \text{ for all } \alpha, \quad \text{where } |\alpha| < |\phi|.$

Consider the computation of X on M with input λ. Since R is a restricted procedure program, the last step in this terminating computation must consist of the application of some operation. It cannot be a test because this would entail the presence of I, standing by itself, in one arm of a conditional expression. This implies that the computation does not depend on the value of the test $T_M(\phi)$. In other words, we have

$$k[X](\lambda) = m[X](\lambda) = \phi.$$

Moreover, since K is a trace machine, it follows that

$$k[X; Y](\lambda) = k[Y] \cdot k[X](\lambda) = k[Y](\phi) = \phi n[Y](\lambda)$$

for any term Y, establishing the lemma.

Proof of Lemma 4

Clearly, if $X \equiv \Omega$ or $Y \equiv \Omega$ then $X; Y \equiv \Omega$. To prove the converse, suppose $X; Y \equiv \Omega$ and $X \not\equiv \Omega$. Let M be a trace machine such that $m[X](\lambda)$ is defined, and let N be an arbitrary trace machine. Let K be the composition of M and N with respect to X, so that

$$k[X; Y](\lambda) = m[X](\lambda)n[Y](\lambda).$$

Since the left hand side of this equation is undefined by supposition, we must have $n[Y](\lambda)$ undefined. Since N was arbitrary, we have shown $Y \equiv \Omega$.

Proof of Lemma 5

In the case that either side is infinite, the conclusion follows at once by Lemma 4. We can therefore assume that both $\theta(X; Y)$ and $\theta(X) + \theta(Y)$ are finite. Suppose M and N are trace machines such that

$$|m[X](\lambda)| = \theta(X) \quad \text{and} \quad |n[Y](\lambda)| = \theta(Y).$$

Let K be the composition of M and N with respect to X. It follows that

$$\theta(X; Y) \leqslant |k[X; Y](\lambda)| = \theta(X) + \theta(Y).$$

Conversely, to show that $\theta(X; Y) \geqslant \theta(X) + \theta(Y)$, let M be a trace machine such that

$$|m[X; Y](\lambda)| = \theta(X; Y).$$

Define N by taking $T_N(\alpha) = T_M(\phi\alpha)$ for all α, where $\phi = m[X](\lambda)$. We have

$$m[X; Y](\lambda) = m[Y] \cdot m[X](\lambda) = m[X](\lambda)n[Y](\lambda)$$

whence

$$\theta(X; Y) = |m[X](\lambda)| + |n[Y](\lambda)| \geqslant \theta(X) + \theta(Y).$$

Finally, to prove Lemma 8 we need the following lemma:

Lemma 12. Suppose X, Y, W, and Z are terms over R. Then

(i) $W \equiv X$ and $Y \equiv Z$ implies $W; Y \equiv X; Z$,

(ii) $Y; X \equiv Z; X$ and $X \not\equiv \Omega$ implies $Y \equiv Z$.

Proof. The proof of (i) follows from the definition of a trace machine and is left as an exercise. In order to prove (ii), we show that for any trace machine M, $m[Y](\lambda)$ is defined only if $m[Z](\lambda)$ is defined and $m[Z](\lambda)$ is an initial substring of $m[Y](\lambda)$. By symmetry, we therefore have $m[Y](\lambda) = m[Z](\lambda)$ whenever either side is defined, and this proves (ii).

Accordingly, suppose M is a trace machine such that $m[Y](\lambda) = \phi$, where $|\phi| < \infty$. Let N be any trace machine such that $n[X](\lambda) = \chi$, where $|\chi| = \theta(X) < \infty$. Let K be the composition of M and N with respect to Y, so that $k[Y; X](\lambda) = \phi\chi$. Suppose $k[Z](\lambda) = \psi$. Since $Y; X \equiv Z; X$ we have

$$k[Z; X](\lambda) = k[X](\psi) = \phi\chi.$$

Since $|k[X](\psi)| \geqslant |\psi| + \theta(X)$ (see Exercise 2.10) we have $|\phi| \geqslant |\psi|$. It follows that ψ is an initial substring of ϕ, and so we must have $k[Z](\lambda) = m[Z](\lambda)$. This shows that $m[Z](\lambda)$ is an initial substring of $m[Y](\lambda)$.

Proof of Lemma 8

First, suppose

$$A_{1,j}; C \equiv B_{1,t} \quad \text{and} \quad A_{(j+1),n} \equiv C; B_{(t+1),m}.$$

Applying Lemma 12 (i) twice, we obtain

$$A_{1,n} \equiv A_{1,j}; C; B_{(t+1),m} \equiv B_{1,m}.$$

To prove the converse result, we must first show how the integer t and term C can be determined.

Suppose $\theta(A_{1,j}) = a$, and choose t so that $\theta(B_{1,t-1}) < a$ and $\theta(B_{1,t}) \geqslant a$, the existence of such a t being guaranteed by the fact that $\theta(A) = \theta(B)$. Since we can compute thicknesses of terms, t can be effectively determined. To fix C, pick any trace machine M such that

$$m[A_{1,j}](\lambda) = \phi, \quad \text{where } |\phi| = \theta(A_{1,j}) = a.$$

(It is left as an exercise to show that such an M can be found.) Consider the computation sequence of $B_{1,t}$ on M with input λ. Suppose it has the form

$$X_0, \psi_0, X_1, \psi_1, \ldots$$

where $X_0 = B_{1,t}$ and $\psi_0 = \lambda$. This sequence cannot terminate at an X_h, ψ_h where $|\psi_h| < a$, as this would contradict the fact that $\theta(B_{1,t}) \geqslant a$. Hence we can determine the unique term X_k in the above sequence for which $|\psi_k| = a$. Set $C = X_k$ and also let $\psi = \psi_k$ for short. It follows that

$$m[B_{1,t}](\lambda) = m[C](\psi).$$

Let N be an arbitrary trace machine, and define K by taking

$$T_K(\psi\alpha) = T_N(\alpha) \text{ for all } \alpha$$

and $\qquad T_K(\alpha) = T_M(\alpha) \text{ for all } \alpha, \text{ with } |\alpha| < a.$

It follows that

$$k[B_{1,t}](\lambda) = k[C](\psi) = \psi n[C](\lambda),$$

whence

$$k[B_{1,m}](\lambda) = \psi n[C; B_{t+1,m}](\lambda).$$

Also we have

$$k[A_{1,n}](\lambda) = \phi n[A_{j+1,n}](\lambda).$$

Now suppose $A_{1,n} \equiv B_{1,m}$, so that $k[A_{1,n}](\lambda) = k[B_{1,m}](\lambda)$. Since $|\psi| = |\phi| = a$, we have $\psi = \phi$, and so

$$n[C; B_{t+1,m}](\lambda) = n[A_{j+1,n}](\lambda).$$

Since N was freely chosen, this proves that $A_{j+1,n} \equiv C; B_{t+1,n}$. To complete the proof, we use Lemma 12(i) to obtain

$$A_{1,n} \equiv A_{1,j}; C; B_{t+1,m} \equiv B_{1,m},$$

and Lemma 12 (ii) to give

$$A_{1,j}; C \equiv B_{1,t},$$

as $B_{t+1,m}$ is proper.

Finally, since strongly equivalent terms must have the same thickness, $\theta(A_{1,j}) = \theta(B_{1,t})$ implies $\theta(C) = 0$, and so in this case C must be the null term.

Exercises

1. Define the machine M as follows:

$X_M = S$, where S consists of every *infinite* sequence over $\{0,1\}$,

$V_M = S \times \{F, G, ...\}^*$

$Y_M = \{F, G, ...\}^*$

$I_M(\beta) = (\beta, \lambda)$

$O_M(\beta, \phi) = \phi$

$F_M(b\beta, \phi) = (\beta, \phi F)$ for all ϕ, β and b, where $b = 0$ *or* 1.

$T_M(b\beta, \phi) = true$ if $b = 1$

   $= false$ if $b = 0$.

Prove that two flowchart programs are strongly equivalent if and only if they are equivalent on M.

2. Translate the following program into a set of labelled compound instructions, each of which has four successors corresponding to every possible outcome of the two tests T_1 and T_2.

   1: **do** F **then goto** *2*

   2: **if** T_1 **then goto** *1* **else goto** *3*

   3: **do** G **then goto** *4*

   4: **if** T_2 **then goto** h **else goto** *1*

3. Prove that $\theta(j) = 1 + \min\{\theta(j_1), \theta(j_2)\}$, where labels j_1 and j_2 are the successors of label j.

4. Why is Lemma 3 incorrect if it is not assumed that P is a simplified set of instructions?

5. Determine whether or not the following flowchart programs are strongly equivalent:

   1: **do** F **then goto** *2*

   2: **if** T **then goto** *3* **else goto** *5*

   3: **do** G **then goto** *4*

   4: **if** T **then goto** *1* **else goto** h

   5: **do** F **then goto** *6*

   6: **if** T **then goto** *7* **else goto** *2*

   7: **do** G **then goto** *8*

   8: **if** T **then goto** *6* **else goto** h

1: **do** F **then goto** 2
2: **if** T **then goto** 3 **else goto** 1
3: **do** G **then goto** 4
4: **if** T **then goto** 1 **else goto** h

6. When translating a list of restricted procedure definitions into standard form, why is it always possible to detect infinite loops of substitutions?
7. Translate the following list of definitions into standard form:

R_1 is (**if** T **then** R_2; (**if** T **then** F **else** R_1) **else** F; G)
R_2 is (**if** T **then** F **else** R_3; R_1)
R_3 is F; R_3.

8   Construct a list of definitions that cannot be transformed into a strongly equivalent list in standard form. Note that it is not sufficient merely to give a set of definitions that makes use of the null expression I, since such a set may still be transformable to standard form.
9. Describe, in greater detail than given in the text, how the problem of determining whether two restricted procedure programs are strongly equivalent can be described as a problem about the strong equivalence of terms. Is it necessary that the initial expressions of the programs also be restricted?
10. Suppose that X is a proper term over a restricted set of definitions, M is an arbitrary trace machine, and ϕ is any string of operation identifiers. Prove that

$$|mX(\phi)| \geqslant |\phi| + \theta(X).$$

11. Prove that, if X, Y and Z are terms over a restricted set of definitions, then

$$X; Y \equiv X; Z \quad \text{and} \quad X \not\equiv \Omega \quad \text{implies} \quad Y \equiv Z.$$

12. Prove Lemma 7
13. With the definitions given after Lemma 7, prove that $A \equiv B$ if and only if each W_r is consistent.
14. In the example after Lemma 9, we split the successors of the pair in U_1 using the special case $j = 2$ of Lemma 8 rather than strictly according to the algorithm. How does the example proceed if we adhere strictly to the algorithm?
15. Prove that the construction of C in Lemma 8 is effective, by showing how to choose a trace machine M such that

$$|m[T](\lambda)| = \theta(T)$$

for a given term T.

Chapter 3

Algorithms and Universal Machines

Up to now we have used the term *algorithm* in a rather loose way to describe any effective general method for determining whether or not a particular property holds for given members of a class of inputs. Our purpose in this chapter is to examine more carefully the concept of algorithm and to attempt to characterize its nature in a formal definition. Apart from the natural desire to be quite clear about every fundamental notion that enters into the subject of computation, there is another reason why this work is important. It is only by having a clear and precise understanding about what constitutes an algorithm that the existence of an algorithm to solve a particular problem, or compute a particular function, can explicitly be denied. Until some formal definition of the term algorithm is given, one must always remain in doubt about the existence of problems with no algorithmic solution. In Chapter 4 we shall prove that such unsolvable problems do exist, but, in order to substantiate the claim, the following investigation into the nature of algorithms is absolutely necessary.

The algorithms given in Chapter 2 are more accurately referred to as *decision* algorithms, because the output is restricted to two possible values only, one to signify that the property in question holds for the input data, and one to indicate that it does not. More generally, of course, we can consider algorithms with a number of possible outputs. As a famous example, Euclid's algorithm takes two positive integers as input and computes their greatest common divisor as output. The proof of Theorem 1.1(ii) contains another example, since it amounts to describing an algorithm whose input is an arbitrary flowchart program and whose output is a strongly equivalent procedure program. It can be seen from these examples that, in coming to grips with algorithms, we are at once confronted with a great number of data spaces over which algorithms may operate. Any attempt to incorporate numbers, strings, programs, and truth values directly into a mathematical model for algorithms is likely to produce such a complicated definition as to make analysis impossible. To get round this problem we shall concentrate exclusively on *numerical* algorithms in which only non-negative integers are used. This restriction is not so drastic as at first sight appears. In Section 1 we show how elements of more complicated data spaces can be coded as non-negative integers in such a way as to ensure that no information is lost. Manipulations of strings, programs, etc., can then be represented by calculations with the appropriately coded numbers.

Among the many possible approaches to the problem of characterizing algorithms, the most natural one in terms of our framework is to identify

47

algorithms with programs for a suitable machine. There are a number of reasons why such an approach is reasonable. First, it is a working hypothesis for Computer Scientists that any algorithm, capable of a precise specification, can be realized as a program for a computer. Limitations of time and space restrict what algorithms can actually be programmed in practice, but this is not a theoretical limitation on the expressive power of programming languages. Second, any attempt at a general description of what we understand by an algorithm sounds in the end very much like the description of some sort of program. The important point is that, whereas a general description of what constitutes an algorithm must of necessity remain vague and intuitive, descriptions of programs can be made precise and unambiguous.

If the identification of algorithms with programs is a reasonable one, then we shall have to consider what sort of machine is necessary for interpreting the programs. On the one hand, it has to be powerful enough to possess all the important features of real computers, but on the other hand, it has to be sufficiently simple in its mode of operation so that its properties can be investigated and some general conclusions drawn about the class of functions that it can compute. If we can argue convincingly that every algorithm can be represented as a program for such a machine, then we call the machine a *universal* machine.

In Section 2 we propose such a machine and consider its status as a universal machine by studying the computations it can carry out with flowchart programs. It should be clearly understood at the outset that there is no possibility of a formal proof that every algorithm can be realized as a program for the proposed machine. Such a proof would depend on an *a priori* formal definition of algorithm, but this is just the *result* we are trying to achieve. In asserting the identity of the two concepts we are stating a *thesis*, and can only amass the evidence in its favour. Broadly speaking, there are two kinds of evidence that we can put forward:

1. *Internal evidence*, which consists of a demonstration that no matter how we try to extend the capabilities of the proposed machine in a constructive manner, we still end up with something that is no more powerful.

2. *External evidence*, which consists of an examination of other historical attempts at defining the notion of algorithm, together with a proof that these models are computationally equivalent.

We shall consider the internal evidence in Section 2, and the external evidence in Section 3.

3.1 Coding

In this section we briefly consider the problem of *coding*, in which members of a variety of data spaces are represented by single non-negative integers. Through-out the chapter we suppose $N = \{0, 1, 2, \ldots\}$; elements of N will be referred to simply as integers or numbers. Suppose X is a given data space. What we seek is a computable one-one mapping from X into N, i.e. a computable function $\sigma: X \to N$ such that $\sigma(x) = \sigma(y)$ implies $x = y$ for all x and y in X. The number $\sigma(x)$ gives the *coding* of x. It is not insisted that every number should be the coding of some element of X, although this may be the case for particular coding functions. Rather than attempt a general treatment we consider two important examples.

(1) Coding of *n*-tuples

Suppose we wish to code a n-tuple $(x_1, x_2, \ldots, x_n)$ of numbers x_j into a single number. Among the many ways this can be done, the following is perhaps the simplest. Define $\sigma^n: N^n \to N$ by

$$\sigma^n(x_1, x_2, \ldots, x_n) = p_1^{x_1} p_2^{x_2} \ldots p_n^{x_n},$$

where $p_1 = 2$, $p_2 = 3$, and, in general, p_n is the nth prime number in order of magnitude. By the fundamental theorem of arithmetic every positive integer is uniquely decomposable into the product of primes, so that σ^n is one-one. If we define $\sigma_j: N \to N$ by

$\sigma_j(x) = $ the exponent of prime p_j in the prime decomposition of x,

then it follows that

$$\sigma_j \cdot \sigma^n = u_j^n \quad \text{for } 1 \leqslant j \leqslant n,$$

where u_j^n is the projection function defined by

$$u_j^n(x_1, x_2, \ldots, x_n) = x_j.$$

(2) Coding of flowcharts

As an important but more complicated example, we consider the problem of coding an arbitrary flowchart program P, defined over operation identifiers $F_1, F_2, \ldots$ and test identifiers $T_1, T_2, \ldots$, as a single number. First, we represent the flowchart P as a set of labelled instructions with label identifiers $0, 1, \ldots n$. We can arrange that 1 is the initial label of the program, and 0 is the unique terminal label if the program has one. Thus instructions have the form

$$j: \textbf{do } F_k \textbf{ then goto } l$$

or $\qquad\qquad j: \textbf{if } T_k \textbf{ then goto } l \textbf{ else goto } m.$

Each such instruction is now represented by a 4-tuple of numbers in the following way.

$(0, k, l, l)$ represents $\quad \textbf{do } F_k \textbf{ then goto } l$

$(1, k, l, m)$ represents $\quad \textbf{if } T_k \textbf{ then goto } l \textbf{ else goto } m.$

Thus, the first number signifies the instruction type, i.e. operation or test, the second number describes the appropriate identifier, and the third and fourth numbers give the next labels. These four numbers can be coded into a single number using the coding described under (1) for 4-tuples.

At this point we have represented the information contained in the flowchart by n integers $j_1, j_2, \ldots j_n$, where

$$j_i = \sigma^4(0, k, l, l) \qquad \text{if } i\colon \textbf{do } F_k \textbf{ then goto } l$$

is an instruction in P

or $\qquad j_i = \sigma^4(1, k, l, m) \qquad \text{if } i\colon \textbf{if } T_k \textbf{ then goto } l \textbf{ else goto } m$

is an instruction in P.

Finally, we code P into the single number p, where

$$p = \sigma^n(j_1, j_2, \ldots, j_n).$$

Note that not every integer is the coding of some program. To see how we can uniquely decode a number into its associated flowchart, consider the number $p = 2^{150}3^{105}$. Since $150 = 2^1 \times 3^1 \times 5^2 \times 7^0$ and $105 = 2^0 \times 3^1 \times 5^1 \times 7^1$, the two instructions of the flowchart P are

1: **if** T_1 **then goto** *2* **else goto** *0*

2: **do** F_1 **then goto** *1*.

In general, we can extract any desired information about the flowchart coded as p by observing that

$$\sigma_j(p) = \text{the code of instruction labelled } j \text{ in } P$$

$$\sigma_1 \cdot \sigma_j(p) = \text{the instruction type,}$$

$$\sigma_2 \cdot \sigma_j(p) = \text{the instruction name,}$$

and $\qquad \left.\begin{array}{l} \sigma_3 \cdot \sigma_j(p) \\ \sigma_4 \cdot \sigma_j(p) \end{array}\right\} = \text{the associated exit labels.}$

3.2 The machine NORMA

We now introduce the machine NORMA and study the question of its universality. NORMA stands for <u>N</u>umber theoretic <u>R</u>egister <u>MA</u>chine, and is a register machine in the sense of Section 1.5. NORMA's input and output set are given by

Input set $= N \qquad$ Output set $= N$,

so NORMA computes 1-place number theoretic functions. The memory set is structured as an infinite set of registers, each of which can contain an arbitrary element of N, i.e. $V = N^\infty$. To avoid using subscripts, the registers will be denoted by $A, B, \ldots, X, Y$. The operations and tests that NORMA defines are those naturally suggested by the following identifiers:

operations $\quad A\colon = A + 1$

$\qquad\qquad\quad A\colon = A - 1 \quad$ for any register A

tests $\qquad\qquad A = 0 \qquad\quad$ for any register A.

The reader is invited to give the formal definitions of the corresponding functions. We shall suppose that the effect of executing an instruction $A := A - 1$ when A contains zero will be to leave A unchanged. The two registers X and Y play a special role. NORMA's input function sets X to contain the input number and initializes all other registers to zero. NORMA's output function extracts the final contents of register Y as the given output.

The object of this section is to review the internal evidence in support of the following thesis.

Thesis.   With suitable coding of the data, every algorithm can be represented as a flowchart program for NORMA.

NORMA meets at least one criterion mentioned at the beginning of the chapter: it is a very simple machine. So simple, in fact, that it appears woefully inadequate to serve as a machine on which every algorithm can be implemented. Nevertheless, it is hoped that, by the end of the chapter, the reader will come to believe in NORMA as a very powerful machine, so powerful that we can justifiably call it a universal machine.

To begin with, let us list some of the obvious criticisms of NORMA as a model of real computers.

Criticism (1)   NORMA does not define enough operations and tests. We also need to be able to add, multiply, subtract, divide, and compare the contents of two registers for many computations.

Criticism (2)   NORMA's memory set is too restricted. There is no provision for the handling of negative or floating point numbers which may be necessary in certain computations.

Criticism (3)   In addition, access to the memory set is too restricted. There is need for the introduction of subscripted variables for handling arrays of numbers.

Criticism (4)   The restriction to flowchart programs is too severe. There may be a need for more general sequencing mechanisms such as is provided by procedure programs. At the very least, one may need to be able to refer to labels indirectly so that subroutines can be constructed.

Criticism (5)   Since there is no concrete representation of the memory values, as say binary strings, there is no way to handle strings or perform any of the so-called 'logical' operations, such as shifting or masking, that one finds in the order code of most real computers.

The plan of campaign is to take up these points one by one and show that each criticism can be answered in a convincing fashion.

Answer to criticism (1)

We answer the first objection by showing how the operations of copy, add, multiply etc., can be defined in terms of NORMA instructions. As perhaps the simplest example, we can define the operation $A: = 0$ by the **while** program

$$\textbf{until } A = 0 \textbf{ do } A: = A - 1.$$

In this way, we can treat the operation $A: = 0$ as a *macro*, and replace it by its definition wherever it may occur. Since every **while** program can be translated into a flowchart, this substitution results in a proper NORMA flowchart. Whenever possible, we shall write macros as **while** programs rather than drawing flowcharts, as this tends to improve the clarity of the definition.

The macro $A: = 0$ can be used to construct macros for $A: = 1, A: = 2$ etc. For example, $A: = 2$ is given by

$$A: = 0; A: = A + 1; A:= A + 1$$

The instruction $A: = A + B$ cannot be defined as a macro without using some further register as work space, and this introduces side-effects. The program

$$\textbf{until } B = 0 \textbf{ do } (A: = A + 1; B: = B - 1)$$

certainly adds the contents of B to A, but unfortunately it also sets B to zero. If it is necessary to preserve the original contents of B, then we must use the more complicated program

$$C: = 0;$$
$$\textbf{until } B = 0 \textbf{ do } (A: = A + 1; C: = C + 1; B: = B - 1);$$
$$\textbf{until } C = 0 \textbf{ do } (B: = B + 1; C: = C - 1).$$

However, this program has the unavoidable side-effect of destroying the original contents of C. To make explicit the fact that the macro has a side-effect, we write its name as follows:

$$A: = A + B \text{ using } C$$

Using macros with side-effects does not affect our contention that programs containing the operation $A: = A + B$ can be replaced by NORMA programs. Suppose P is a flowchart program in which the operation $A: = A + B$ occurs. By inspection, choose some register C which does not appear in P and replace $A: = A + B$ by $A: = A + B$ *using* C wherever it occurs. The resulting program is a NORMA flowchart program equivalent to P.

Given the macro $A: = A + B$ *using* C, we can define a macro $A: = B$ *using* C as follows:

$$A: = 0;$$
$$A: = A + B \text{ using } C$$

The definition of a macro for $A: = A \times B$ is more complicated since it requires two extra registers. Define $A: = A \times B$ *using* C, D as follows:

$$C: = 0;$$
$$\textbf{until } A = 0 \textbf{ do } (C: = C + 1; A: = A - 1);$$
$$\textbf{until } C = 0 \textbf{ do } (A: = A + B \text{ using } D; C: = C - 1)$$

As a final example of macro construction, we construct a program for

$$A: = \text{PRIME}(B)$$

which has the effect of storing the bth prime number in A, where b is the contents of B. For completeness, we suppose that the 0th prime number is 1. The program takes the form

> $A: = 1; C: = B;$
> **until** $C = 0$ **do**
> $\quad (C: = C - 1; A: = A + 1;$
> $\quad$ **until** $prime(A)$ **do** $A: = A + 1),$

where the test $prime(A)$ yields *true* if the contents of A is a prime number, and *false* otherwise. To construct this test, we determine whether A is divisible by any of the numbers $A - 1, A - 2, \ldots, 2$. The macro is

> **(if** $A < 2$ **then** *false*
> **else** $D: = A;$
> $\quad D: = D - 1;$
> $\quad$ **until** $div(D, A)$ **do** $D: = D - 1;$
> $\quad D: = D - 1;$
> $\quad$ **(if** $D = 0$ **then** *true* **else** *false*)),

where $div(D, A)$ is a further test which yields *true* if the contents of D divides into the contents of A, and *false* otherwise. When translating the above program into a set of labelled instructions, the constants *true* and *false* have, of course, to be replaced by jumps to the appropriate label. We leave the reader to fill in the necessary details, and also provide definitions for the tests $A < 2$ and $div(D, A)$. By taking the special case

$$Y: = \text{PRIME}(X)$$

of the macro, we have shown how to compute the prime number function on NORMA.

To summarize the above discussion, the criticism that NORMA defines insufficient arithmetical operations is answered by the fact that these operations can be defined as programs over the basic set of instructions. These operations can then be replaced by the associated programs wherever they occur.

Answer to criticism (2)

The criticism that NORMA cannot handle negative integers is easily answered. An arbitrary integer m can always be represented as an ordered pair (n, d) of nonnegative integers, where

> $n = |m|$ (the absolute value of m), and
> $d = 0 \quad$ if $m \geqslant 0,$
> $\quad = 1$ otherwise, (the sign of m).

Each arithmetic operation on integers corresponds to an operation on ordered pairs. For example, to add one to an integer $m = (n, d)$ we set

$$(n, d) + 1 = (n + 1, 0) \quad \text{if } d = 0,$$
$$= (0, 0) \qquad\quad \text{if } d = 1 \text{ and } n = 1,$$
$$= (n - 1, 1) \quad \text{otherwise.}$$

One simple way to simulate an integer operation $A := A + 1$ on NORMA is to associate two registers A_1 and A_2 with A, the first to hold n and the second to hold d, and define $A := A + 1$ to be

$$\textbf{(if } A_2 = 0 \textbf{ then } A_1 := A_1 + 1 \textbf{ else}$$
$$A_1 := A_1 - 1;$$
$$\textbf{(if } A_1 = 0 \textbf{ then } A_2 := A_2 - 1 \textbf{ else } I)).$$

The other operations can be treated in a similar fashion. Extra tests such as $A \geqslant 0$ can easily be defined in terms of the appropriate tests on A_2.

Using a very similar idea, arithmetic on arbitrary *rational* numbers can be simulated by NORMA. A non-negative rational r can be represented as an ordered pair (a, b) of natural numbers, where $b > 0$ and $r = a/b$. The representation is not unique as, for example, 0.75 is represented by $(3, 4)$ and $(6, 8)$ among many others, but this is not too important. Since arithmetic on rationals conforms to the rules:

$$(a, b) \pm (c, d) = (ad \pm bc, bd)$$
$$(a, b) \times (c, d) = (ac, bd)$$
$$(a, b) \div (c, d) = (ad, bc) \text{ provided } c \neq 0$$
$$(a, b) = (c, d) \text{ if and only if } ad = bc,$$

there is no problem in constructing the appropriate NORMA program.

Answer to criticism (3)

In order to answer the third criticism satisfactorily, we must give a reasonable definition of an array handling machine and show how, in the sense of Definition 1.3, it can be simulated by NORMA. Accordingly, let us define a machine SAM (Simple Array Machine) which augments NORMA by possessing the *array* of registers $A(1), A(2), \ldots$ in addition to the standard registers $A, B, \ldots, I, J, \ldots X, Y$, which we shall now call *index* registers. The operations defined by SAM for these index registers are exactly the same as those given by NORMA, but SAM also defines the following operations and tests:

operations	$A(J) := A(J) + 1$
	$A(J) := A(J) - 1$, where J is any index register
	$A(n) := A(n) + 1$
	$A(n) := A(n) - 1$, where n is any positive integer
tests	$A(J) = 0 \quad \text{and} \quad A(n) = 0.$

Thus SAM can access its array both directly and indirectly, through index registers. SAM's input function and output function is the same as in NORMA, but the input function initializes each array register to zero as well.

The result we are after is worth stating as a theorem.

Theorem 1.   NORMA can simulate SAM.

Proof.   We have to show how any given program P for SAM can be translated into a NORMA program Q such that

$$normaQ = samP.$$

The way to do it is to use coding to pack the whole of SAM's array into a single NORMA register. Thus, if at some stage during a computation of P the array $A(1), A(2), \ldots$ contains the numbers $a_1, a_2, \ldots$, then at the same stage during the corresponding computation of Q one particular register, say A, will contain the number a, where

$$a = p_1^{a_1} p_2^{a_2} \ldots, \quad p_j = j\text{th prime}.$$

Since SAM's input function initializes the array to zero, only a finite number of the quantities $a_1, a_2, \ldots$ will be different from zero. Hence a is always a well defined finite number.

To define Q from P, we translate each SAM instruction into a sequence of NORMA instructions, on a step by step basis, as follows: ·

(i)   index register instructions are left unchanged.

(ii)   an operation $A(J): = A(J) + 1$ is translated into the sequence

$$B: = \text{PRIME}(J); \ A: = A \times B,$$

where PRIME is the prime number function defined previously. Similarly, the operation $A(J): = A(J) - 1$ is translated as the sequence

$$B: = \text{PRIME}(J); \ A: = A/B,$$

where / is the special integer division operation defined by

$$a/b = a \div b \quad \text{if } b \text{ divides into } a,$$
$$= a \qquad \text{otherwise.}$$

To translate the test $A(J) = 0$, we again invoke the operation $B: = \text{PRIME}(J)$, and then test whether or not $div(B, A)$, where $div(B, A)$ is *true* when B divides into A, and *false* otherwise. The test $div(B, A)$ will give *true* just in the case that $A(J) \neq 0$.

(iii)   The operations $A(n): = A(n) + 1$ and $A(n): = A(n) - 1$ are dealt with by making use of the appropriate prime number. Thus $A(n): = A(n) + 1$ is translated as

$$A: = A \times p_n$$

and $A(n)$: $= A(n) - 1$ is translated as

$$A: = A/p_n.$$

The test $A(n) = 0$ uses the test $div(p_n, A)$ to determine the correct exit.

Of course, each operation and test appearing in Q must now be replaced by the correct NORMA macro, but we have already seen how to do this. Finally, we must ensure that Q initially sets A equal to 1 to represent the input condition of SAM's array. The simulation clearly works correctly, and the theorem is therefore proved.

If the reader has carefully followed and understood the details of the above proof, then he may begin to suspect that NORMA is not perhaps the simplest possible universal machine. Surely the same trick of coding infinitely many registers into one register can be worked with NORMA itself, and will result in an equally powerful machine but possessing far fewer registers? To show that this suspicion is well founded, let us define two more machines: NORMA2 and IRMA.

NORMA2 is in all respects identical with NORMA, except that it has only two registers X and Y. The machine IRMA has a single register X and defines the following operations and tests:

$$operations \quad X: = k \times X, \quad X: = X/k$$
$$tests \quad\quad\, k \,|\, X,$$

where k is an arbitrary positive integer. The test $k \,|\, X$ is another way of writing $div(k, X)$ and gives *true* when k divides the contents of X, and *false* otherwise. IRMA's input and output function respectively initializes X to some non-negative integer, and extracts its final contents.

Theorem 2. Using simulation in the sense of Definition 1.4:

(i) IRMA can simulate NORMA, and

(ii) NORMA2 can simulate NORMA.

Proof. (i) Note first the dependence of the theorem on the definition of simulation. Definition 1.4 says that, in order to show IRMA can simulate NORMA, we are allowed to construct coding and decoding functions $c: N \to N$ and $d: N \to N$, and then prove that each NORMA program P can be translated into an IRMA program Q such that

$$d \cdot irmaQ \cdot c = normaP.$$

The functions c and d are given as follows:

$$c(x) = 2^x \quad \text{and}$$

$$d(x) = \sigma_2(x) = \text{the exponent of } p_2(= 3) \text{ in the prime decomposition of } x.$$

The reasoning behind this choice of coding and decoding functions will become apparent in a moment, although other choices are possible.

As in the previous theorem, we code a typical configuration $(x, y, a, b, \ldots)$ of the NORMA registers $X, Y, A, B, \ldots$ into a single number

$$p_1^x p_2^y p_3^a \ldots.$$

which is stored in the IRMA register X. We suppose that the NORMA registers can be ordered in sequence, with X as the first register, Y as the second, and so on. To effect the translation of P into Q, the NORMA identifiers are replaced by IRMA identifiers as follows:

$$N := N + 1 \quad \text{becomes} \quad X := p_n \times X$$
$$N := N - 1 \quad \text{becomes} \quad X := X/p_n$$

and $\qquad N \neq 0 \qquad \text{becomes} \quad p_n \mid X,$

where N is the nth register in the ordering. For the last replacement to be well defined we must first transform all identifiers of the form $N = 0$ into tests $N \neq 0$, by switching over the relevant exit labels or conditional expressions. The resulting program will be of the same type, i.e. flowchart, **while**, or procedure program, as the initial program.

It can now be seen why the coding and decoding were chosen in the way they were. The combined effect of the coding function, followed by IRMA's input function, is to initialize X to

$$2^x = p_1^x p_2^0 p_3^0 \ldots,$$

which is just what is required in order to get the simulation under way. Similarly, the choice of d ensures that the correct final value of Y is extracted from the coded configuration.

(ii) To prove the second assertion we show how to translate a given IRMA program P into a NORMA2 program Q such that

$$norma2Q = irmaP.$$

In other words, we prove that NORMA2 can simulate IRMA in the sense of Definition 1.3. Combining the translations under (i) and (ii) produces the desired result. For simplicity, we consider only the problem of translating flowcharts into flowcharts.

Each instruction in the IRMA program P is replaced as follows.

(1) Replace

by the program

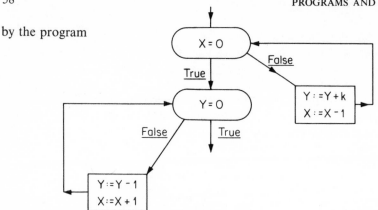

Since k is a given constant, the instruction $Y: = Y + k$ can be replaced by k operations of the form $Y: = Y + 1$. Provided Y is initially zero, this program will multiply the contents of X by k and leave Y zero.

(2) Replace

by the program

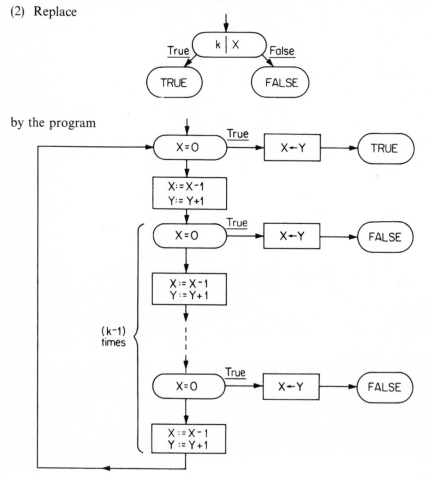

where $X \leftarrow Y$ is the transfer operation defined by

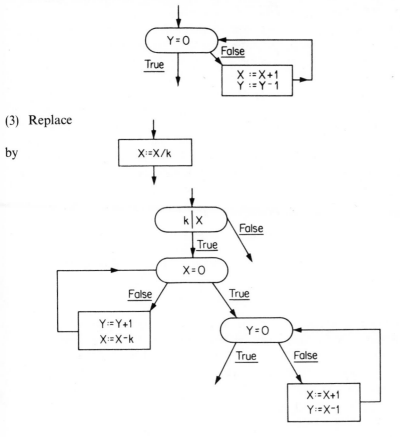

(3) Replace

by

where the test $k \mid X$ is expanded as in (2). If we recall that

$$x/k = x \text{ if } k \text{ does not divide } x$$
$$= x \div k, \text{ otherwise,}$$

then it is easy to see that the above program works.

This nearly completes the proof. We finally have to arrange that the contents of X are transferred into Y just before termination; this ensures that the coded configuration is in the right register for output.

Note that the simulation of NORMA by IRMA does not work if the more restricted Definition 1.3 is used, since there is no apparent way to initialize X, i.e. change x to 2^x, for the ensuing computation. The only way round this difficulty appears to be to take c and d as IRMA's input and output function. Some further consequences of this type of simulation are explored in the exercises at the end of the chapter.

Answer to criticism (4)

The fourth criticism claims that flowchart programs do not provide a sufficiently versatile sequencing mechanism for controlling the course of computations. It has been shown in Chapter 1 that every flowchart program can be translated into a strongly equivalent procedure program, which means that the class of computations that can be carried out by procedure programs on NORMA is certainly no smaller than the class of computations defined by flowcharts. Moreover, it may even be larger. Even if we retain the framework of labels and **gotos**, there is apparently no way of using labels indirectly in so-called *computed jumps*. Such a mechanism is certainly necessary for the construction of subroutines. Let us consider this latter problem first.

Suppose P is a flowchart program represented as a set of labelled instructions with labels chosen from the set of numerals. We can define a simple computed jump facility by allowing two more instruction types in P:

$$l: \textbf{do } F \textbf{ then goto } A$$
$$l: \textbf{if } T \textbf{ then goto } A \textbf{ else goto } B,$$

where F and T are NORMA identifiers, and A and B are NORMA registers. The effect of the command

$$\textbf{goto } A$$

is simply a jump to the instruction with label a, where a is the contents of A. If no such instruction exists, then a is a terminal label and the program stops.

Suppose P is a set of labelled instructions, with labels from the set $\{0, 1, \ldots k\}$, which may include these extra types. The simplest way to remove the computed jumps is to include in P an extra piece of program for each register A appearing in P. This piece of program has the entry label *table A* and is defined by the flowchart of Figure 4.

We can now remove the extra instruction types by replacing

$$l: \textbf{do } F \textbf{ then goto } A$$

by $l: \textbf{do } F \textbf{ then goto } table\ A,$

and $l: \textbf{if } T \textbf{ then goto } A \textbf{ else goto } B$

by $l: \textbf{if } T \textbf{ then goto } table\ A \textbf{ else goto } table\ B.$

It is clear that the resulting program is NORMA—equivalent to P.

Now let us deal with procedure programs. As an example of the extra power of procedures, consider the instruction $A := B$. We stated previously that there is no way of expanding this instruction in terms of NORMA operations without using an extra register as work space. This is not quite true. There is certainly no way of writing $A := B$ as a *flowchart* program over NORMA operations, but it *can* be done with a procedure program. For example:

COPY **where**

COPY **is** $A := 0;\ ADD,$

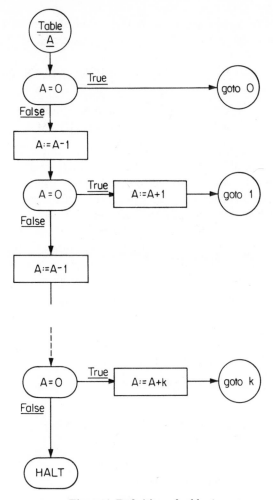

Figure 4. Definition of *table A*

ADD **is (if** $B = 0$ **then** I **else**
$$B: = B - 1; \ A: = A + 1; \text{ADD}; \ B: = B + 1)$$

To see that the above procedure gives the desired result, note that the effect of ADD is the same as performing $A: = A + B$. The extra power of procedures is used to 'remember' the original contents of B so that B can be restored to its initial value.

As another cunning example, consider

SQUARE **where**

SQUARE **is (if** $X = 0$ **then** I **else**
$$X: = X - 1; \ A: = A + 1; \text{SQUARE}; \text{ADD}),$$

ADD **is (if** $A = 0$ **then** I **else**
$$A: = A - 1; \ Y: = Y + 1: ADD; \ A: = A + 1).$$

The effect of ADD is to perform $Y := Y + A$, so the effect of SQUARE is to set $A := X$ and then execute $Y := Y + A$ exactly X times. Hence SQUARE computes $Y := X^2$.

These examples may suggest that criticism (4) is a valid one. Nevertheless the following result is true.

Theorem 3. Given any procedure program P for NORMA, we can find a flowchart program Q for NORMA such that Q is NORMA-equivalent to P.

Proof. The way we prove the theorem is just a simplified version of the traditional implementation of recursion. P is translated into a flowchart program for SAM, and then Theorem 1 is used to translate the resulting program into a NORMA flowchart. In order to translate procedure calls, we need the mechanism of a *stack* on which to store the appropriate return address. The stack will be just SAM's array $A(1), A(2), \ldots$, and a special index register K will be used as the stack pointer. Rather than give the formal translation, we can see the pertinent ideas by translating the program SQUARE defined above. As a first step, we translate SQUARE into the following set of labelled instructions:

1: **if** $X = 0$ **then goto** *6* **else goto** *2*

2: **do** $X := X - 1$ **then goto** *3*

3: **do** $A := A + 1$ **then goto** *4*

4: **do** SQUARE **then goto** *5*

5: **do** ADD **then goto** *6*,

and ADD into:

7: **if** $A = 0$ **then goto** *12* **else goto** *8*

8: **do** $A := A - 1$ **then goto** *9*

9: **do** $Y := Y + 1$ **then goto** *10*

10: **do** ADD **then goto** *11*

11: **do** $A := A + 1$ **then goto** *12*.

The instructions involving the identifiers SQUARE and ADD are now expanded into the appropriate subroutine calls. We replace

    (a) 4: **do** SQUARE **then goto** *5*

by

        4: **do** $A(K) := 5$ **then goto** *41*   (set return address)

      41: **do** $K := K + 1$ **then goto** *1*,   (increase stack pointer
                                        and jump to entry label
                                        of SQUARE).

    (b) 5: **do** ADD **then goto** *6*

by   5: **do** $A(K) := 6$ **then goto** *51*   (set return address)

      51: **do** $K := K + 1$ **then goto** *7*,   (increase stack pointer
                                          and jump to ADD)

and (c)   10: **do** ADD **then goto** *11*

by   10: **do** $A(K)$: = 11 **then goto** *101*

          101: **do** K: = $K + 1$ **then goto** *7*.

To ensure that the subroutines SQUARE and ADD return control to the appropriate label, the following instructions are added to the translated program:

      6: **do** K: = $K - 1$ **then goto** *61*

     61: **if** $K = 0$ **then goto** *0* **else goto** $A(K)$

and   12: **do** K: = $K - 1$ **then goto** *61*.

When SQUARE reaches its terminal label 6, the return address is computed from the stack and becomes the label of the next instruction. If the stack is empty, then the program halts on terminal label 0. An identical return sequence is obeyed when ADD reaches its terminal label 12. It remains to initialize the stack pointer, so we include, as the first instruction of the program, the assignment

start: **do** K: = 1 **then goto** *1*.

The final translated program is not quite a SAM program as computed jumps are used. These can be removed by first copying $A(K)$ into an index register, and then using the previously described method for dealing with computed jumps. The remaining details are left to the reader.

It is worth mentioning, in passing, a much simpler way of translating SQUARE into a flowchart program. The trick is to see that the procedure

R **is** (**if** T **then** F; R; G **else** I)

can directly be turned into a **while** program by making use of a register C to count the number of procedure calls. The result is the following **while** program:

    C: = 0;
    while T **do** (F; C: = $C + 1$);
    until $C = 0$ **do** (G; C: = $C - 1$).

As long as C does not interfere with the operations F and G, the above program is equivalent to the procedure R. Using this counter method, SQUARE can be translated directly as

    C: = 0;
    until $X = 0$ **do** (X: = $X - 1$; A: = $A + 1$; C: = $C + 1$);
    until $C = 0$ **do**
        (D: = 0;
        until $A = 0$ **do** (A: = $A - 1$; Y: = $Y + 1$; D: = $D + 1$);
        until $D = 0$ **do** (A: = $A + 1$; D: = $D - 1$);
        C: = $C - 1$).

Answer to criticism (5)

In order to answer the fifth criticism convincingly, we have to define a simple string processing machine and show that it can be simulated by NORMA. Exactly such a machine was defined by Turing in another approach to the problem of making the notion of algorithm mathematically precise. Rather than repeat the work here, we leave it to the next section which reviews the external evidence in favour of the thesis that every algorithm can be represented as a flowchart program for NORMA.

3.3   The machine TURING

The second type of evidence in support of our thesis is historical in nature. Over the past forty years various formalizations of the concept of an algorithm have been proposed, each with its own particular emphasis and basis in reality. For instance, hindsight apart, the NORMA approach depends for its intuitive appeal on a familiarity with the basic features of digital computers and programming languages. It is clearly essential for the validity of these formalizations that each should turn out to be computationally equivalent. If such were not the case, and one formulation turned out to describe a different class of computations than another, then it would be impossible to continue to believe that both properly modelled the same intuitive concept. By showing that the NORMA approach is equivalent to the other methods, we adduce further convincing evidence in favour of the NORMA thesis.

We shall discuss, somewhat briefly and with slight modification, just one of these other formulations, given by Turing in 1936, approximately 20 years before the advent of digital computers.

Turing's point of departure was to analyse the situation in which a human being X, equipped with a writing implement and an eraser, is performing a calculation on a supply of paper. As a result of this analysis, Turing arrived at the notion of a simple mechanical device capable of carrying out such calculations, and used this device as a basis for giving a precise specification of the general computational process. We shall retrace the main steps of Turing's analysis, although we shall arrive at a modified formulation of Turing's original model.

At the start of the calculation, we may suppose that X is confronted with a supply of paper, ruled into squares, on which is inscribed only the initial data for the problem. Observing X at work, we see him perform a sequence of simple operations of the following sort:

(a) changing a symbol in a particular square,

(b) determining what symbols a particular square or squares contain, and

(c) moving his eyes to another square or group of squares.

Finally, when some satisfactory representation of the desired answer has been reached, X terminates his calculations.

Concerning this situation, we make the following plausible assumptions:

(1) The two-dimensional nature of the paper is not an essential requirement for the calculation, hence we may assume that the supply of paper consists of an infinite one-dimensional tape ruled into squares.

(2) We can assume that the alphabet of symbols is finite. Since X can always use sequences of symbols in place of single symbols, this assumption is justified.

(3) We can assume that the number of 'states of mind' that X may enter during the course of a calculation is finite. Moreover, among these states of mind are two in particular: 'I am about to begin' and 'I have finished', which X enters at the beginning and at the end of the calculation respectively.

(4) We can assume that X's behaviour at any moment is strictly determined only by his present state of mind and the symbol or symbols on which he currently has his attention.

(5) Finally, we can assume that X is able to observe and change symbols only one square at a time, and can only transfer his attention to a neighbouring square. This means that at each moment of time, X can perform only the following operations:

   (i) observation of the symbol in the currently scanned square,
   (ii) possible change of this symbol for another one,
   (iii) possible change of state of mind,
   (iv) possible transfer of attention to the square immediately to the left or right of the scanned square.

At this point, a formal model of the above situation can be proposed. It consists of an infinite linear *tape* ruled into squares, on which a read–write head rests. The head, which is capable of traversing the tape in either direction, is attached to a black-box capable of entering any one of a finite number of states. Each basic operation of the device is governed by the current state q of the black box and the symbol a under the reading head. In Turing's original formulation, each basic operation took the form

$$(q, a) \rightarrow (b, p, D),$$

where q and p are states, a and b are symbols, and $D \in \{left, right, stay\}$, and described the following action:

'If the current state is q and the square under scan contains the symbol a, then replace a by b, change state to p, and move the reading head one square to the left (if $D = left$), or one square to the right (if $D = right$), or leave the reading head where it is (if $D = stay$)'.

To ensure a deterministic mode of operation, each non-terminal state q and symbol a is associated with a *unique* basic operation. Given such a device, and assuming a suitable input and output convention for representing the initial data and final results on the tape, the computation proceeds in a straightforward step by step fashion. At each moment of time the basic operation associated with the current state and symbol under scan is applied, until the terminal state is entered, if it ever is, when the computation terminates. The output is then taken from the final configuration of the tape.

To give one reasonable input and output convention for computations with non-negative integers, suppose that among the alphabet of symbols there occurs a 0 (or blank symbol) and a 1 (or stroke symbol). To input an integer $x \geqslant 0$, we can initialize the tape in the form

$$\ldots 001^x 00 \ldots$$

$$\triangle$$

start

indicating that the tape is everywhere blank except for a sequence of x strokes immediately to the left of the square initially under scan, and the initial state of the black-box is the *start* state.

To output an integer $y \geqslant 0$, we can suppose that the terminal configuration of the tape has the form

$$\ldots \text{anything } 0 \; 1^y \; 0 \text{ anything} \ldots$$

$$\triangle$$

halt

Regarding these devices, which he called machines, Turing proposed the following thesis: *with suitable representation of the data, every algorithm can be realized as a Turing machine.*

Note that Turing machines are not machines in the sense we have been using this word. Rather, each Turing machine corresponds to the idea of a program-machine pair in which an underlying machine and a fixed program are considered together as one operational unit. We shall reformulate Turing's model within our standard framework, in order to bring this underlying machine to the surface.

Definition. The machine TURING consists of a single register K, capable of containing an arbitrary positive or negative integer, and an array $\ldots S(-2)$, $S(-1), S(0), S(1), \ldots$ each element of which can contain an arbitrary non-negative integer. The input function, for argument $x \geqslant 0$, initializes

$$S(-t) = 1 \quad \text{for } 1 \leqslant t \leqslant x,$$

and sets all other registers to zero. The output function extracts y from the memory set, where

$$S(t) = 1 \quad \text{for } 1 \leqslant t \leqslant y \quad \text{and} \quad S(y + 1) = 0.$$

(These functions correspond to the conventions described above). In addition, TURING defines the following operations and tests:

$$\text{operations} \quad K := K + 1, \; K := K - 1 \quad \text{and}$$
$$S(K) := n$$
$$\text{tests} \quad \quad S(K) = n,$$

where n is an arbitrary non-negative integer.

We now claim that an equivalent formulation of Turing's model results from replacing the idea of a Turing machine with the idea of a *flowchart program* for TURING. The array S corresponds to the tape, and the register K indicates the current position of the read–write head. The operations and tests on $S(K)$ correspond to reading and printing a symbol n. The set of such symbols is clearly finite for each given TURING flowchart P, since no arithmetic operations are allowed on the array elements. Moreover, each label in P corresponds to a state of the black box and vice-versa. We have merely broken up the notion of a basic operation into the four constituent actions:

$$K: = K + 1 \quad \text{'move right'}$$
$$K: = K - 1 \quad \text{'move left'}$$
$$S(K): = n \quad \text{'print } n\text{'}$$
$$S(K) = n \quad \text{'read } n\text{'}.$$

The result we wish to prove can now be stated.

Theorem 4. TURING is equivalent to NORMA.

Proof. To prove that TURING can simulate NORMA, we shall show that TURING can simulate NORMA2 and appeal to Theorem 2. Strictly speaking, this method of proof is unsatisfactory since it only shows that TURING can simulate NORMA in the sense of Definition 1.4 which allows the use of coding and decoding functions. Nevertheless, the following proof is easily extended to a direct simulation of NORMA by TURING.

The contents x and y of NORMA2's registers X and Y is coded in TURING's memory by taking

$$S(-t) = 1 \quad \text{for } 1 \leqslant t \leqslant x, \qquad S(t) = 1 \quad \text{for } 1 \leqslant t \leqslant y$$

and all other registers zero. TURING's input function initializes the array in the desired manner, and the output function extracts the contents of Y. We shall indicate the nature of the simulation, by programming the operations $X: = X + 1$ and $Y: = Y - 1$.

The former translates as

$$K: = K - 1;$$
$$\textbf{until } S(K) = 0 \textbf{ do } K: = K - 1;$$
$$S(K): = 1;$$
$$\textbf{until } S(K) = 0 \textbf{ do } K: = K + 1,$$

which changes the array element $S(-x - 1)$ to 1 and returns K to its original value zero. The operation $Y: = Y - 1$ translates as

$$K: = K + 1;$$
$$(\textbf{if } S(K) = 0 \textbf{ then } K: = K - 1$$
$$\textbf{else until } S(K) = 0 \textbf{ do } K: = K + 1;$$

$$K := K - 1; S(K) := 0; K := K - 1;$$
$$\textbf{until } S(K) = 0 \textbf{ do } K := K - 1),$$

which, provided $y > 0$, changes the array element $S(y)$ to 0 and resets K to zero. Further details are omitted.

To prove that NORMA can simulate TURING, we code each array configuration $\ldots, s_{-2}, s_{-1}, s_0, s_1, \ldots$ into three numbers

$$a = p_1^{s_{-1}} p_2^{s_{-2}} \ldots,$$
$$b = s_0,$$

and
$$c = p_1^{s_1} p_2^{s_2} \ldots,$$

which are stored in three NORMA registers, A, B, and C. The contents of TURING's index register K, which may take on negative values, is stored in two NORMA registers S and T, and contains the sign and absolute value of K respectively. With this representation, an operation $K := K + 1$ translates into the code

$$\textbf{(if } S = 0 \textbf{ then } T := T + 1 \textbf{ else}$$
$$\textbf{(if } T = 1 \textbf{ then } T := 0; S := 0$$
$$\textbf{else } T := T - 1)).$$

An operation $S(K) := n$ is translated as

$$\textbf{(if } T = 0 \textbf{ then } B := n$$
$$\textbf{else } P := \text{PRIME}(T);$$
$$\textbf{(if } S = 0 \textbf{ then } \text{SET}(A) \textbf{ else } \text{SET}(C))),$$

where SET(A), for example, is defined as

$$\textbf{while } div(P,A) \textbf{ do } A := A/P;$$
$$A := P \times A; A := P \times A; \ldots; A := P \times A \quad (n \text{ times}).$$

In a similar fashion, the other operations can be programmed for NORMA. To initialize the NORMA registers, we must include the program

$$T := 1; A := 1; C := 1;$$
$$\textbf{until } X = 0 \textbf{ do}$$
$$(P := \text{PRIME}(T); A := A \times P; T := T + 1; X := X - 1);$$
$$T := 0,$$

which ensures that the initial value a of A is

$$a = p_1 p_2 \ldots p_x.$$

To extract the final result, a similar program has to be executed before the simulation terminates, but we shall leave its construction, and those of the other operations, to the reader. This completes a rather sketchy proof.

Theorem 4 convincingly demonstrates the equivalence of the two different approaches to the problem of defining algorithms, and increases our confidence in the validity of the NORMA thesis.

3.4 A universal program

As a final test of NORMA's abilities, consider the following problem. Given any NORMA flowchart P and some input x, we can construct the computation of P on NORMA with input x, and, provided it terminates, discover the value of $normaP(x)$. In other words, there is a simple partial algorithm which, given a program P and integer x as inputs, will determine the value of $normaP(x)$, provided the value is defined. We call the algorithm *partial*, since for some inputs the process may not terminate. The problem is to program this algorithm for NORMA, i.e. to find a NORMA program I such that

$$normaI(c(P,x)) = normaP(x),$$

for each program P and integer x, where c is some suitable coding function. I can therefore be regarded as a *universal* NORMA program which is capable of interpreting every other NORMA program. Recalling the definition of a control machine from Section 1.6, it is clear that an equivalent formulation of the problem is given in the statement of the following theorem.

Theorem 5. NORMA can simulate its control machine.

Proof. Since the input set of $C(\text{NORMA})$, the control machine of NORMA, consists of pairs (P, x) of flowchart programs P and integers x, and is consequently different from NORMA's input set, we must first define a suitable coding function c. Once we have coded P into an integer p, the function c can be defined by

$$c(P, x) = 2^p 3^x,$$

so we are left with the problem of finding a representation of flowchart programs as single integers. Section 1 tells us how to do this. We represent the flowchart as a set of labelled instructions, choosing labels from the set $\{0, 1, \ldots, n\}$, where 1 is the initial label and 0 is the unique terminal label. Next, each instruction is coded as four numbers (a, b, c, d), where c and d are labels, and a and b are specified according to the following table:

a—instruction type	b—register involved
0 test instruction	1 input register X
1 increment operation	2 output register Y
2 decrement operation	3 register A_1
	4 register A_2, etc.

Thus, for example, the instruction **if** $A_2 = 0$ **then goto** 3 **else goto** 4 is coded as $(0, 4, 3, 4)$. For operation instructions we suppose $c = d$. If (a_j, b_j, c_j, d_j) are the four numbers associated with instruction labelled j, then we define

$$i_j = \sigma^4(a_j, b_j, c_j, d_j)$$

and take

$$p = \sigma^n(i_1, i_2, \ldots, i_n).$$

To define the simulation, we have to show how a typical memory configuration (P, l, v) of $C(\text{NORMA})$, where P is a flowchart, l is a label, and v is a typical NORMA memory configuration, can be coded into NORMA registers. We use three registers:

P to hold p the code of flowchart P,

L to hold l

V to hold $p_1^x p_2^y p_3^{a_1} p_4^{a_2} \ldots$ where $v = (x, y, a_1, a_2, \ldots)$ is an element of NORMA's memory set.

Now, $C(\text{NORMA})$ defines one test TERMINAL and one operation NEXTSTEP. The test TERMINAL is translated simply as the test $L = 0$. To translate NEXTSTEP (see Section 1.6 for its meaning), we use the following macros:

$$A: = B \times C$$

$$A: = B/C$$

$A: = \text{PRIME}(B)$ set $a = p_b$, where B contains b.

$A: = \sigma(J, B)$ set $a = $ exponent of p_j in the prime decomposition of b, where J contains j and B contains b,

and $A: = \sigma_j(B)$ similar to above, except that j is a given integer.

NEXTSTEP can now be translated into the following NORMA program:

if $L = 0$ **goto** *out*	: do nothing if l is a terminal label
$I: = \sigma(L, P)$	: find code of instruction l in P
$A: = \sigma_1(I)$	: find instruction type
$B: = \sigma_2(I)$	: find register involved
$C: = \sigma_3(I)$	: find exit labels
$D: = \sigma_4(I)$	
if $A \neq 0$ **goto** *op*	: jump if operation instruction
$E: = \sigma(B, V)$	: find contents of register
if $E = 0$ **goto** *zero*	
$L: = D$	: set $l = d$ if contents non-zero
goto *out*	
zero: $L: = C$	: set $l = c$ if contents zero

goto *out*

op: **if** $A \neq 1$ **goto** *dec*   : jump if decrement operation

       $E: = \text{PRIME}(B)$: increment exponent of p_b in v by 1

       $V: = V \times R$

       $L: = C$: set $l = c$

       goto *out*

dec: $E: = \text{PRIME}(B)$: decrement exponent of p_b in v by 1

       $V: = V/E$

       $L: = C$: set $l = c$

out:

In addition, we have to initialize P, L and V before each computation. This is achieved by the instructions

$$L: = 1; P: = \sigma_1(X); V: = \sigma_2(X); V: = 2^v.$$

Finally, we have to arrange that Y contains the terminal value at the end of each computation. This is achieved by the instruction

$$Y: = \sigma_2(V).$$

Applying this translation to the program

until TERMINAL **do** NEXTSTEP,

yields the NORMA program I for which

$$normaI(c(P, x)) = normaP(x).$$

Exercises

1. Prove that $\sigma(x, y) = 2^x(2y + 1)$ is a coding function for pairs of natural numbers. Construct the two inverse functions, and show how σ can be extended to code arbitrary n-tuples of natural numbers.

2. Show how the instructions

       j: **if** $A < 2$ **then goto** k **else goto** m

   and j: **if** $div(A, B)$ **then goto** k **else goto** m

   can be constructed as NORMA macros.

3. Program the arithmetic operations

$$A: = B + C \qquad A: = B - C$$
$$A: = B \times C \qquad A: = B/C$$

   for NORMA.

4. Construct the operations

   $A: = \sigma(J, B)$: set $a = \sigma_j(b)$ where J contains j

   $A: = \sigma_j(B)$: set $a = \sigma_j(b)$

   as **while** programs for NORMA.

5. The machine NORMAN is in all respects identical to NORMA except that it can store negative integers in its registers. Prove that for every NORMAN flowchart program we can find an equivalent NORMA flowchart program which uses no extra registers.

6. Suppose that in the definition of SAM we replace the array operations by the set

$$A(J): = K \quad \text{and} \quad K: = A(J).$$

Prove that NORMA can simulate this version of SAM.

7. In the proof of Theorem 2(i), show that it is possible to choose any of the following decoding functions:

$$d(x) = \sigma_1(x)$$
$$d(x) = \lfloor \log_2 x \rfloor$$
$$d(x) = \lfloor \log_3 x \rfloor,$$

where $\lfloor x \rfloor$ is the integer part of the real number x.

8. Complete the proof of Theorem 2(ii) by showing that for each IRMA procedure program we can find an equivalent NORMA2 procedure program. Is it possible to translate IRMA **while** programs into NORMA2 **while** programs?

9. Construct the operations

$$X: = k \uparrow X \quad \text{and} \quad X: = \lfloor \log_2 X \rfloor$$

as procedure programs for NORMA, without making use of any other registers as work space. ($\uparrow$ denotes exponentiation). Hence show that for any NORMA procedure program we can find an equivalent NORMA2 procedure program.

10. The machine NORMA1 is in all respects identical to NORMA except that it possesses only one register X, and the output is taken from X. Investigate the class of functions computable on NORMA1 by

    (a) **while** programs
    (b) flowchart programs
    (c) procedure programs.

11. Prove that every NORMA flowchart program can be translated into an equivalent NORMA **while** program.

12. Call a **while** program *simple* if it does not contain conditional statements. Show that every NORMA **while** program can be translated into an equivalent simple NORMA **while** program.

13. Construct a TURING program to square a given number.

14. Fill in the details of the proof of Theorem 4.

Chapter 4

Unsolvable Decision Problems

The previous chapter was concerned with the positive aspects of NORMA's capabilities; this one is concerned with some of the things that NORMA programs cannot do. In the following sections we shall describe a number of decision problems, and prove in each case that the associated function is not NORMA-computable. On the basis of our thesis that every algorithm can be realized as a NORMA program, we can then conclude that none of these problems is solvable by any algorithmic process.

Some of the decision problems concern properties of NORMA programs themselves, while others are of a purely combinatorial nature. One important example of the former sort is the problem of deciding, given a NORMA program P, whether or not P terminates for all inputs. Its unsolvability means that no effective general method for deciding termination can exist, even though particular methods may exist for particular programs. The existence of practically important, but algorithmically unsolvable, decision problems about programs not only demonstrates the theoretical limitations of programming, but also shows that we cannot hope to develop general methods for deciding properties of the programs we can construct.

4.1 More on coding

In Sections 3.1 and 3.4 we showed how to code each NORMA flowchart program P into a unique positive integer p. As a result, decision problems about programs can be translated into decision problems about integers. One disadvantage of our choice of coding function (which we shall denote by *code*) is that not every non-negative integer is the coding of some program. This technical inconvenience can be removed by introducing a new coding function *ncode*. In order to define *ncode*, consider the sequence of integers

$$p_0, p_1, p_2, \cdots$$

formed by arranging the set of coded programs (using *code*) in order of magnitude. If the code of program P appears as p_n in this sequence, i.e. if $code(P) = p_n$, then we define $ncode(P) = n$. In this manner, every program P is associated with a unique non-negative integer n, and conversely. We now show how the new coding function can be calculated.

In order to calculate $ncode(P)$ for a given P we first compute $p = code(P)$, and then take $ncode(P)$ to be the number of integers in the set $\{0, 1, \ldots, p - 1\}$ that

73

code programs under *code*. Since we can decide whether or not a given integer is the code of some program, say by a test *iscode*, this process is described by the following algorithm:

$$p: = code(P), \quad n: = 0;$$
$$\textbf{until } p = 0 \textbf{ do}$$
$$(p: = p - 1;$$
$$\textbf{if } iscode(p) \textbf{ then } n: = n + 1 \textbf{ else } I)$$

Conversely, to discover the program *P* coded under *ncode* by a given integer *n*, we perform the following computation:

$$n: = n + 1; \quad p: = 0;$$
$$\textbf{until } n = 0 \textbf{ do}$$
$$(p: = p + 1;$$
$$\textbf{if } iscode(p) \textbf{ then } n: = n - 1 \textbf{ else } I);$$
$$P: = decode(p).$$

Here, *decode(p)* gives the program *P* for which *code(P) = p*.

Henceforth, when we say that *p* is the code of *P*, we mean that $p = ncode(P)$.

4.2 The Self-Applicability problem

In this section we establish the unsolvability of a particular decision problem about NORMA programs called the Self-Applicability problem. While the Self-Applicability problem (abbreviated: the SA-problem) has a highly artificial nature, and possesses little practical interest, it is nevertheless the basis from which every other unsolvable result in the chapter is derived. It can be stated in the following form:

> to decide, given an arbitrary NORMA flowchart program *P*, whether or not *normaP(p)* is defined, where *p* is the code of *P*.

In other words, the SA-problem is to decide of an arbitrary NORMA flowchart *P*, whether or not the computation of *P* on NORMA with input *p* is terminating.

To show that the SA-problem is unsolvable, suppose that there does exist an algorithm which, when supplied with a description of *P*, returns the answer 0 if *normaP(p)* is defined, and the answer 1 otherwise. The form of the output is clearly not important as long as there are two distinct values. Using our thesis, we can therefore suppose that there exists a NORMA flowchart program *Q* such that

$$normaQ(p) = 0 \quad \text{if } normaP(p) \text{ is defined,}$$
$$= 1 \quad \text{otherwise.}$$

Here, we are making use of the same coding of programs into integers to represent the input program to *Q*. Since every integer corresponds to some program (see Section 1), there is no need to cater for the possibility that the input to *Q* is not a coded program.

Now, let us modify this hypothetical program Q a little, by adding an apparently innocuous loop at the end. Define R to be the program

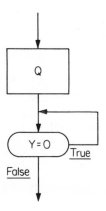

Thus R carries out each computation of Q but, before terminating, tests the output value of Q. If it is zero, then R fails to terminate, otherwise R terminates normally. To avoid drawing flowcharts for similar constructions on future occasions, we can mix the syntax of flowcharts and **while** programs a little, and define R as

$$Q;\ \textbf{while}\ Y = 0\ \textbf{do}\ (I).$$

Clearly,

$$normaR(x) = normaQ(x) \quad \text{if } normaQ(x) \neq 0,$$
$$= \text{undefined otherwise.}$$

So far, so good. But now let us try and determine the value of $normaR(r)$, where r is the coding of R:

(1) Suppose the value of $normaR(r)$ is undefined. From the definition of R it follows that $normaQ(r) = 0$, since Q always terminates. However, by the definition of Q, $normaQ(r) = 0$ just in the case that $normaR(r)$ is defined. This is a contradiction, and so $normaR(r)$ must be defined.

(2) Suppose then that the value of $normaR(r)$ is defined. From the definition of R we have that $normaQ(r) \neq 0$. But now, by the definition of Q, we must have $normaR(r)$ is undefined. Again we have a contradiction.

The only way out of this impasse is to drop our assumption that R can indeed be constructed. But R can certainly be constructed if Q can, and so Q cannot exist either. Hence no algorithm can exist and the Self-Applicability problem is unsolvable.

It is important to see exactly where the above argument depends upon acceptance of our thesis. What we have *formally* proved can be stated in the following way. Say that a set S is NORMA-*decidable* if there exists a NORMA flowchart program Q such that

$$normaQ(x) = 0 \quad \text{if } x \in S$$
$$= 1 \quad \text{otherwise.}$$

We have shown the following to be true.

Theorem 1.   The set $\{p: normaP(p)$ is defined$\}$ is not NORMA-decidable.

The conclusion we draw from Theorem 1, on the basis of our thesis, is that the set $\{p: normaP(p)$ is defined$\}$ is not decidable in any intuitive sense either.

4.3   Decision problems about programs

Many other decision problems about NORMA programs are unsolvable. In this section we shall establish the unsolvability (formally, the NORMA-undecidability) of every problem on the following list.

Name of problem	Input	To determine whether
Halting problem	P, x	$normaP(x)$ is defined.
Zero input halting problem	P	$normaP(0)$ is defined.
Emptiness problem	P	$normaP(x)$ is defined for at least one x.
Totality problem	P	$normaP(x)$ is defined for every x.
Equivalence problem	P, Q	$normaP = normaQ$

In each case, the unsolvability is derived by using the following important *reduction principle*:

(1) Let A and B be two decision problems. Suppose we can show how to modify any given algorithm for solving problem B into an algorithm for solving problem A. In other words, suppose we can *reduce* problem A to problem B.

(2) Suppose we already know that problem A is unsolvable.

(3) We can conclude that problem B is also unsolvable.

The validity of the reduction principle is fairly evident. As a result of step (1), we can conclude that problem A is solvable if problem B is solvable; but since A is known to be unsolvable, it follows that B is unsolvable as well. By reducing any known unsolvable problem to a given problem B, we can therefore establish the unsolvability of B. Of course, in reducing problems to others in this way, there must be no doubt that the modification can actually be carried out. Loosely speaking, we shall only modify algorithms by preprocessing the input. More formally, suppose P is a NORMA program for deciding B. The NORMA program Q for deciding A will always have the form

$$\text{Preprocess}(X); \ P$$

Provided that the preprocessing is a computable translation of the input, Q can always be constructed if P can.

As a simple application of the reduction principle, take B = Halting problem, the first problem on our list. Suppose there is a NORMA flowchart Q which will decide, given a suitable representation of each pair (P, x), whether or not $normaP(x)$ is defined. In fact, we can always design Q to interpret every input z in the form

$$z = 2^p 3^x \dots,$$

where p is the code of P. Let R be the program

$$X: = 6^X; Q.$$

Given any input p, R will set the input register X to the value $2^p 3^p$ and then enter Q. It is easy to see that R will decide whether or not $normaP(p)$ is defined, and so R is a program which solves the SA-problem. Since the SA-problem is unsolvable, so is the Halting problem.

In a similar fashion, we can reduce the SA-problem to the Zero input halting problem (abbreviated: the 0-Halting problem). For each NORMA flowchart P, let P' be the program

$$X: = p; P,$$

where p is the code of P. P' is easily constructed from P, and so the function f, for which $f(p) = p'$ where p' is the code of P', is clearly total and computable, if rather complicated. Suppose now Q is a program to decide the 0-Halting problem. Take R to be the program

$$X: = f(X); Q.$$

We claim that R will decide the SA-problem. To see why, consider the computation of R on NORMA with input p. If $f(p) = p'$, then from the definition of f,

$normaP'(0)$ is defined if and only if $normaP(p)$ is defined.

Since Q decides whether or not $normaP'(0)$ is defined, it follows that R will decide the SA-problem.

Exactly the same construction works in the reduction of the SA-problem to either the Emptiness or Totality problem. Look again at the definition of f. If $f(p) = p'$, then

(a) $normaP(p)$ is defined if and only if $normaP'(x)$ is defined for at least one x,

(b) $normaP(p)$ is defined if and only if $normaP'(x)$ is defined for every x.

Essentially, every computation of P' reduces after the first step to just one computation, the computation of P with input p. No matter what the original input to P' is, the first step immediately overwrites the contents of the input register X with p, and then continues with P. It follows that any program for deciding either the Emptiness problem or the Totality problem can at once be modified into a program for deciding the SA-problem. Hence these problems too are unsolvable.

As a final example, we reduce the Emptiness problem, now known to be unsolvable, to the Equivalence problem. Let LOOP denote the program

while $X = 0$ **do** (I); **while** $X \neq 0$ **do** (I).

It is clear that $normaLOOP(x)$ is undefined for every x. Moreover for any program P,

$P \equiv$ LOOP on NORMA if and only if $normaP(x)$ is undefined for every x.

Thus, given a program to decide the Equivalence problem, we can construct a program to decide the Emptiness problem. Hence the Equivalence problem is also unsolvable.

Formally, the above discussion has established the truth of the following theorem.

Theorem 2.   None of the following sets are NORMA-decidable:

(a) $\{2^p3^x: normaP(x)$ is defined$\}$,

(b) $\{p: normaP(0)$ is defined$\}$,

(c) $\{p: normaP(x)$ is defined for at least one $x\}$,

(d) $\{p: normaP(x)$ is defined for every $x\}$,

(e) $\{2^p3^q: normaP = normaQ\}$.

While each of the above decision problems concerned properties of NORMA programs, it is easy to see that similar results hold for any machine that can simulate NORMA. Suppose M is a machine that can simulate NORMA in the sense of Definition 1.3. This means that given any program P for NORMA, we can effectively find a program Q for M such that $mQ = normaP$. It follows that any algorithm for solving one of the above problems for M-programs can immediately be used for deciding the same problem about NORMA programs. In this way we can show, for example, that there is no algorithm to determine whether two ALGOL programs are equivalent.

If coding functions are allowed in the simulation, then we have to be a bit careful. For example, recall from Section 3.2 that both IRMA and NORMA2 can simulate NORMA, provided we allow the coding function $c(x) = 2^x$. Since $c(0) = 1$ it follows that we can reduce the 0-halting problem for NORMA to the 1-halting problem for either IRMA or NORMA2, and so these latter problems too are unsolvable. However, while the 0-halting problem for NORMA2 is undecidable (why?), there is a simple method for deciding if $irmaP(0)$ terminates for a given IRMA program P (see Exercise 4.9). The 0-halting problem for NORMA2 is used in the reduction to be described in the next section, and the 1-halting problem for IRMA in Section 4.5. Together they constitute perhaps the simplest unsolvable decision problems about programs that we could ever hope to achieve.

4.4 Post Normal Systems and the Post Correspondence Problem

In this section we establish the unsolvability of two decision problems of a combinatorial nature. They were originally formulated and proved unsolvable by the logician Emil Post. The first is surprisingly simple to state.

Post Correspondence Problem

Given two arbitrary sequences $(x_1, x_2, \ldots, x_n)$ and $(y_1, y_2, \ldots, y_n)$, of strings of symbols from some alphabet A, to determine whether or not there is a non-empty sequence of integers $i_1, i_2, \ldots i_k$ such that

$$x_{i_1} x_{i_2} \ldots x_{i_k} = y_{i_1} y_{i_2} \ldots y_{i_k}.$$

Such a sequence is called a *solution* to the correspondence problem.

Let us consider some examples. Suppose $A = \{a, b\}$, and let a^m abbreviate the string $aa \ldots a$ (m times).

Example 1

x	b^3	ab	b^2
y	b^2	bab^2	a^2b^2

Here we are representing the given sequences by a table, where $x_1 = b^3$, $y_1 = b^2$, $x_2 = ab$, $y_2 = bab^2$, etc. By inspection, we can see that

$$x_1 x_2 x_1 = b^3 abb^3 = y_1 y_2 y_1.$$

So, for this example, there is a solution to the correspondence problem.

Example 2

x	a	b^2a	a^2b	ab
y	ba	a^3	b	b^2a

Since each pair x_j, y_j begin with different symbols, no solution is possible.

Example 3

x	b	ab^2	a^2	b	ba
y	ba	bab	ab^2	a	aba

In this example, note that $|x_j| \leqslant |y_j|$ for $1 \leqslant j \leqslant 5$. Hence, for a solution

$$x_{i_1} x_{i_2} \ldots x_{i_k} = y_{i_1} y_{i_2} \ldots y_{i_k}$$

to exist, we must have $|x_{i_j}| = |y_{i_j}|$ for $1 \leqslant j \leqslant k$. However, $|x_j| = |y_j|$ only for $j = 2$ and 4, and the pairs (x_2, y_2) and (x_4, y_4) begin with different symbols. Hence no solution is possible.

We shall prove that, under the assumption that A contains at least two symbols, the Post Correspondence Problem (abbreviated: PCP) is unsolvable. It is left to the reader to formulate an effective necessary and sufficient condition to test whether two sequences of strings over a single-letter alphabet possess a correspondence solution.

The second combinatorial problem is closely related to the PCP. In fact, we shall establish its unsolvability first, and then reduce it to the PCP. First, we need to say what a Post Normal System is.

Post Normal Systems

Given an alphabet A, a Post Normal System consists of a designated string α_0 over A, called the *axiom*, together with a finite number of *productions* of the form

$$[\phi_i, \psi_i] \quad 1 \leqslant i \leqslant n,$$

where ϕ_i and ψ_i are strings over A. We say that a string β can be *derived* from a string α, and write $\alpha \Rightarrow \beta$, if $\alpha = \phi_i \gamma$ and $\beta = \gamma \psi_i$ for some production $[\phi_i, \psi_i]$. We write $\alpha \Rightarrow *\beta$ if there exists a sequence of strings $\gamma_0, \gamma_1, \ldots, \gamma_k$ such that $\alpha = \gamma_0, \gamma_j \Rightarrow \gamma_{j+1}$ for $0 \leqslant j < k$, and $\gamma_k = \beta$. A string β is *terminal* if for no γ can we have $\beta \Rightarrow \gamma$. Finally, we say that a PNS *terminates* if $\alpha_0 \Rightarrow *\beta$ for some terminal β, where α_0 is the axiom of the PNS.

The Post Normal System Problem (PNSP) is to determine whether or not a given PNS terminates.

Example 4. Suppose $A = \{0, 1\}$. Take $\alpha_0 = 101$, and the productions to be

$$[00, 0] \quad [01, 101]$$
$$[10, 11] \quad [11, 0].$$

Notice the set of productions have the property that, given any string α, at most one production can be applied to α, and so at most one terminal string can be derived from α. In such a case, the PNS is said to be *monogenic*. Since

$$101 \Rightarrow 111 \Rightarrow 10 \Rightarrow 11 \Rightarrow 0$$

and 0 is terminal, the PNS terminates.

In order to prove that the PNSP is unsolvable for an alphabet of more than one symbol, we reduce the 0-halting problem for NORMA2 flowchart programs to it. That is, we show how to construct for each NORMA2 flowchart P, a PNS which terminates if and only if $norma2P(0)$ is defined. Since the 0-halting problem for NORMA2 flowcharts is known to be unsolvable from Section 2, it follows that the PNSP too is unsolvable.

Suppose P is the given NORMA2 flowchart, written as a set of labelled instructions with labels in the set $\{0, 1, \ldots, n\}$, where 1 is the initial label and 0 is the unique terminal label. We are going to construct a *monogenic* PNS over the alphabet

$$\{0, a_0, a_1, \ldots, a_n, b_0, b_1, \ldots, b_n, c_0, c_1, \ldots, c_n\}$$

which will simulate P in the following sense: when P, at the kth step of its computation is about to execute the instruction labelled j on the contents (x, y) of

NORMA2's memory, then the PNS, at the kth step of its unique derivation, will have derived the string

$$\alpha_k = a_j 0^x b_j 0^y.$$

We take $\alpha_0 = a_1 b_1$ to be the axiom of the PNS, since this represents the initial configuration of P. Each instruction of P is translated into a set of productions as follows.

(1) if j: **do** $X := X + 1$ **then goto** k is in P, then construct the set of productions

$$[a_j, a_k 0], \quad [b_j, b_k] \quad \text{and} \quad [0, 0].$$

Applying these productions to a string $a_j 0^x b_j 0^y$, we obtain

$$a_j 0^x b_j 0^y \Rightarrow 0^x b_j 0^y a_k 0 \Rightarrow^* b_j 0^y a_k 0^{x+1} \Rightarrow^* a_k 0^{x+1} b_k 0^y.$$

(2) if j: **do** $Y := Y + 1$ **then goto** k is in P, then construct the set

$$[a_j, a_k], \quad [b_j, b_k 0] \quad \text{and} \quad [0, 0],$$

whose effect is analogous to (1), but 'increments' the second register.

(3) if j: **do** $X := X - 1$ **then goto** k is in P, then construct the set of productions

$$[a_j 0, a_k], \quad [a_j b_j, a_k b_k], \quad [b_j, b_k] \quad \text{and} \quad [0, 0].$$

Applying these productions to a string $a_j 0^x b_j 0^y$, where $x > 0$, we obtain

$$a_j 0^x b_j 0^y \Rightarrow 0^{x-1} b_j 0^y a_k \Rightarrow^* a_k 0^{x-1} b_k 0^y,$$

whereas if $x = 0$, then we obtain

$$a_j b_j 0^y \Rightarrow 0^y a_k b_k \Rightarrow^* a_k b_k 0^y,$$

in accordance with the effect of $X := X - 1$ when X is empty.

(4) if j: **do** $Y := Y - 1$ **then goto** k is in P, then construct the following set of productions:

$$[a_j, a_k], \quad [b_j 0, b_k], \quad [b_j a_k, c_j a_k], \quad [c_j, b_k] \quad \text{and} \quad [0, 0].$$

Here the simulation is not so straightforward. If $y \neq 0$ then, as a result of these productions,

$$a_j 0^x b_j 0^y \Rightarrow^* b_j 0^y a_k 0^x \Rightarrow 0^{y-1} a_k 0^x b_k \Rightarrow^* a_k 0^x b_k 0^{y-1},$$

and everything is simple. If however $y = 0$, then

$$a_j 0^x b_j \Rightarrow^* b_j a_k 0^x \Rightarrow 0^x c_j a_k \Rightarrow^* c_j a_k 0^x \Rightarrow a_k 0^x b_k,$$

which arrives at the desired derived string, but only by 'cycling' through the original string once again after the fact that $y = 0$ has been discovered.

(5) if j: **if** $X = 0$ **then goto** k **else goto** l is in P, then construct the productions

$$[a_j 0, a_l 0], \quad [b_j, b_l], \quad [a_j b_j, a_k b_k] \quad \text{and} \quad [0, 0].$$

Here we have

$$a_j 0^x b_j 0^y \Rightarrow 0^{x-1} b_j 0^y a_l 0 \Rightarrow^* a_l 0^x b_l 0^y,$$

provided $x > 0$, and

$$a_j b_j 0^y \Rightarrow^* a_k b_k 0^y$$

if $x = 0$.

(6) Finally, if j: **if** $Y = 0$ **then goto** k **else goto** l is in P, then construct the productions

$$[a_j, a_l], \quad [b_j 0, b_l 0], \quad [b_j a_l, c_j a_k], \quad [c_j, b_k] \quad \text{and} \quad [0, 0].$$

Supposing $y \neq 0$, we have

$$a_j 0^x b_j 0^y \Rightarrow^* b_j 0^y a_l 0^x \Rightarrow 0^{y-1} a_l 0^x b_l 0 \Rightarrow^* a_l 0^x b_l 0^y,$$

and if $y = 0$, then we have

$$a_j 0^x b_j \Rightarrow 0^x b_j a_l \Rightarrow^* b_j a_l 0^x \Rightarrow 0^x c_j a_k \Rightarrow^* c_j a_k 0^x \Rightarrow a_k 0^x b_k.$$

Provided we keep only one production of the form $[0, 0]$, the resulting PNS is clearly monogenic and has the desired properties. The derivation from $a_1 b_1$ will only terminate if a string of the form $a_0 0^x b_0 0^y$ is derived, in which case the original NORMA2 program P terminates also. Hence we have succeeded in reducing the 0-halting problem for NORMA2 flowcharts to the PNSP for a general alphabet A, and consequently the PNSP is unsolvable.

To get down to a two symbol alphabet we proceed as follows. Let P be a PNSP over an alphabet $A = \{a_1, a_2, \ldots, a_n\}$. Code each symbol $a_j \in A$ as a string α_j, where

$$\alpha_j = 0^j 1,$$

over a binary alphabet $B = \{0, 1\}$. If we code each string appearing in the definition of P by replacing each symbol from A with its binary encoding, then we obtain another PNSP over B which terminates if and only if P terminates. It follows that the PNSP for a two symbol alphabet is also unsolvable.

Finally, we establish the unsolvability of the Post Correspondence Problem. Consider again an arbitrary NORMA2 program P. We can easily arrange that, if P terminates with input 0, then it does so with final contents $(0, 0)$ of the two NORMA2 registers. Let Q be the Post Normal System constructed from P in the manner described above. We know that Q is monogenic, has axiom $a_1 b_1$, and if it terminates, then it does so on the terminal string $a_0 b_0$; i.e. Q terminates if and only if

$$a_1 b_1 \Rightarrow^* a_0 b_0.$$

For each production $[\phi_i, \psi_i]$ in Q, where $1 \leqslant i \leqslant n$, define the pair of strings Φ_i and Ψ_i as follows:

(a) Φ_i is ϕ_i with a new letter X inserted *after* every symbol of ϕ_i,

(b) Ψ_i is ψ_i with the new letter X inserted *before* every symbol of ψ_i.

We claim that Q terminates just in the case that the following correspondence problem has a solution:

x	X	Φ_1	Φ_2	$\ldots$	Φ_n	$a_0 X b_0 X$
y	$X a_1 X b_1$	Ψ_1	Ψ_2	$\ldots$	Ψ_n	X

To see why this claim is justified, consider the possible form of a solution $x_{i_1} x_{i_2} \ldots x_{i_k} = y_{i_1} y_{i_2} \ldots y_{i_k}$ of the correspondence problem. The first pair (x_{i_1}, y_{i_1}) must be $(X, X a_1, X b_1)$, since this is the only pair in the set that begins with the same letter, namely X. It follows that in the second pair (x_{i_2}, y_{i_2}), the string x_{i_2} must be an initial substring of $a_1 X b_1 \alpha$ for some string α. However, Q is monogenic, which means that there can only be one string x_{i_2} satisfying this requirement. Hence (x_{i_2}, y_{i_2}) is uniquely determined. Continuing in this fashion, it can be seen that each pair of the correspondence solution is uniquely determined. Moreover, if the solution does indeed exist, then the last pair must be $(a_0 X, b_0 X, X)$ since this is the only pair which ends with the same letter, namely X again. Remembering that Q simulates the computation of P with input 0, we can see that the solution of the PCP follows the course of the computation of P, transcribing the steps of P into one long string of symbols from Q interspersed with Xs. This string is finite if and only if the computation of P with input 0 terminates. In other words, the PCP has a solution if and only if $norma2P(0)$ is defined.

To see the process at work, let us consider a simple example. Consider the program P given by

$$1: \textbf{do } X: = X + 1 \textbf{ then goto } 2$$
$$2: \textbf{do } X: = X - 1 \textbf{ then goto } 0$$

Clearly, $norma2P(0)$ is defined and the final contents of both registers are zero with this computation. The Post Normal System Q associated with P has alphabet

$$\{0, a_0, a_1, a_2, b_0, b_1, b_2, c_0, c_1, c_2\},$$

axiom $a_1 b_1$, and the following productions:

$$[0, 0]$$

$$\left.\begin{array}{l} [a_1, a_2 0] \\ [b_1, b_2] \end{array}\right\} \text{for instruction 1}$$

$$\left.\begin{array}{l} [a_2 0, a_0] \\ [a_2 b_2, a_0 b_0] \\ [b_2, b_0] \end{array}\right\} \text{for instruction 2.}$$

Q terminates since

$$a_1 b_1 \Rightarrow b_1 a_2 0 \Rightarrow a_2 0 b_2 \Rightarrow b_2 a_0 \Rightarrow a_0 b_0.$$

The PCP associated with Q is given by the table

x	X	$0X$	a_1X	b_1X	a_2X0X	a_2Xb_2X	b_2X	a_0Xb_0X
y	Xa_1Xb_1	$X0$	Xa_2X0	Xb_2	Xa_0	Xa_0Xb_0	Xb_0	X

The unique solution, up to repetition, of the PCP is

$$x_1x_3x_4x_5x_7x_8$$
$$= y_1y_3y_4y_5y_7y_8$$
$$= Xa_1Xb_1Xa_2X0Xb_2Xa_0Xb_0X.$$

If we suppress the Xs and space out the solution, then we obtain

$$a_1b_1 \quad a_20b_2 \quad a_0b_0,$$

which transcribes the terminating computation

$$(1,(0,0)), \quad (2,(1,0)), \quad (0,(0,0))$$

of P.

4.5 An unsolvable equivalence problem

In this section we describe an unsolvable problem concerning register machine equivalence, partly because of the interesting construction involved, and partly to show how fine the dividing line between solvability and unsolvability can be. In 1971, Malcolm Bird discovered an algorithm to determine of any two flowchart programs, defined over the two operations and tests

$$R_j: = f(R_j), \quad p(R_j) \quad \text{for } 1 \leqslant j \leqslant 2,$$

whether or not they were equivalent on *all* register machines (i.e. under all interpretations of the identifiers f and p). However, if we allow just one extra operation

$$R_2: = f(R_1),$$

then the corresponding problem becomes unsolvable. Moreover, we only need this extra operation to occur in just one place, right at the beginning of the program, in order to establish unsolvability. The result was actually established in 1966 by Luckham and Park (see Luckham, Park and Paterson [1970]), although the proof that follows is different.

Let us say that P is a *simple* program if P is a flowchart over the identifiers

$$R_j: = f(R_j), \quad p(R_j) \quad \text{for } 1 \leqslant j \leqslant 2,$$

except that its first two instructions are the pair of assignments

$$R_2: = f(R_1); R_1: = f(R_1).$$

To avoid drawing flowcharts, we shall specify simple programs using **while** program constructions augmented with **goto** statements. Given any register machine M, the effect of the first two instructions of a simple program is to set both R_1 and R_2 equal to the same value x, whatever this value might be. Furthermore, the termination of a simple program P is dependent solely on the sequence of values of the tests

$$p_M(x), p_M(f_M x), p_M(f_M^2 x), \dots$$

By taking 0 for *false* and 1 for *true*, we can consider this sequence, uniquely determined by M and x, as an infinite sequence of 0s and 1s. If the computation of P on M with input n is terminating, and x is given by

$$x = f_M \cdot u_1^2 \cdot I_M(n),$$

i.e. x is the common value in R_1 and R_2 after the first two assignments in the computation sequence with input n, then the above sequence is said to be a *trace sequence for P*. Thus, P possesses a trace sequence if and only if there is some machine M and input n such that the computation of P on M with input n terminates. Let LOOP be the program

while $p(R_1)$ **do** (I); **until** $p(R_1)$ **do** (I).

It follows that

$$P \equiv \text{LOOP}$$

on all register machines, just in the case that P does *not* possess a trace sequence. The plan of attack can now be formulated. We are going to show how to associate with each IRMA program Q, a simple program P such that P has a trace sequence if and only if $irmaQ(1)$ is defined. Since the 1-halting problem for IRMA is unsolvable, it follows that the equivalence problem for simple programs is also unsolvable. The trace sequence of P, if it exists, will have the form

$$0^{a_1}10^{a_2}1\dots0^{a_n}1\alpha,$$

where α is arbitrary, $a_1 = 1$, and, in general, a_j is the contents of IRMA's register immediately before the execution of the jth step of Q. The integer n is determined by the fact that Q terminates after $(n - 1)$ steps.

To shorten the description of P, let us abbreviate the programs

while $p(R_2)$ **do** (I); $R_2 := f(R_2)$ by ZERO

and   **until** $p(R_2)$ **do** (I); $R_2 := f(R_2)$ by ONE

ZERO only terminates if the value of $p(R_2)$ is *false*, which corresponds to a zero in the trace sequence, and ONE only terminates if the value of $p(R_2)$ is *true*, corresponding to a one in the trace sequence.

The simple program P starts off with the code

$$R_2 := f(R_1); R_1 := f(R_1); \text{ZERO}; \text{ONE}.$$

This piece of program ensures that if P has a trace sequence, then it must be one beginning with the sequence 01. If the trace sequence began with a 1, then the value of $p(R_2)$ would be *true* on entry to ZERO, and so ZERO would fail to terminate. Similarly, ONE only terminates if the next symbol in the sequence is 1. Consider now the situation which arises if and when the above program terminates. The value of the test $p(R_1)$ at this point must be 0; it cannot be 1 since there are no assignments to R_1 in ZERO or ONE, and so R_1 still contains the original value of R_2. Moreover, we also know that the value of $p(f(R_1))$ is 1, since the program has successfully passed through the program ONE. The situation can therefore be pictured as follows:

$$p(x) \qquad p(fx) \qquad p(f^2x)$$
$$0 \qquad\quad 1 \qquad\quad ?$$
$$\uparrow p(R_1) \qquad\qquad \uparrow p(R_2)$$

This picture describes the essence of the simulation. The value of $p(R_2)$ always 'keeps ahead' of $p(R_1)$, and consequently determines the future values of $p(R_1)$. At the same time, the program can 'remember' past values of $p(R_2)$ by referring to the current value of $p(R_1)$.

The rest of P is determined by the instructions of Q as follows:

(1) if Q contains j: **do** $X := 2 \times X$ **then goto** k, then P contains

j: **until** $p(R_1)$ **do**
$\qquad$ (ZERO; ZERO; $R_1 := f(R_1)$);
$\qquad$ ONE; $R_1 := f(R_1)$; **goto** k

This segment of P determines further values of the trace sequence as follows: if on entry to the segment the picture is

$$\overbrace{}^{n}$$
$$0\,0...0\,1\,?$$
$$\uparrow \qquad\ \uparrow$$
$$p(R_1) \quad p(R_2)$$

and if the segment terminates, then on exit the picture will be

$$\overbrace{}^{n}\ \overbrace{}^{2n}$$
$$0\,0...0\,1\,0\,0...0\,1\,?$$
$$\uparrow \qquad\qquad \uparrow$$
$$p(R_1) \qquad p(R_2)$$

In order to 'multiply' by an arbitrary constant, we simply need to include an appropriate number of ZERO instructions in the segment.

(2) if Q contains j: **do** $X := X/2$ **then goto** k, then P contains

j: **until** $p(R_1)$ **do**
$\qquad$ ($R_1 := f(R_1)$; (**if** $p(R_1)$ **then** I **else** ZERO
$\qquad\qquad\qquad\qquad\qquad$ $R_1 := f(R_1)$));

$$\text{ONE}; R_1: = f(R_1); \textbf{goto } k$$

Here, we are supposing $X/2 = \lfloor X/2 \rfloor$, if 2 does not divide X.

(3) if Q contains j: **if** $2|X$ **then goto** k **else goto** l, then P contains

j: **until** $p(R_1)$ **do**
$$(\text{ZERO}; R_1: = f(R_1);$$
$$(\textbf{if } p(R_1) \textbf{ then } \text{ONE}; R_1: = f(R_1); \textbf{goto } l$$
$$\textbf{else } \text{ZERO}; R_1: = f(R_1)));$$
$$\text{ONE}; R_1: = f(R_1); \textbf{goto } k$$

The translations under (2) and (3) are easily generalized in the case of division by an arbitrary constant. Translation (3), because it contains a jump out of a **while** loop, is the only translation not corresponding to a proper **while** program. With a little thought, since this type of curious simulation takes some getting used to, it will be seen that P does indeed have the desired properties.

Exercises

1. How can we code NORMA flowchart programs so that each program is represented by a unique *positive* integer, and conversely?

2. Show that the problem of deciding, given a NORMA flowchart P, whether or not $normaP(x) = 0$ for some x, is unsolvable.

3. Construct a fixed program P such that the problem of deciding, given x, whether or not $normaP(x)$ is defined, is unsolvable.

4. Suppose P and Q are two NORMA flowcharts. Say that P *includes* Q if $normaQ(x) = normaP(x)$ for all x such that $normaQ(x)$ is defined. In other words, P includes Q if the function $normaP$ is a possibly trivial extension of $normaQ$. Prove that the problem of deciding, given P and Q, whether or not P includes Q, is unsolvable.

5. Prove that S is NORMA-decidable if and only if $\bar{S}$, the complement of S, is NORMA-decidable.

6. Say that a set of S of positive integers is NORMA-*enumerable* if there exists a NORMA flowchart P such that $normaP$ is total and
$$S = \{normaP(x): normaP(x) > 0\}.$$

Prove that S is NORMA-decidable if and only if S and $\bar{S}$ are both NORMA-enumerable.

7. Let $T = \{p: normaP \text{ total}\}$ and $S = \{p: normaP(p) \text{ is defined}\}$, where the coding of programs is into positive integers, as described in Exercise 1. Show that S is NORMA-enumerable, but T is not.

8. Let M be any number theoretic machine with the ability to test the output value for zero. Show that the set $\{p: mP(p) \text{ is defined}\}$ is not M-decidable.

9. Show: (a) the 0-halting problem for NORMA2 is unsolvable, (b) the 0-halting problem for IRMA is solvable.

10. Give algorithms to decide: (a) whether or not a Post Correspondence problem over a single symbol alphabet has a solution, (b) whether or not a Post Normal System over a single symbol alphabet terminates.

Chapter 5
The Correctness of Programs

We have seen in the previous chapter that many decision problems connected with programs are unsolvable. This is an unfortunate situation, since a number of these problems are important to the practical activity of program construction. For instance, a programmer who designs a program to carry out a particular task usually wishes to know that his program terminates under certain stated assumptions about the input; he may also want to know that his program is equivalent to a second, possibly less efficient, program. Both termination and equivalence can be regarded as aspects of the problem of program *correctness*, i.e. the problem of determining that a program actually carries out its designer's intention. However, for NORMA programs at least, both the termination and equivalence problems are algorithmically unsolvable.

In attempting to overcome the phenomenon of unsolvability, two basic approaches are possible. The first is to discover suitable restrictions on the class of programs and machines under which the decision problem in question becomes solvable. However, it is apparent that the restrictions would have to be fairly drastic, since some very simple machines, e.g. IRMA and NORMA2, are universal machines even with the most basic types of program structure, and so possess the same unsolvability characteristics as more general machines and languages. Since the programs we encounter in practice are unlikely to conform to the restrictions, such an approach, while theoretically interesting, is of limited practical value.

The second approach, which we shall elaborate on at some length in the remaining chapters, is to abandon the goal of an algorithmic solution, and try instead to discover general mathematical techniques useful in the task of proving properties of particular programs. The hope is to be able to create a sufficiently general framework of deductive techniques, within which particular properties can be shown to hold for particular programs, even though the proofs cannot be constructed in a purely mechanical fashion.

The purpose of this chapter is to examine in more detail the problem of program correctness, and to describe an axiomatic approach for proving the correctness of a given program. In Chapters 6 and 7 we shall develop a second method for proving correctness, based on the idea of interpreting programs as recursively defined functions.

5.1   Termination, equivalence and correctness

The particular program properties with which we shall be mainly concerned are the properties of termination, equivalence and correctness. The first two have been described previously, but it is convenient to give the definitions again. Suppose P and Q are given programs, and M is a machine with input set X. We say that

$$P \text{ terminates on } M \text{ if } mP(x) \text{ is defined for all } x \in X,$$

and

$$P \text{ is equivalent to } Q \text{ on } M \text{ if } mP(x) = mQ(x) \text{ for all } x \in X.$$

To simplify subsequent definitions, we shall often omit explicit reference to the machine M when it is clear from the context that a particular machine is being understood.

In practice, we may be interested in the termination or equivalence of programs only for those inputs x which satisfy a given condition $\phi(x)$. For example, ϕ may be given by

$$\phi(x): x \text{ is a prime number greater than 2}$$

or

$$\phi(x, y): x \text{ and } y \text{ are positive integers with } x \leqslant y.$$

The definitions of termination and equivalence can be generalized to deal with assumptions about the input, as follows:

P terminates with respect to ϕ (on M) if $mP(x)$ is defined for all $x \in X$ such that $\phi(x)$ is true;

P is equivalent to Q with respect to ϕ (on M) if $mP(x) = mQ(x)$ for all $x \in X$ such that $\phi(x)$ is true.

In order to define the correctness condition of a given program P, it is necessary to find some way of describing precisely what it is that P is intended to do. Broadly speaking, there are three ways in which this can be done:

(a)   by giving a second program Q which is already known to be correct, so that the correctness of P is expressed as the condition that P is equivalent to Q on the appropriate machine;

(b)   by writing down an assertion $\psi(x, y)$ which describes the intended relation between the input value x and the output value y on termination of P;

(c)   by directly describing the function f which P is supposed to compute.

The basic distinction between the assertion method (b) and the functional method (c) lies in the different types of language required for expressing the correctness condition. For the assertion method we require a suitable language for writing down meaningful and useful assertions, i.e. true–false statements, possibly expressing such assertions as combinations of simpler ones, while in the functional approach the need is for a language for describing a whole variety of functions. The task of constructing a language for defining functions simply and succinctly is an interesting one, and Chapters 6 and 7 are devoted to the subject. One of the advantages of the functional method is that it often allows the correctness condition to be stated in a form which corresponds more directly to intuition, especially when the question of termination is involved. In the assertion method, with which the rest of this chapter is concerned, it is usually more convenient to prove correctness and termination in two separate stages. This division of the problem of correctness into two parts is captured in the following two definitions:

> *P is partially correct with respect to ϕ and ψ (on M)* if $\psi(x,mP(x))$ is true for every $x \in X$ such that $\phi(x)$ is true and $mP(x)$ is defined.

> *P is totally correct with respect to ϕ and ψ (on M)* if $mP(x)$ is defined and $\psi(x, mP(x))$ is true for every $x \in X$ such that $\phi(x)$ is true.

Partial correctness is thus a weaker condition than total correctness, since the question of termination is not involved. In fact, one can easily see that a program P is totally correct with respect to ϕ and ψ if and only if P is partially correct with respect to ϕ and ψ and P terminates with respect to ϕ.

In practice, proofs of termination, and hence of total correctness, can be extremely difficult. For example, many famous unsolved problems in Number Theory can be formulated as termination problems of quite simple programs. As an illustration, consider the unsolved problem of determining whether or not there exists infinitely many perfect numbers, where a natural number x is *perfect* if the sum of its divisors, including 1 but excluding x itself, adds up to x. It is easy to write a short program for generating the nth perfect number, if it exists, given input n. Clearly, such a program terminates for all inputs if and only if there does indeed exist an infinite number of perfect numbers. As an even simpler demonstration of the difficulty of proving termination, consider the program

> **while** $x \neq 1$ **do**
>> **if** $2 \mid x$ **then** $x: = x \div 2$ **else** $x: = 3x + 1$.

No-one has yet succeeded in showing that this program terminates for all inputs $x \geqslant 1$.

These examples illustrate the difficulty of total correctness proofs, and show why we shall concentrate on the weaker condition of partial correctness. Nevertheless, this problem too is unsolvable; there is no algorithm to determine, given P, ϕ and ψ, whether or not P is partially correct with respect to ϕ and ψ. To see this, recall from Chapter 4 that the problem of determining whether a given NORMA program P halts with input 0 is unsolvable. Now, *normaP*(0) is *not* defined just in the case that P is partially correct with respect to ϕ and ψ, where

$$\phi(x): x = 0$$
$$\psi(x, y): \textit{false.}$$

Hence if we can solve the problem of partial correctness for NORMA programs, then we can solve the 0-input termination problem, and this is impossible.

Before we can develop a method for dealing with the partial correctness of particular programs, it is necessary to first introduce some simple notation, drawn from mathematical logic, for describing assertions such as ϕ and ψ in a short and convenient form.

5.2 Notation from the Predicate Calculus

Many mathematical statements can be expressed as suitable combinations of simpler statements. For example, the assertion

x is a prime greater than 2

can be expressed in the equivalent form

x is a prime and x is greater than 2.

Here, use is made of the basic propositional connective *and* to combine two simple statements into a more complicated one. Apart from *and*, there are a number of other basic connectives, such as *or*, *not*, *implies*, etc., which occur with sufficient frequency that it is useful to introduce special symbols for them.

Suppose P and Q are statements; we define

(i) $P \wedge Q$ (read: *P and Q*) to be the statement which is true just in the case that both P and Q are true;

(ii) $P \vee Q$ (read: *P or Q*) to be the statement which is true just in the case that at least one of P and Q is true;

(iii) $P \supset Q$ (read: *P implies Q*) to be the statement which is false just in the case that P is true and Q is false;

(iv) $\sim P$ (read: *not P*) to be the statement which is true just in the case that P is false.

There is one further useful propositional connective which combines three statements into one:

(v) $(P \rightarrow Q, R)$ (read: *if P then Q else R*)—the statement which is true just in the case that either both P and Q are true, or both $\sim P$ and R are true.

When writing down compound statements involving two or more connectives, parentheses can be used to resolve possible ambiguity. Thus, for example, we would write $P \wedge (Q \supset R)$ or $(P \wedge Q) \supset R$ rather than the ambiguous $P \wedge Q \supset R$. However, the use of parentheses can be minimized by adopting a conventional order of precedence among the connectives, just as in ordinary arithmetic expressions in which multiplication ($\times$) is regarded as more binding than addition ($+$). We shall regard negation ($\sim$) as more binding than conjunction ($\wedge$) and disjunction ($\vee$), and these in turn as more binding than implication ($\supset$). Thus,

$$\sim P \wedge Q \quad \text{means} \quad (\sim P) \wedge Q,$$

$$P \wedge Q \supset R \quad \text{means} \quad (P \wedge Q) \supset R$$

and
$$P \supset Q \vee R \quad \text{means} \quad P \supset (Q \vee R).$$

Notice that some propositional connectives can be defined in terms of others. For example, $P \vee Q$ is equivalent to $\sim(\sim P \wedge \sim Q)$, and $(P \to Q, R)$ is equivalent to $(P \wedge Q) \vee (\sim P \wedge R)$. In fact, if we suppose that T and F denote statements which are always true and false respectively, then each of the first four connectives can be described solely in terms of the fifth connective as follows:

(i) $P \wedge Q$ is equivalent to $(P \to Q, F)$

(ii) $P \vee Q$ is equivalent to $(P \to T, Q)$

(iii) $P \supset Q$ is equivalent to $(P \to Q, T)$

(iv) $\sim P$ is equivalent to $(P \to F, T)$

As it stands, the assertion

$$x \text{ is prime} \wedge (x > 2)$$

is not a true–false statement, since it refers to an unknown quantity x. Only when appropriate substitutions are made for x—in this case natural numbers—does the statement yield a truth value. Such statements are called *predicates*, and are denoted by $P(x), Q(x)$, etc. In the definition of a predicate $P(x)$, the set S of possible values of the free variable x is implicitly understood. There are two important operations associated with predicates, which we can define as follows:

universal quantification: if $P(x)$ is a predicate involving the free variable x, then

$$\forall x \in S . P(x)$$

(read: *for all $x \in S$, $P(x)$*) describes the statement which is true if and only if $P(x)$ is true for every $x \in S$.

existential quantification: if $P(x)$ is a predicate involving the free variable x, then

$$\exists x \in S . P(x)$$

(read: *there exists an $x \in S$ such that $P(x)$*) describes the statement which is true if and only if $P(x)$ is true for at least one $x \in S$.

When the definition of S is clear from the context, we can write more simply $\forall x . P(x)$ and $\exists x . P(x)$. Notice the distinction between the variables x and y in the statement

$$\forall x . P(x, y).$$

Here, y is a free variable since we are free to make arbitrary substitutions for y. On the other hand, x is a dummy or *bound* variable, since such substitutions are not possible for x. In other words, $\forall x . P(x, y)$ is a predicate involving the variable y alone.

The operations of universal and existential quantification are very flexible, as the following examples show:

1. The statement

$$\exists x . \forall y . P(y) \supset y = x$$

asserts that the predicate $P(x)$ holds for *at most one* x. Notice that, by the definition of $\supset$, the statement remains true in the case that $P(x)$ holds for no x.

2. The statement

$$\exists x . [P(x) \wedge \forall y . [P(y) \supset y = x]]$$

on the other hand, asserts that there is *exactly one* x such that $P(x)$ holds. Here, square brackets have been used to improve the clarity of the expression by delimiting the scope of each quantified variable. Note that

$$Q \wedge \forall x . P(x) \quad \text{and} \quad \forall x . [Q \wedge P(x)]$$

are equivalent expressions, provided that Q does not depend on x. Thus, an equivalent formulation of unique existence is

$$\exists x . \forall y . [P(x) \wedge [P(y) \supset y = x]].$$

3. Consider how the predicate 'x is prime' may be expressed in terms of simpler predicates. By definition, a natural number x is prime if x is greater than 1 and the only divisors of x are 1 and x itself. The phrase 'the only divisors of x are 1 and x itself' can be rendered symbolically as

$$\forall y . [y \ divides \ into \ x \supset y = 1 \vee y = x].$$

Furthermore, we can give the condition that y divides into x in the form

$$\exists z . y \times z = x,$$

and so express the primality of x in the form

$$(x > 1) \wedge \forall y . [\exists z . y \times z = x \supset y = 1 \vee y = x].$$

4. Finally, consider the assertion 'y is the maximum element in the set $\{x(1), x(2), \ldots, x(n)\}$'. This can be formulated as

$$\exists j . [1 \leq j \leq n \wedge x(j) = y] \wedge \forall j . [1 \leq j \leq n \supset x(j) \leq y]$$

combining the conditions that y must be a member of the set, and also an upper bound.

5.3   Proof of partial correctness

We shall now describe the axiomatic method, due to Floyd and Hoare, for proving the partial correctness of programs. We shall only be concerned with the method as it applies to the class of **while** programs defined in Chapter 1. The first step is to introduce a simple piece of notation for expressing a generalized version of the partial correctness condition.

Suppose P is a program and M is a machine with input set X and memory set V, and suppose $A(x, v)$ and $B(x, v)$ are predicates involving $x \in X$ and $v \in V$. By definition, the assertion

$$\{A(x, v)\} P\{B(x, v)\}$$

means that if $A(x, v)$ is true prior to the computation of P on M with input x and initial contents v of V, and if, moreover, this computation terminates, then $B(x, v)$ is true on completion of the computation, where v now denotes the *final* contents of V. Thus the two occurrences of v describe different memory contents. Unlike v, the value of the input variable x never changes once it is given; its presence is useful because it enables one to describe relationships between the original input and the current contents of the memory set. Another way of describing the meaning of the notation can be given if we let $P(v)$ denote the final contents of V after the computation of P with initial contents v of V, the machine M being understood. The assertion $\{A(x, v)\} P\{B(x, v)\}$ is then equivalent to

$$\forall w . [A(x, v) \wedge P(v) = w \supset B(x, w)].$$

It is easy to express the partial correctness of a program P in terms of the notation $\{A\} P\{B\}$: P is partially correct with respect to ϕ and ψ if and only if the assertion

$$\{\phi(x) \wedge v = I_M(x)\} P\{\psi(x, O_M(v))\}$$

holds for all $x \in X$ and $v \in V$.

At the heart of the axiomatic method is an axiom for generating true assertions of the form

$$\forall x, v . \{A(x, v)\} P\{B(x, v)\},$$

when P consists of a single operation identifier. The most general formulation of this axiom is as follows:

operation axiom (for a machine M):

$$\vdash \{A(x, F_M(v))\} F\{A(x, v)\}.$$

In the statement of the axiom, F denotes any operation identifier, and A is any predicate. The symbol $\vdash$ is read as 'it is true that ....' or 'it can be deduced that ....'. Since x and v are not specified and so can take any value, the axiom actually states

$$\vdash \forall x, v . \{A(x, F_M(v))\} F\{A(x, v)\},$$

but for simplicity we shall usually omit the universal quantifiers. The axiom can be justified by observing that if $A(x, v)$ is to be true of the values x and v after the operation F_M has been performed, then the statement $B(x, v)$, where $B(x, v) = A(x, F_M(v))$, must have been true beforehand.

When M is a register machine, as in practice will always be the case, the operation axiom can be stated in a slightly more convenient form. Suppose M is a register machine with registers $R_1, R_2, \ldots, R_n$, so that individual operations are assignment instructions of the form

$$R_j := f(R_1, R_2, \ldots, R_n).$$

In such a case, the operation axiom can be stated as follows:

assignment axiom

$$\vdash\{A(x, r_1, \ldots, r_{j-1}, f_M(r_1, \ldots, r_n), r_{j+1}, \ldots, r_n)\}$$
$$R_j := f(R_1, R_2, \ldots, R_n)\{A(x, r_1, \ldots, r_n)\}$$

In addition to the assignment or operation axiom, the axiomatic method also provides certain *rules of inference*, also called *deduction rules*, for enabling assertions about a program P to be deduced from similar assertions about the various parts of P. The complete list of basic deduction rules is as follows:

1. *composition rule:*

   if $\vdash\{A\}P_1\{B\}$ and $\vdash\{B\}P_2\{C\}$, then $\vdash\{A\}P_1; P_2\{C\}$

2. *conditional rule:*

   if $\vdash\{A \wedge T\}P_1\{B\}$ and $\vdash\{A \wedge \sim T\}P_2\{B\}$,

   then $\vdash\{A\}$ **if** T **then** P_1 **else** $P_2\{B\}$

3. *empty rule:*

   if $\vdash A \supset B$, then $\vdash\{A\}I\{B\}$, where I denotes the empty program

4. *while rule:*

   if $\vdash\{A \wedge T\}P\{A\}$, then $\vdash\{A\}$ **while** T **do** $P\{A \wedge \sim T\}$

Most of these rules are self evident. Notice that in the empty rule, the statement $A \supset B$ is a purely logical implication. Such a statement should be regarded as an abbreviation for

$$\forall x, v . A(x, v) \supset B(x, v).$$

In the while rule, the assertion $\{A \wedge T\}P\{A\}$ essentially means that the predicate A is an *invariant* of the program **while** T **do** P, i.e. if A is true prior to the execution of the while loop, then A remains true, of the appropriate memory contents, no matter how many times the body of the loop is executed. Thus, if and when execution of the loop terminates, both A and the exit condition $\sim T$ will be true.

In practice it is often useful to combine the above deduction rules into a number of derived rules. These are as follows:

5. *assignment rule:*

   if $\vdash A(x, v) \supset B(x, F(v))$, then $\vdash\{A(x, v)\}F\{B(x, v)\}$

6. *repeated assignments rule:*

   if $\vdash A(x, v) \supset B(x, F_n(F_{n-1}(\ldots F_1(v)\ldots)))$,

   then $\vdash\{A(x, v)\}F_1; F_2; \ldots; F_n\{B(x, v)\}.$

7. *derived composition rule:*

   if $\vdash\{A\}P\{B\}$, $\vdash\{C\}Q\{D\}$, and $\vdash B \supset C$,

   then $\vdash\{A\}P; Q\{D\}.$

8. *derived while rule:*

    if $\vdash A \supset B$, $\vdash\{B \wedge T\}P\{B\}$, and $\vdash B \wedge \sim T \supset C$,

    then $\vdash\{A\}$ **while** T **do** $P\{C\}$.

Each of these new rules can be derived from the basic deduction rules by using the fact that $P; I = I; P = P$ for every program P, where I is the null program (see Exercise 5.4).

Let us now consider a simple example of the use of the axiomatic method. Suppose we wish to prove that the NORMA program

    while $X \neq 0$ **do**

        begin $X: = X - 1$; $Y: = Y + 1$ **end**

computes the identity function whenever it terminates. In order to write down the partial correctness condition of this program P, we must be careful to avoid using the same variable for both the initial input and the current contents of the register X. Since it is logical to use x and y for the contents of X and Y respectively, we shall let x_0 denote the input integer, i.e. the initial contents of X. The assertion we have to prove is the following:

$$\{x_0 \geqslant 0 \wedge x = x_0 \wedge y = 0\}P\{y = x_0\}$$

The first parenthesized statement in this assertion expresses the fact that x_0 is non-negative and the initial memory state of NORMA, as far as X and Y are concerned, is $(x_0, 0)$. Since P is a **while**-statement, the derived while rule tells us that the desired assertion will be proved if we can find a statement A such that for all x and y

  (i) $(x_0 \geqslant 0 \wedge x = x_0 \wedge y = 0) \supset A(x_0, x, y)$

  (ii) $\{A(x_0, x, y) \wedge x \neq 0\}X: = X - 1$; $Y: = Y + 1\{A(x_0, x, y)\}$

and

  (iii) $(A(x_0, x, y) \wedge x = 0) \supset y = x_0$.

At this point, the essentially creative rather than mechanical nature of the axiomatic method becomes apparent. It is only by 'understanding' the way in which P works that we can formulate the right statement A which enables the proof to go through. Since P is very simple, it is easily seen that the correct choice is to take $A(x_0, x, y)$ to be the statement

$$x + y = x_0.$$

With this choice, the proofs of (i) and (iii) are immediate. The final condition (ii) can be proved by using the repeated assignments rule: we have only to show that the implication

$$A(x_0, x, y) \wedge x \neq 0 \supset A(x_0, x - 1, y + 1)$$

holds. Since this is obvious by the definition of A, the proof is complete.

Let us now consider a second example of a similar sort. We want to prove that the NORMA program

while $X \neq 0$ **do**

    begin $X := X - 1$; $A := A + 1$; $B := A + 1$;

        while $A \neq 0$ **do**

            begin $A := A - 1$; $Y := Y + 1$ **end**;

        $A := B$

end

which we shall denote by P, satisfies

$$normaP(n) = x^2$$

whenever $normaP(n)$ is defined.

The assertion we have to prove is

$$\{x_0 \geqslant 0 \wedge a = 0 \wedge b = 0 \wedge y = 0 \wedge x = x_0\} P \{y = x_0^2\}.$$

Since P is of the form

$$\textbf{while } X \neq 0 \textbf{ do } Q,$$

the derived while rule tells us to look for a statement C such that

(i) $(x_0 \geqslant 0 \wedge a = 0 \wedge b = 0 \wedge y = 0 \wedge x = x_0) \supset C(x_0, a, b, x, y)$

(ii) $\{C(x_0, a, b, x, y) \wedge x \neq 0\} Q \{C(x_0, a, b, x, y)\}$

(iii) $(C(x_0, a, b, x, y) \wedge x = 0) \supset y = x_0^2$.

Here, the correct choice of C is the statement

$$a = 2(x_0 - x) \wedge a = b \wedge y = (x_0 - x)^2.$$

Assertions (i) and (iii) are immediate, so we can concentrate on proving (ii). We have to find a statement D such that

(iv) $\{C(x_0, a, b, x, y) \wedge x \neq 0\} X := X - 1; A := A + 1; B := A + 1$
    $\{D(x_0, a, b, x, y)\}$

(v) $\{D(x_0, a, b, x, y) \wedge a \neq 0\} A := A - 1; Y := Y + 1 \{D(x_0, a, b, x, y)\}$

(vi) $\{D(x_0, a, b, x, y) \wedge a = 0\} A := B \{C(x_0, a, b, x, y)\}$.

We take $D(x_0, a, b, x, y)$ to be

$$b = 2(x_0 - x) \wedge a + y = (x_0 - x)^2.$$

Using the assignment rules, we now have to show that the following three implications hold:

$C(x_0, a, b, x, y) \wedge x \neq 0 \supset D(x_0, a + 1, a + 2, x - 1, y)$

$D(x_0, a, b, x, y) \wedge a \neq 0 \supset D(x_0, a - 1, b, x, y + 1)$

$D(x_0, a, b, x, y) \wedge a = 0 \supset C(x_0, b, b, x, y)$.

In each case, the proof is straightforward, and so the partial correctness of P is established.

In Section 5 we shall give one further example of a partial correctness proof using the axiomatic approach. In addition to being more complicated, the program contains assignments involving array elements. In the next section we turn to the problem of proving termination of **while** programs.

5.4 Proof of termination

While the axiomatic method described in the last section is a useful tool for proving partial correctness, it is not directly applicable to the problem of total correctness. A proof of total correctness can, however, be obtained by combining a partial correctness proof with a proof of termination. In this section we consider one way in which termination of programs can be demonstrated.

The only type of program statement which causes trouble in termination proofs is the loop

while T **do** P.

A minimal requirement for this loop to terminate is that P must change the contents of the memory in such a way that after a finite number of executions of P, condition T can no longer be satisfied. One simple way of showing that this must be the case is to construct a function $E: X \times V \to N$, called a *potential* function, whose values decrease with each execution of P. Since E takes values in the set of non-negative integers N, and no infinite decreasing sequence of non-negative integers can exist, it must follow that the number of executions of P is finite, and so termination is assured. If P itself contains a loop, then a second potential function has to be constructed for the inner loop, and so on. Thus, in order to show that the program

while T **do**
    begin Q;
        while T' **do** S;
        R
    end

terminates, we have to construct a potential function E_1 which decreases with each execution of Q; **while** T' **do** S; R, and a potential function E_2 which decreases with each execution of S.

Actually, it is not necessary to insist that E must take non-negative values. If we allow E to assume arbitrary integer values, positive or negative, and can prove

$$T(v) \supset E(x, v) > 0,$$

then the fact that E decreases with each execution of P also guarantees the eventual termination of the loop **while** T **do** P.

In order to formulate this idea more precisely, recall the notation

$$P(v) = w$$

to express the fact that the computation of P (on some implicitly understood machine M) with initial contents v of the memory set, terminates with final value w. Clearly, P terminates with respect to ϕ just in the case that

$$\phi(x) \wedge v = I_M(x) \supset \exists w . P(v) = w$$

holds for all inputs x.

The idea of using potential functions can now be made precise in the following deductive rule:

if $\vdash T(v) \supset E(x, v) > 0,$

and $\vdash T(v) \supset \exists w . [P(v) = w \wedge E(x, v) > E(x, w)],$

where E is some integer valued function, then

$$\vdash \exists w . (\textbf{while } T \textbf{ do } P)(v) = w$$

In this and subsequent rules, each condition should be regarded as having its free variables universally quantified. For the sake of simplicity, this universal quantification will usually be omitted.

As it stands, the above rule is not sufficiently general for practical use. In the first place, we may only wish to prove termination under certain assumptions about x and v, and in the second place, we usually need to prove more than just the fact that **while** T **do** P terminates, if this program is part of some larger loop. The full termination rule for while statements (omitting explicit universal quantification of the free variables) is as follows:

while-termination rule:

if   (i) $\vdash T(v) \supset E(x, v) > 0$

       (ii) $\vdash A(x, v) \wedge T(v) \supset \exists w . [P(v) = w \wedge B(x, v, w) \wedge E(x, v) > E(x, w)],$

       (iii) $\vdash B(x, v, w) \wedge T(w) \supset A(x, w),$

       (iv) $\vdash B(x, u, v) \wedge B(x, v, w) \supset B(x, u, w),$

and   (v) $\vdash A(x, v) \wedge \sim T(v) \supset B(x, v, v),$

then $\vdash A(x, v) \supset \exists w . [(\textbf{while } T \textbf{ do } P)(v) = w \wedge B(x, v, w) \wedge \sim T(w)].$

In order to explain this seemingly complicated rule, let us consider the purpose of each condition:

1. Condition (i) ensures that the integer valued function E has a positive value whenever T is true. This means that as soon as E is negative, the test T must become false, and so terminate the loop **while** T **do** P.

2. Condition (ii) ensures that if $A(x, v)$ is satisfied and $T(v)$ is true, then the execution of P on v will terminate, decrease the value of E, and establish B.

3. Condition (iii) is necessary to ensure that, at the end of the execution of P, the condition $A(x, v)$ is again satisfied if $T(v)$ is true, where v now denotes the

new memory value. This is just what is needed to enable condition (ii) to be applied again, and so establish the truth of B for all subsequent executions of P.

4. Condition (iv), which essentially asserts the transitive nature of B, is needed to make sure that $B(x, u, v)$ holds, where v is the final memory value obtained by applying P any finite number of times to original value u.

5. Finally, condition (v) is needed to establish B when P is not executed at all.

In order to be able to apply the while-termination rule, we need to have further rules for establishing assertions of the form

$$A(x, v) \supset \exists\, w \,.\, P(v) = w \wedge B(x, v, w),$$

when P is not itself a while statement. These rules are as follows:

assignment rule:

> if $\vdash A(x, v) \supset B(x, v, F(v))$,
>
> then $\vdash A(x, v) \supset \exists\, w \,.\, [F(v) = w \wedge B(x, v, w)]$,
>
> where F is any operation identifier.

empty rule:

> if $\vdash A(x, v) \supset B(x, v, v)$,
>
> then $\vdash A(x, v) \supset \exists\, w \,.\, [I(v) = w \wedge B(x, v, w)]$,
>
> where I denotes the null program.

conditional rule:

> if $\vdash A(x, v) \wedge T(v) \supset \exists\, w \,.\, [P(v) = w \wedge B(x, v, w)]$
>
> and $\vdash A(x, v) \wedge \sim T(v) \supset \exists\, w \,.\, [Q(v) = w \wedge B(x, v, w)]$,
>
> then $\vdash A(x, v) \supset \exists\, w \,.\, [(\textbf{if } T \textbf{ then } P \textbf{ else } Q)(v) = w \wedge B(x, v, w)]$

composition rule:

> if $\vdash A(x, v) \supset \exists\, w \,.\, [P(v) = w \wedge B_1(x, v, w)]$,
>
> $\vdash B(x, v) \supset \exists\, w \,.\, [Q(v) = w \wedge B_2(x, v, w)]$,
>
> $\vdash B_1(x, v, w) \supset B(x, w)$,
>
> and $\vdash B_1(x, u, v) \wedge B_2(x, v, w) \supset B(x, u, w)$,
>
> then $\vdash A(x, v) \supset \exists\, w \,.\, [(P; Q)(v) = w \wedge B(x, v, w)]$.

In the definition of the composition rule, the condition $B_1(x, v, w) \supset B(x, w)$ is needed for the execution of Q, and the final condition is needed to relate the intermediate memory state v resulting from the execution of P on u, to the final state w resulting from the execution of $P; Q$.

Let us now see the method at work on an example. Suppose P is the following program:

$$
\left.
\begin{array}{l}
\textbf{while } x < n \textbf{ do} \\
\qquad
\left.
\begin{array}{l}
\textbf{begin if } y < n \textbf{ then} \\
\qquad
\left.
\begin{array}{l}
\textbf{while } x \leqslant y \textbf{ do } x := x + 1
\end{array}
\right]S \\
\qquad \textbf{else } x := x + 1; \\
\qquad y := y + 1 \\
\textbf{end}
\end{array}
\right]R
\end{array}
\right]Q
$$

In the program x and y are variables and n is some fixed positive integer. We wish to prove that P terminates for all integers x and y (ambiguously using x and y both as the register names and as their respective contents).

Since P takes the form **while** $x < n$ **do** Q, the first step in the proof is to apply the while-termination rule. We can prove the desired result

$$\exists\, x', y'.\ (\textbf{while } x < n \textbf{ do } Q)(x, y) = (x', y'),$$

by finding an integer valued function $E(x, y)$ such that the following conditions are satisfied:

(1) $x < n \supset E(x, y) > 0$

(2) $x < n \supset \exists\, x', y'.\ [Q(x, y) = (x', y') \land E(x, y) > E(x', y')]$

(Here, we have taken $A = B = \textit{true}$ in the definition of the while-termination rule). We define E as follows:

$$
\begin{aligned}
E(x,y) &= 2n - (x + y) &&\text{if } \ y \leqslant n \\
&= n - x &&\text{if } \ y \geqslant n.
\end{aligned}
$$

With this definition, (1) is obvious.

Since Q is the composition of program R and assignment $y := y + 1$, condition (2) can be proved by using the composition and assignment rules. We have to find predicates B, B_1 and B_2 such that

(3) $x < n \supset \exists\, x', y'.\ [R(x, y) = (x', y') \land B_1(x, y, x', y')],$

(4) $B(x, y) \supset B_2(x, y, x, y + 1),$

(5) $B_1(x, y, x', y') \supset B(x', y'),$

and (6) $B_1(x, y, x', y') \land B_2(x', y', x'', y'') \supset E(x, y) > E(x'', y'').$

We choose B to be the constant predicate $\textit{true}$, and B_1 and B_2 to be the following predicates:

$$B_1(x, y, x', y'):\quad (y' \geqslant n \to E(x, y) > E(x', y'),\ E(x, y) \geqslant E(x', y'))$$

$$B_2(x, y, x', y'):\quad (y \geqslant n \to E(x, y) \geqslant E(x', y'),\ E(x, y) > E(x', y')),$$

where we make use of the propositional connective $(p \to q, r)$ discussed in Section 2. To prove (4) we must show $B_2(x, y, x, y + 1)$ holds for all x and y. This is proved by using the fact that

$$E(x, y) = n - x = E(x, y + 1) \quad \text{if } y \geqslant n,$$

and $\quad E(x, y) = 2n - (x + y) > 2n - (x + y + 1) = E(x, y + 1) \quad \text{if } y < n.$

Condition (5) is immediate by our choice of B, and (6) is straightforward.

At this stage, we are left with the proof of condition (3). Since R is a conditional statement, it is sufficient to show

(7) $\quad x < n \wedge y < n \supset \exists x', y' . [S(x, y) = (x', y') \wedge B_1(x, y, x', y')],$

and $\quad$ (8) $\quad x < n \wedge y \geqslant n \supset B_1(x, y, x + 1, y).$

Since

$$E(x, y) = n - x > n - (x + 1) = E(x + 1, y)$$

if $y \geqslant n$, condition (8) is satisfied. Using the fact that program S does not change the value of y, i.e. $y' = y$, we can prove (7) by proving the stronger condition

(9) $\quad \exists x', y' . [S(x, y) = (x', y') \wedge E(x, y) \geqslant E(x', y')].$

Since the relation $E(x, y) \geqslant E(x', y')$ is reflexive and transitive, the while-termination rule shows that (9) will be established if we can find a potential function D such that

(10) $\quad x \leqslant y \supset D(x, y) > 0,$

and $\quad$ (11) $\quad x \leqslant y \supset E(x, y) \geqslant E(x + 1, y) \wedge D(x, y) > D(x + 1, y)$

A simple choice of D, which immediately yields (10) and (11) is to take

$$D(x, y) = 1 + y - x.$$

Since conditions (1)–(11) have all been satisfied, the proof of the termination of P is complete.

5.5 Partial correctness of *in situ* permutation

In this section we apply the axiomatic method developed in Section 3 to prove the partial correctness of a somewhat more complicated program. In Chapter 8, a different proof of its partial correctness will be given.

One of the reasons for the additional complexity is that the program deals with an array, and contains assignments to array elements. The axiom for array assignments can be stated in the form

$$\vdash \{A(x, v, X')\} X(k) := e\{A(x, v, X)\},$$

where X and X' are arrays, and X' is defined by the conditions

$$X'(j) = X(j) \quad \text{for } j \neq k, \ X'(k) = e.$$

As a simple example of the use of this axiom, suppose we wish to prove

$$\{A(X)\} X(k) := X(j) \{A(X)\},$$

where $A(X)$ is the predicate

$$\forall i . X(i) \leqslant n,$$

n being some fixed constant. The assignment rule shows that it is sufficient to prove the implication $A(X) \supset A(X')$, where X' is defined by the conditions

$$X'(i) = X(i) \quad \text{for } i \neq k, \ X'(k) = X(j).$$

In other words, we have to show

$$\forall i . X(i) \leqslant n \supset \forall i . (i = k \to X(j) \leqslant n, \ X(i) \leqslant n).$$

Since

$$\forall i . X(i) \leqslant n \supset X(j) \leqslant n$$

for any j, the result follows at once.

Now let us turn to the definition of the program P. P is designed to permute the elements of a given array *in situ* i.e. using only a finite amount of memory in addition to that required to store the array. The inputs to P consist of an integer $N \geqslant 1$, an array $X(1), X(2), \ldots, X(N)$, and a permutation f of the integers $\{1, 2, \ldots, N\}$; the intended effect of P is to replace $X(1), X(2), \ldots, X(N)$ by $X(f1), X(f2), \ldots, X(fN)$. The rearrangement of X is carried out by using the cycle structure of the permutation f in the following way. Let us say that j is a *cycle-leader* of f if $j \leqslant f^n j$ for all $n \geqslant 0$, i.e. if j is numerically the least element in the cycle to which it belongs. Each cycle of f has a unique leader, and P carries out the permutation cycle by cycle, when each leader is detected. The program, incorporating brief comments to show the stages of the method, is as follows:

1	$j := 1;$
2	**while** $j \leqslant N$ **do**
3	**begin comment** *the permutation has been*
4	*carried out over all cycles whose leader is*
5	*less than* $j;$
6	$k := f(j);$
7	**while** $j < k$ **do** $k := f(k);$
8	**if** $k = j$ **then**
9	**begin comment** j *is a cycle leader*;
10	$y := X(j);$
11	**while** $j \neq f(k)$ **do**
12	**begin** $X(k) := X(f(k)); \ k := f(k)$ **end**;
13	$X(k) := y$
14	**end**;
15	$j := j + 1$
16	**end**

Let us now write down the partial correctness condition of P. Let $perm\ (f, N)$ abbreviate the predicate

$$\forall x.[1 \leqslant x \leqslant N \supset 1 \leqslant fx \leqslant N] \land$$
$$\forall x, y.[1 \leqslant x, y \leqslant N \land fx = fy \supset x = y],$$

which asserts that f is a permutation on the set $\{1, 2, \ldots, N\}$, and let $A(1), A(2), \ldots, A(N)$ denote the initial values of $X(1), X(2), \ldots, X(N)$. The partial correctness condition of P is

$$\{\text{INPUT}\}P\{\text{OUTPUT}\},$$

where INPUT is an abbreviation for the predicate

$$N \geqslant 1 \land perm\ (f, N) \land \forall x.[1 \leqslant x \leqslant N \supset X(x) = A(x)],$$

and OUTPUT is an abbreviation for

$$\forall x.[1 \leqslant x \leqslant N \supset X(x) = A(fx)].$$

We can ease the notation slightly by assuming throughout that the variable x is restricted to the set $\{1, 2, \ldots N\}$, and so express predicates of the form

$$\forall x.[1. \leqslant x \leqslant N \supset Q(x)]$$

more simply by $\forall x. Q(x)$.

Notice first that neither N or f are changed by P, so that the relation

$$N \geqslant 1 \land perm\ (f, N)$$

obviously holds at each point during the course of computation. There is thus no need to formally establish its invariance, and it can be assumed as an implicit condition whenever necessary.

Since P takes the form

$$j: = 1; \textbf{ while } j \leqslant N \textbf{ do } P_{3,15},$$

where $P_{3,15}$ describes the program given by lines 3–15 of P, the first step in the proof of partial correctness is to look for a predicate $L(j, X)$ such that

(1) $\{\text{INPUT}\}\ j: = 1\{L(j, X)\}$

(2) $\{L(j, X) \land j \leqslant N\}\ P_{3,15}\{L(j, X)\}$

and (3) $L(j, X) \land j > N \supset \text{OUTPUT}$

To define $L(j, X)$, let $C(x)$ denote the leader of the cycle of f to which x belongs. The comment in lines 3–5 of P suggests that the correct choice of $L(j, X)$ is the predicate:

$$\forall x. (C(x) < j \rightarrow X(x) = A(fx), X(x) = A(x)).$$

Since $1 \leqslant C(x) \leqslant N$ if $1 \leqslant x \leqslant N$, the proofs of (1) and (3) are straightforward. To prove (2), we use various derived deduction rules and look for assertions D and

E so that the following conditions are satisfied:

(4) $\{L(j, X) \wedge j \leqslant N\}k\colon = f(j)\{D\}$

(5) $\{D \wedge j < k\}k\colon = f(k)\{D\}$

(6) $\{D \wedge j = k\}P_{10,13}\{E\}$

(7) $D \wedge j > k \supset E$

(8) $\{E\}j\colon = j + 1\{L(j, X)\}$.

We choose E to be $L(j + 1, X)$ since this immediately establishes (8) by the assignment axiom. We define D to be

$$L(j, X) \wedge \exists n . [n > 0 \wedge k = f^n j \wedge \forall m . [0 < m < n \supset j < f^m j]].$$

With this definition of D, condition (4) is straightforward (take $n = 1$ in the definition of D), and (5) can be verified by a short argument. Furthermore, if D holds and $j > k$, then there exists an n such that $j > f^n j$, and so j cannot be a cycle leader. In this case, $L(j, X)$ implies $L(j + 1, X)$ and so (7) is established.

At this stage, we are left with the proof of condition (6). Note first that if D holds with $j = k$, then we have

$$\exists n . [n > 0 \wedge j = f^n j \wedge \forall m . [0 < m < n \supset j < f^m j]].$$

This condition simply states that j is a cycle leader. Since j is unaltered by $P_{10,13}$, we can assume for the rest of the proof that j remains a cycle leader. To prove (6) we have to find an assertion F such that the following further conditions are satisfied:

(9) $\{D \wedge j = k\}y\colon = X(j)\{F\}$

(10) $\{F \wedge j \neq fk\}X(k)\colon = X(fk); \ k\colon = fk\{F\}$

(11) $\{F \wedge j = fk\}X(k)\colon = y\{E\}$.

We take F to be

$$y = A(j) \wedge \exists t . [k = f^t j \wedge \forall x . B(X(x), x, j, t)],$$

where $B(z, x, j, t)$ is given by

$$(C(x) < j \vee \exists r . [0 \leqslant r < t \wedge x = f^r j] \to z = A(fx), z = A(x)).$$

Condition (9) is easily established by taking the value $t = 0$ in F. For condition (11) we have to prove $F \wedge j = fk \supset E'$, where E' is derived from E by replacing the array X by X', defined by $X'(x) = X(x)$ for $x \neq k$ and $X'(k) = y$. Recalling that E is $L(j + 1, x)$, we find that E' is

$$\forall x \neq k . (C(x) \leqslant j \to X(x) = A(fx), X(x) = A(x))$$
$$\wedge (C(k) \leqslant j \to y = A(fk), y = A(k)).$$

Now from $F \wedge fk = j$ we can deduce that $C(k) = j$ and $y = A(fk)$; this establishes the second conjunction of E'. Moreover, if $j = fk$ and $k = f^t j$, then the condition $\exists r . [0 \leqslant r < t \wedge x = f^r j]$ reduces to $C(x) = j$ provided $x \neq k$, and so the first part may also be proved.

Finally, we are left with condition (10). We have to verify the implication $F \land j \neq fk \supset F'$, where F' is derived from F by first substituting fk for k, and then array X' for X, where X' is defined by the conditions $X'(x) = X(x)$ if $x \neq k$ and $X'(k) = X(fk)$. Assertion F' turns out to be

$$y = A(j) \land \exists t . [fk = f^t j \land \forall x \neq k . B(X(x), x, j, t) \land B(X(fk), k, j, t)].$$

Suppose s is the least positive value of t which satisfies F; we show that F' can be satisfied by taking $t = s + 1$. If $x \neq k = f^s j$, then $\exists r . [0 \leqslant r < s \land x = f^r j]$ if and only if $\exists r . [0 \leqslant r < s + 1 \land x = f^r j]$, so that F implies $B(X(x), x, j, s + 1)$ for all $x \neq k$. Taking the case $x = fk$ in F, and observing that $\exists r . [0 \leqslant r < s \land fk = f^r j]$ implies $k = f^{r-1} j$, for some $r \geqslant 1$ (because $j \neq fk$), contradicting the minimality of s, we can deduce that $F \land j \neq fk \supset X(fk) = A(fk)$. Finally, since $B(X(fk), k, j, s + 1)$ reduces to

$$(\exists r . [0 \leqslant r < s + 1 \land k = f^r j] \to X(fk) = A(fk), X(fk) = A(k)),$$

and thus to $X(fk) = A(fk)$, the proof of partial correctness is complete.

Exercises

1. Show that P is equivalent to Q with respect to ϕ if and only if for all assertions ψ, P is partially correct with respect to ϕ and ψ if and only if Q is partially correct with respect to ϕ and ψ.

2. Give an alternative formulation of the statement that the predicate $P(x)$ holds for at most one x.

3. Express the following predicates symbolically:

    (i) the greatest common divisor of x and y is z;

    (ii) the array $x(1), x(2), \ldots, x(n)$ is in increasing order;

    (iii) $P(x)$ is true for every x except y.

4. Derive the rules (5)–(8) of Section 5.3 from the basic deduction rules.

5. Let P be given by

$$z: = 1;$$
    while $y \neq 0$ **do**
        begin if odd (y) **then**
            begin $y: = y - 1; z: = z \times x$ **end**;
            $x: = x^2$;
            $y: = y/2$
    end

    Prove that $\{x_0 \geqslant 0 \land y_0 \geqslant 0\} P \{z = x_0^{y_0}\}$

6. Let P be given by

$$x: = 1; y: = n;$$

while $x \neq y$ **do**

      begin $z: = \lfloor (x + y)/2 \rfloor;$

      if $a \leq A[z]$ **then** $y: = z$ **else** $x: = z + 1$

      end

Suppose the inputs to P satisfy the following conditions:

(a) $n \geq 1$

(b) $\forall i, j . [1 \leq i \leq j \leq n \supset A[i] \leq A[j]]$

(c) $\exists i . [1 \leq i \leq n \wedge a = A[i]]$.

Prove that P, if it terminates, will yield an output z such that $1 \leq z \leq n$ and $a = A[z]$.

7. Let P be the program

$$x: = n - 1;$$

$$y: = n;$$

$$z: = n;$$

while $x \neq 0$ **do**

      begin while $x \leq y$ **do** $y: = y - x;$

               if $y = 0$ **then** $z: = z - x;$

               $y: = n; x: = x - 1$

      end.

Prove that P is partially correct with respect to ϕ and ψ, where

$\phi(n)$: $n > 0$

$\psi(n, z)$: $z = 0$ if and only if n is a perfect number.

(See Section 5.1 for the definition of a perfect number.)

8. Let P be given by

while $x \neq y$ **do**

      begin while $x > y$ **do** $x: = x - y;$

               while $y > x$ **do** $y: = y - x$

      end;

      $z: = x$

Prove that P is totally correct with respect to ϕ and ψ, where

$\phi(x, y)$: $x > 0 \wedge y > 0$

$\psi(x, y, x)$: z is the greatest common divisor of x and y.

9. Prove that the following program terminates for all integers x, y and z:

> **while** $x > 0$ **do**
> > **begin** $z: = z - 1$;
> > > **while** $x \leqslant y$ **do begin** $x: = x + 1$; $z: = z - 1$ **end**;
> > > **while** $z \leqslant x$ **do** $x: = x - 1$
> >
> > **end**.

10. The following program is another version of *in situ* permutation (see Section 5.5). Prove its partial correctness

> $j: = 1$;
> **while** $j \leqslant N$ **do**
> > **begin** $k: = f(j)$;
> > > **while** $k < j$ **do** $k: = f(k)$;
> > > $y: = X(j)$; $X(j): = X(k)$; $X(k): = y$;
> > > $j: = j + 1$
> >
> > **end**

Chapter 6
The Definition of Functions by Recursion

In the last chapter we mentioned that one way of stating the correctness condition of a program was to directly describe the function which the program was supposed to compute. Unlike the description of a program, the description of a function has only to indicate the correspondence between argument values and function values, and not necessarily how the function values can actually be obtained. In this chapter and the next, we shall develop a language for defining functions. This language is based upon the idea of recursion. It turns out that recursion is a compact and natural way to define many functions, and at the same time powerful enough to describe every intuitively computable function. In particular, we shall show how the function computed by a given program can be defined recursively, so that statements about the correctness or equivalence of programs can be formulated as statements about recursively defined functions.

Of course, an important task is to make precise what we mean by recursion. In this chapter we shall define recursion as a computational process, in which functional expressions are evaluated according to certain rules. In Chapter 7, recursively defined functions are interpreted within a mathematical theory of partial functions as fixed points. This latter viewpoint leads to the discovery of an important induction rule for proving facts about recursively defined functions. As we shall see, the alliance of recursion, as a definition technique, with induction, as a proof technique, establishes a powerful methodology for the formulation and proof of statements about programs.

6.1 Functions

Throughout this chapter we shall be concerned with *partial* functions, i.e. functions that are not necessarily defined at every point of their domain. The mathematics of partial functions is not so straightforward as at first sight may appear; certain difficulties concerning the existence of defined values have to be recognized and overcome. Some of these difficulties will be made clear in the next section, although they will not be satisfactorily resolved until Chapter 7. In this section, however, we only wish to introduce the concept of a function *type*, and describe some useful notation.

Consider the following three functions, where the variables x and y range over the set N of non-negative integers:

$$f(x) = x^2$$
$$g(x, y) = (x^2, y + x)$$
$$h(f, x) = f(f(x)).$$

The first function f is a straightforward 1-place number-theoretic function; the *type* of f is therefore $(N \to N)$. This fact is usually written as follows:

$$f : N \to N.$$

The second function g is a function from the set of pairs of non-negative integers into itself, and so the type of G is

$$g : (N \times N) \to (N \times N),$$

or more briefly,

$$g : N^2 \to N^2$$

The third function h is an example of a function which takes another function as one of its arguments. The type of h is given by

$$h : ((N \to N) \times N) \to N.$$

Such functions of 'higher' type will usually be referred to as *functionals*, according to normal mathematical terminology. Functionals arise quite naturally in consideration with the functions computed by programs. For example, consider a program P that inputs an array A and an integer n, and computes the maximum of the integers $A(1)$, $A(2), \ldots, A(n)$. We can regard the array A as specifying a (finite) function, so the function f computed by P is given by

$$f(A, n) = \max \{A(j) : 1 \le j \le n\},$$

the type of f being the same as h above.

Functionals can sometimes be usefully employed as replacements for functions of more than one argument. Consider the functions g' and h' defined by

$$g'(x)(y) = (x^2, y + x) \quad \text{and} \quad h'(f)(x) = f(f(x)).$$

The function g' is a functional, which for each integer x defines a function $g'(x)$ as its value. Thus the type of g' is given by

$$g' : N \to (N \to N^2).$$

Although the type of g' is different from that of g, the two functions are identical in their effect. The same is true for h and h', the type of h' being

$$h' : (N \to N) \to (N \to N).$$

In this way, we can regard many-place functions as one-place functionals, a device that sometimes simplifies notation and helps in the manipulation of expressions.

The distinction between functions and their values is often blurred in common mathematical notation and can give rise to confusion. Functions are usually written down in one of three ways: between its (two) arguments (*infix* notation), after its argument (*postfix* notation), or before its arguments (*prefix* notation). As examples, consider the way we usually write down the addition, factorial, and logarithmic functions:

$$x + y \quad \text{infix}$$
$$x! \quad \text{postfix}$$
$$log\,x \quad \text{prefix.}$$

Ambiguity can arise when using infix or postfix notation which is avoided with the consistent use of prefix notation. Does $x!$ denote the factorial function itself, or merely the value of this function for the argument x? In other words, the problem is to distinguish between

$$x!: N \rightarrow N \quad \text{and} \quad x!: N$$

Using prefix notation, the problem can be avoided: log describes the function, and $log\,x$ describes the value for argument x. Since it is important to be able to decide the type of a given mathematical expression, we must find some way of resolving the ambiguity. One solution is to invent suggestive prefix names for functions, e.g.

add, mult, fact, succ, pred

to denote the addition, multiplication, factorial, successor, and predecessor functions respectively. For frequently occurring functions this is a satisfactory solution. Another solution is to employ the *λ-notation* of Church which amounts to a general method for constructing prefix names for functions. In this notation, the phrase

'that function which for arbitrary argument x gives the value $x!$'

is rendered symbolically in the form

$$\lambda x . x!$$

In other words, $\lambda x . x!$ is a prefix name for the factorial function. The expression

$$(\lambda x . x!)(a)$$

is synonymous with the value $a!$. To indicate that the variable x can range over N, we can write

$$\lambda x \in N . x!$$

In λ-notation, the addition function is written as

$$\lambda(x, y) . (x + y),$$

or as $\qquad \lambda(x, y) \in N^2 . (x + y)$

in the extended notation. To improve readability, we shall sometimes omit the first pair of parentheses and write

$$\lambda x, y . (x + y)$$

instead.

Functions of higher type can also be described by λ-notation; for example,

$$\lambda f . \lambda x . f(f(x))$$

denotes a function of type $(N \to N) \to (N \to N)$. The distinction between

$$\lambda f, x . f(f(x)) \quad \text{and} \quad \lambda f . \lambda x . f(f(x))$$

is just the distinction between h and h' mentioned previously.

Note that both

$$\lambda x, y . (x + y) \quad \text{and} \quad \lambda u, v . (u + v)$$

denote the addition function; the actual identifiers used in the λ-expression are not important as long as some simple rules are observed. Of these rules, the only one that need concern us is that the identifiers should be distinct; the expression

$$\lambda x, x . (x + x)$$

is regarded as meaningless.

6.2   Recursion

In mathematics, many notational devices are used to define new functions in terms of given functions and values. Considering only number theoretic functions for the moment, let us list some of the more common methods:

(a)   arithmetic operations, e.g.

$$h(x) = f(x) + g(x),$$
$$h(x) = f(x) \times g(x).$$

(b)   simple composition, e.g.

$$h(x) = f(g(x)).$$

(c)   summation, e.g.

$$h(x) = \sum_{y=0}^{x} f(y).$$

(d)   definition by cases, e.g.

$$h(x) = f(x) \quad \text{if} \quad p(x)$$
$$= g(x) \text{ otherwise,}$$

where p is some predicate, i.e. truth function.

(e) minimization and maximization, e.g.

$$h(x) = \text{the least } y \text{ such that } p(x, y),$$
$$h(x) = \min \{ f(x, y): 0 \leqslant y \leqslant g(x) \}$$
$$h(x) = \max \{ f(x, y): 0 \leqslant y \leqslant g(x) \}.$$

(f) recursion, e.g.

$$x! = 1 \text{ if } x = 0$$
$$= x \times (x - 1)! \quad \text{if } x > 0.$$

In this section we shall see how each of the above definition methods can be reduced to just two: definition by composition and definition by recursion. In order to do this, we introduce the important concept of a *conditional expression*. A conditional expression takes the form

$$(p \rightarrow e_1, e_2),$$

where e_1 and e_2 are arbitrary expressions and p is a predicate expression taking just the values *true* and *false*. Conditional expressions can be viewed as a generalization of the conditional connective $(p \rightarrow q, r)$ introduced in Section 5.2. There, both q and r were also predicate expressions, whereas now they can be arbitrary. The formal definition of a conditional expression will be given in the next section; the examples which follow should make the general idea clear. The value of the conditional expression $(p \rightarrow e_1, e_2)$ is defined to be the value of e_1 if the value of p is *true*, and the value of e_2 if the value of p is *false*. It is also important to say what the value of the conditional expression is in the case that one or more of the values of p, e_1 or e_2 are undefined. In the case that p is undefined, so is the value of the conditional expression; if p is *true*, then the value of the conditional expression is equal to the value of e_1, *whether or not e_2 has a value*. Similarly, if p is *false*, then the value of the conditional expression is the value of e_2, whether or not e_1 has a value. Thus we can regard the expression $(p \rightarrow e_1, e_2)$ as another way of writing the Algol expression

if p **then** e_1 **else** e_2.

To appreciate the use of conditional expressions, consider the definition of the factorial function:

$$fact(x) = (x = 0 \rightarrow 1, x \times fact(x - 1)).$$

Clearly, our intention is to ensure that $fact(0) = 1$; according to the definition of *fact* we have

$$fact(0) = (0 = 0 \rightarrow 1, 0 \times fact(0 - 1)).$$

We can now see why it is important to provide a value for the conditional expression when the predicate expression, in this case $0 = 0$, has the value *true*, even though the second expression $0 \times fact(0 - 1)$ does not possess a value, since $(0 - 1)!$ is undefined.

As another example of definition by recursion, consider the definition of multiplication in terms of addition:

$$mult(x, y) = (x = 0 \to 0, mult(x - 1, y) + y)$$

It is even possible to define addition in terms of the simple successor function:

$$add(x, y) = (x = 0 \to y, add(x - 1, y) + 1).$$

In this way, we can start off with some very simple functions, such as $\lambda x . x + 1$ and $\lambda x . x - 1$, and define a whole host of new functions by recursion. Of course, recursion does not always have to be invoked; the equation

$$h(x) = mult(f(x), g(x))$$

is an example of a definition without the use of recursion. Here the function h is defined by a generalized version of *composition* in terms of *mult*, f and g.

The definition of functions by summation can also be expressed as a definition by recursion; for example

$$h(x) = (x = 0 \to f(0), h(x - 1) + f(x))$$

is another way of saying

$$h(x) = \sum_{y=0}^{x} f(y).$$

The formalism allows us to define functionals just as easily; for instance, we can restate summation in the form

$$h(f, x) = (x = 0 \to f(0), h(f, x - 1) + f(x))$$

to emphasize the functional dependence of h on f.

In order to give a recursive definition of the function h, where

$$h(x) = \min \{ f(x, y) : 0 \leqslant y \leqslant g(x) \},$$

we first construct the function k by

$$k(x, z) = (z = 0 \to f(x, 0), f(x, z) < k(x, z - 1) \to f(x, z), k(x, z - 1)),$$

and then define

$$h(x) = k(x, g(x)).$$

The same trick can be used in other similar cases. Notice the use of

$$(p_1 \to e_1, p_2 \to e_2, e_3)$$

as an unambiguous abbreviation for the conditional expression

$$(p_1 \to e_1, (p_2 \to e_2, e_3)).$$

The above examples indicate the general nature of the formalism we shall adopt. We start with a given collection F of functions and predicates, e.g. for number theoretic functions we may take $F = \{\lambda x . x = 0, \lambda x . x + 1, \lambda x . x - 1\}$, and build new functions from them by using definition by recursion and composition. The class of functions that can be defined in this way is denoted by $C(F)$. However, we shouldn't be too confident at this stage that we really understand the meaning of definition by recursion and composition. Consider, for example, the following three number theoretic functions:

$$mult(x, y) = (x = 0 \to 0, mult(x - 1, y) + y)$$
$$div(x, y) = (x < y \to 0, div(x - y, y) + 1)$$
$$h(x, y) = mult(y, div(x, y)).$$

Intuitively, the first equation defines the multiplication function by recursion, and the second defines div, where

$$div(x, y) = \lfloor x/y \rfloor \text{ provided } y > 0$$
$$= undefined \text{ if } y = 0.$$

Thus h apparently satisfies the equation

$$h(x, y) = y \times \lfloor x/y \rfloor.$$

The problem is to state what value the definition of h gives to $h(x, 0)$. Do we have

$$h(x, 0) = mult(0, div(x, 0)) = 0$$

or $\qquad h(x, 0) = mult(0, div(x, 0)) = undefined?$

In normal mathematical practice, a function value is only considered to be defined if each argument value to the function is defined. Applying this principle to the definition of h, we should expect

$$h(x, 0) = mult(0, undefined) = undefined.$$

However, the principle can cause trouble when combined with the usual interpretation of equality. How are we to understand the definition

$$C(x, y, z) = (x = 0 \to y, z)?$$

Mathematical equations assert equality between the object on the left hand side of the equation and the object on the right. According to the above principle concerning defined values, $C(x, y, z)$ is only defined if each of x, y and z possess defined values. But we have already stated that this is not true of the expression $(x = 0 \to y, z)$ on the right hand side. Moreover the stated interpretation of $(x = 0 \to y, z)$ is absolutely essential for the mechanism of recursive definition. The trouble lies with the interpretation of the equals sign as mathematical equality. This arises with recursive definitions too; consider

$$mult(x, y) = (x = 0 \to 0, mult(x - 1, y) + y).$$

If we try to understand this definition as a mathematical equation—somehow, a defining equation for $mult$—then we have to think of $mult$ as a fixed point of a certain functional. Restated, the equation asserts that

$$mult = \lambda x, y \,.\, (x = 0 \to 0, mult(x - 1, y) + y)$$

and as such has the form

$$mult = F(mult).$$

We can even say what F is:

$$F = \lambda f \,.\, \lambda x, y \,.\, (x = 0 \to 0, f(x - 1, y) + y)$$

Now the equation $mult = F(mult)$ simply says that $mult$ is *fixed point* of F. But how do we know that F has any fixed points and what if it has more than one?

The computational answer to these problems is to replace $=$ by *is*, and treat a definition such as

$$mult(x, y) \; is \; (x = 0 \to 0, mult(x - 1, y) + y)$$

as a purely formal sequence of symbols with no inherent meaning, except that it enables values to be attached to $mult(x, y)$ through the consistent use of a stated *rule of evaluation*. Problems such as whether $mult(0, div(x, 0))$ possesses a defined value or not are then resolved by inspecting the order of evaluation implied by the rule. The mathematical answer, on the other hand, is to construct a theory of partial functions through which it is possible to consider defined values for undefined arguments, and then to study the question of the existence of fixed points. The main disadvantage with the computational approach is that manipulations with formal definitions have no intuitive meaning; for example, we cannot be sure, without looking closely at the rule of evaluation, that the definitions

$$f(x, y) \; is \; (x = 0 \to 1, h(x, f(x - 1, y))),$$

where $\quad h(x, y) \; is \; (y = 0 \to 0, f(y - 1, x)),$

and $\quad f(x, y) \; is \; (x = 0 \to 1, f(x - 1, y) = 0 \to 0, f(f(f(x - 1, y) - 1, x))$

in fact describe the same function f. Nevertheless, the computational approach is more readily available to us, and, provided the rules of evaluation are reasonably straightforward, simple to comprehend. This computational approach is developed at some length in Sections 6.3 and 6.4, while the mathematical approach is taken up in Chapter 7.

6.3 Recursive definitions

We now formalize the concept of a recursive definition introduced in the last section. The first task is to say exactly what is meant by an expression.

Suppose $V_1, V_2, \ldots$ is some collection of types. We suppose that in this collection occurs the special type $T = \{true, false\}$ of truth values. Associated with each type V are two sets of identifiers:

(a) *constants* $a_1, a_2, \ldots$, which denote particular elements of V, and

(b) *variables*, $x_1, x_2, \ldots$, which denote arbitrary elements of V.

We suppose that it can be determined of each identifier whether or not it is a constant or a variable, and also its associated type.

As a simple example, we can take the set of constants of type N to be the *numerals* $0, 1, 2, \ldots$ etc., and the set of variables to be the letters $x, y, \ldots$ etc. It is important to realize the logical distinction between a constant identifier and the abstract object it denotes. Only in the case of type T do we allow the two constant identifiers, *true* and *false*, to denote themselves.

Relative to the given collection of types, the class of *expressions* and their associated types, is defined recursively as follows:

(1) each constant or variable of type V, standing by itself, is an *expression* of *type* V.

(2) If $e_1, e_2, \ldots, e_n$ are expressions of types $V_1, V_2, \ldots, V_n$ respectively, and f is a constant or variable of type $V_1 \times V_2 \times \cdots \times V_n \to U$, then $f(e_1, e_2, \ldots, e_n)$ is an *expression* of *type* U,

(3) if p is an expression of type T, and e_1 and e_2 are both expressions of type V, then $(p \to e_1, e_2)$ is an *expression of type* V.

Thus the class of expressions is built up from constant and variable expressions, by forming applicative expressions and conditional expressions.

Having defined what expressions are, we can now construct recursive definitions. The simpler case of a single recursive definition is given first.

Suppose e is an expression of type U such that:

(i) the only variables appearing in e are among the set $\{x_1, x_2, \ldots, x_n, f\}$,

(ii) x_j is of type V_j for $1 \leqslant j \leqslant n$, and

(iii) f is of type $V_1 \times V_2 \times \cdots \times V_n \to U$.

In such a case, the definition

$$f(x_1, x_2, \ldots, x_n) \text{ is } e$$

is said to be a *recursive definition of* f.

Notice that not every variable in $\{x_1, x_2, \ldots x_n, f\}$ has to occur in e; in particular, if f does not occur, then the above definition is also said to be a definition of f by *composition*.

More generally, we may define a number of functions simultaneously. Suppose $e_1, e_2, \ldots, e_k$ are expressions of type $U_1, U_2, \ldots, U_k$ respectively, such that for each j:

(i) the only variables appearing in e_j are among the set $\{x_1^{(j)}, x_2^{(j)}, \ldots, x_{n_j}^{(j)}, f_1, f_2, \ldots, f_k\}$,

(ii) $x_m^{(j)}$ is of type $V_m^{(j)}$ for $1 \leqslant m \leqslant n_j$, and

(iii) f_j is of type $V_1^{(j)} \times V_2^{(j)} \times \cdots \times V_{n_j}^{(j)} \to U_j$.

Then we say that

$$f_1(x_1^{(1)}, \ldots, x_{n_1}^{(1)}) \ is \ e_1$$
$$f_2(x_1^{(2)}, \ldots, x_{n_2}^{(2)}) \ is \ e_2$$
$$\cdots\cdots\cdots\cdots$$
$$f_k(x_1^{(k)}, \ldots, x_{n_k}^{(k)}) \ is \ e_k$$

is a set of *simultaneous recursive definitions of* $f_1, f_2, \ldots, f_k$.

The above definitions are very general, and it is instructive to see how they can be tailored to meet the requirements of a particular case. For instance, let us consider an interesting class of recursive definitions of number-theoretic functions and predicates, based upon a few simple constant functions, in which functionals and propositional variables (i.e. variables of type T) do not appear. We shall refer to this class as the *number-theoretic formalism.*

Definition of the number-theoretic formalism

The basic collection of types consists of N, T, and derived types of the form $N^n \to N$ and $N^n \to T$. The various identifiers are described as follows:

(1) For N, we assume as constants, the numerals $0, 1, 2, \ldots$ etc., and as variables, the letters $x, y, x_1, y_1, \ldots$ etc.

(2) For T, the only identifiers are the constants *true* and *false* which denote themselves.

(3) For $N \to T$, the only identifier is the constant *zero* which denotes the function $\lambda x . x = 0$.

(4) For $N \to N$, the only constant identifiers are *succ* and *pred* which denote the functions $\lambda x . x + 1$ and $\lambda x . (x = 0 \to 0, x - 1)$ respectively (in other words the successor function and the (total) predecessor function).

(5) Finally, for variables of type $N^n \to N$ or $N^n \to T$ we use the letters $f, g, \ldots$ etc.

There are two types of expressions, *numerical* and *predicate expressions* of types N and T respectively, which are defined as follows

numerical expressions:

(1) each constant or variable of type N standing by itself is a numerical expression,

(2) if $e_1, e_2, \ldots, e_n$ are numerical expressions and f is a constant or variable of type $N^n \to N$, then $f(e_1, e_2, \ldots, e_n)$ is a numerical expression

(3) if p is a predicate expression (see below), and e_1 and e_2 are numerical expressions, then $(p \to e_1, e_2)$ is a numerical expression.

predicate expressions:

(1) the constants *true* and *false* standing by themselves are predicate expressions

(2) if e is a numerical expression, then $zero(e)$ is a predicate expression

(3) if p_1, p_2 and p_3 are predicate expressions, then so is $(p_1 \to p_2, p_3)$.

To define the class of recursive definitions suppose $e_1, e_2, \ldots, e_k$ are expressions such that for each j, e_j is of type V_j, where $V_j = N$ or T, and the variables appearing in e_j are among $\{x_1^{(j)}, x_2^{(j)}, \ldots x_{n_j}^{(j)}, f_1, f_2, \ldots, f_k\}$, where $x_m^{(j)}$ is of type N for each m, and f_j is of type $N^{n_j} \to V_j$ for $1 \leqslant j \leqslant k$. Then the set of definitions

$$f_1(x_1^{(1)}, \ldots, x_{n_1}^{(1)}) \ is \ e_1$$

$$\cdots \cdots \cdots \cdots$$

$$f_k(x_1^{(k)}, \ldots, x_{n_k}^{(k)}) \ is \ e_k$$

is said to be a set of simultaneous recursive definitions of the number theoretic functions and predicates $f_1, f_2, \ldots f_k$. As an example of a recursive definition in the number theoretic formalism, consider

$$f(x) \ is \ (zero(x) \to succ(x), \ succ(f(pred(x))))).$$

Recalling the definitions of $zero$, $succ$ and $pred$, we can see that the above definition is the formal version of

$$f(x) \ is \ (x = 0 \to x + 1, f(x - 1) + 1).$$

6.4 Rules of evaluation

In order to be able to say exactly what functions are described by recursive definitions, we need to specify a *rule of evaluation* for associating function values with given arguments. Among many possible rules, the two we shall describe are called the *eaf-rule* and the *eal-rule*. The letters *eaf* stand for 'evaluate arguments first' and the *eaf*-rule corresponds roughly with the Algol 60 call-by-value mechanism. Its basic feature is that in any recursive call of the function or functions being defined, the arguments associated with the call are always evaluated first. The letters *eal* stand for 'evaluate arguments last' and the *eal*-rule resembles the Algol 60 call-by-name concept. In the *eal*-rule, the arguments associated with a given recursive call of the function being defined are passed across in an unevaluated form. If and when these arguments are later needed to continue the evaluation, they are then evaluated as required. Thus in the *eal*-rule the evaluation of arguments is delayed until the last possible moment.

It is as well to have some intuitive understanding about the effect of these two rules before passing to a formal definition.

Suppose we wish to evaluate $f(1, 0)$ from the definition

$$f(x, y) \ is \ (x = 0 \to 0, f(x - 1, f(x, y))).$$

Roughly speaking, the values 1 and 0 are substituted for x and y in the defining expression, giving

$$(1 = 0 \to 0, f(1 - 1, f(1, 0))),$$

and this variable-free expression is then evaluated. Since $1 = 0$ evaluates to *false*, the process of evaluation is continued by evaluating the expression

$$f(1 - 1, f(1,0)).$$

Here, the distinction between the *eaf* and *eal*-rules of evaluation comes into play. According to the *eaf*-rule, we must evaluate the arguments $(1 - 1)$ and $f(1, 0)$ in order to proceed with the evaluation of $f(1 - 1, f(1,0))$. The first argument evaluates to 0, but the evaluation of $f(1, 0)$ involves starting the whole process again, which thereby continues without end. Thus, under the *eaf*-rule:

$$f(1, 0) = undefined.$$

According to the *eal*-rule on the other hand, the expressions $(1 - 1)$ and $f(1, 0)$ are not evaluated but are substituted directly into the defining expression of f; thus the next step in evaluating $f(1 - 1, f(1,0))$ is the evaluation of

$$(1 - 1 = 0 \rightarrow 0, f((1 - 1) - 1, f((1 - 1), f(1, 0)))).$$

Since the evaluation of $1 - 1 = 0$ gives *true*, the evaluation terminates with the value 0. Under the *eal*-rule therefore:

$$f(1, 0) = 0.$$

This example illustrates an important point about rules of evaluation: the process of evaluation is carried out by manipulating expressions and not strictly speaking with the abstract quantities that the expressions represent. This means that the constant functions, have to be interpreted as functions from constant expressions to constant expressions, e.g. the function $\lambda x . x - 1$ in the above example has to be interpreted as a function from numerals to numerals rather than from N to N.

To simplify the formal treatment, we shall only give a precise definition of the *eaf* and *eal*-rules as they relate to a single recursive definition

$$f(x_1, x_2, \ldots, x_n) \text{ is } E,$$

where x_j is of type V_j and f is of type $V_1 \times V_2 \times \cdots \times V_n \rightarrow U$, where U is the type of E. Suppose that for each type V, the set $C(V)$ consists of all constant identifiers (i.e. constant expressions), one for each element of V. Both the rules show how to associate with elements $(a_1, a_2, \ldots, a_n)$ of $C(V_1) \times C(V_2) \times \cdots \times C(V_n)$, a possible element b of $C(U)$ which represents the value, if it exists, of $f(a_1, a_2, \ldots, a_n)$. For this process to work, we have to suppose that each constant function $g : V \rightarrow W$ can be interpreted as a function of type $C(V) \rightarrow C(W)$.

Apart from constant expressions, it is necessary to consider free expressions. A *free expression* is any expression in which no variable appears except possibly for the variable f itself.

Definition of eaf-rule

(1) To evaluate f for the argument $(a_1, a_2, \ldots, a_n)$, where $a_1, a_2, \ldots, a_n$ are free expressions, substitute a_j for x_j throughout the expression E for $1 \leqslant j \leqslant n$,

and then evaluate the resulting free expression e according to the following rules:

(2) If e is of the form $(p \to e_1, e_2)$ then evaluate p according to rules (1)–(5). If the result of this evaluation is *true*, then take the value of e to be the result of evaluating e_1. If the evaluation of p gives *false*, then take the value of e to be the result of evaluating e_2. If the process of evaluating p does not terminate, then the value of e is undefined.

(3) If e is of the form $g(e_1, e_2, \ldots, e_k)$, where g is a constant function, then evaluate $e_1, e_2, \ldots, e_k$ in sequence. If this process terminates, resulting in constant expressions $b_1, b_2, \ldots, b_k$, then the value of e is the value of g applied to $(b_1, b_2, \ldots, b_k)$.

(4) If e is of the form $f(e_1, e_2, \ldots, e_n)$, then evaluate $e_1, e_2, \ldots, e_n$ in sequence. If this process terminates, resulting in expressions $b_1, b_2, \ldots, b_n$, then take the value of e to be the result of evaluating f with the new arguments $b_1, b_2, \ldots, b_n$, as described by rule (1).

(5) If e has none of the above forms, then take the value of e to be e itself.

Definition of eal-rule

In order to define the *eal*-rule, we make the following change to rule (4):

(4′) If e is of the form $f(e_1, e_2, \ldots, e_n)$, then take the value of e to be the result of evaluating f with the new free expressions $e_1, e_2, \ldots, e_n$, as described by rule (1).

Since constant expressions are particular cases of free expressions, and subexpressions of free expressions are also free expressions, the above rules are consistent and adequate to describe the evaluation of f with given constant arguments $x_1, x_2, \ldots, x_n$. In order to deal with the general case of a set of simultaneous recursive definitions of $f_1, f_2, \ldots, f_k$, only slight changes have to be made to rules (1), (4) and (4′). In the general case, a free expression will be any expression in which no variables appear apart possibly for $f_1, f_2, \ldots, f_k$.

Both rules can be effectively applied provided that the constant functions are computable functions of their arguments so that rule (3) can actually be carried out. Notice that such constant functions are always applied to evaluated arguments; it is only arguments to the recursively defined function, or functions, that can be passed across unevaluated. To see the rules at work, consider again the troublesome example of the Section 6.2:

$$mult(x, y) \text{ is } (x = 0 \to 0, \, mult(x - 1, y) + y)$$
$$div(x, y) \text{ is } (x < y \to 0, \, div(x - y, y) + 1)$$
$$h(x, y) \text{ is } mult(y, \, div(x, y)).$$

More formally, we should have written expressions such as $x < y$, $x + y$ and so on, in prefix form, but such liberties with the notation are not too serious and do improve readability. To evaluate $h(1, 0)$ according to the *eaf*-rule, rule (1) tells us to evaluate

$$mult(0, div(1, 0)).$$

This is an application of a recursively defined function *mult* (here, of course, we have a set of simultaneous recursive definitions), and rule (4) applies. This means that the arguments 0 and $div(1, 0)$ have to be evaluated. The constant expression 0 evaluates as 0, according to rule (5); to evaluate $div(1, 0)$ we have to evaluate

$$(1 < 0 \rightarrow 0, div(1 - 0, 0) + 1)$$

by rule (1). By rule (2), we have to evaluate

$$div(1 - 0, 0) + 1.$$

This is an application of the constant successor function, so by rule (3) we have to evaluate $div(1 - 0, 0)$. Thus by rule (4), we again have to evaluate $div(1, 0)$, and so the process of evaluation continues indefinitely without end. Thus under the *eaf*-rule,

$$h(1, 0) = undefined.$$

Turning to the *eal*-rule, we have more shortly:

$h(1, 0)$

$\Rightarrow mult(0, div(1, 0))$ by rule (1),

$\Rightarrow (0 = 0 \rightarrow 0, mult(0 - 1, div(1, 0)) + div(1, 0))$ by rule (4'),

$\Rightarrow 0$ by rule (2) and rule (5).

Hence under the *eal*-rule,

$$h(1, 0) = 0.$$

As another example, this time involving functionals, consider the following definitions:

$$f_1(x) \, is \, f_2(f_3, x)$$
$$f_2(g, x) \, is \, g(x, g(x, 0))$$
$$f_3(x, y) \, is \, (x = 0 \rightarrow y, f_1(x - 1)),$$

where x is a variable of type N. This is a properly formed set of simultaneous recursive definitions under the following type assignments:

$$f_1 : N \rightarrow N$$
$$f_2 : (N^2 \rightarrow N) \times N \rightarrow N$$
$$f_3, g : N^2 \rightarrow N.$$

The evaluation of $f_1(1)$ by the *eaf*-rule proceeds as follows:

$$f_1(1) \Rightarrow f_2(f_3, 1)$$ by rule (1).

Since both f_3 and 1 evaluate to themselves by rule (5), we have

$$f_2(f_3, 1) \Rightarrow f_3(1, f_3(1, 0)) \quad \text{by rule (4)}.$$

Now 1 evaluates to 1, and

$$
\begin{aligned}
f_3(1, 0) &\Rightarrow (1 = 0 \rightarrow 0, f_1(1 - 1)) && \text{by rule (1)}, \\
&\Rightarrow f_1(0) && \text{by rules (2) and (3)}, \\
&\Rightarrow f_2(f_3, 0) && \text{by rule (1)}, \\
&\Rightarrow f_3(0, f_3(0, 0)) && \text{by rules (5) and (1)}.
\end{aligned}
$$

Furthermore,

$$
\begin{aligned}
f_3(0, 0) &\Rightarrow (0 = 0 \rightarrow 0, f(0 - 1)) && \text{by rule (1)}, \\
&\Rightarrow 0 && \text{by rule (2)}.
\end{aligned}
$$

Hence $\quad f_3(1, 0) \Rightarrow f_3(0, 0) \Rightarrow 0,$

and so $\quad f_2(f_3, 1) \Rightarrow f_3(1, f_3(1, 0)) \Rightarrow f_3(1, 0) \Rightarrow 0.$

Thus we have

$$f_1(1) = 0.$$

Turning to the evaluation of $f_1(1)$ by the *eal*-rule, we have:

$$
\begin{aligned}
f_1(1) &\Rightarrow f_2(f_3, 1) \\
&\Rightarrow f_3(1, f_3(1, 0)) && \text{by rule (4')} \\
&\Rightarrow (1 = 0 \rightarrow f_3(1, 0), f_1(1 - 1)) && \text{by rule (4')} \\
&\Rightarrow f_1(1 - 1) && \text{by rule (2)} \\
&\Rightarrow f_2(f_3, 1 - 1) && \text{by rule (4')} \\
&\Rightarrow f_3(1 - 1, f_3(1 - 1, 0)) && \text{by rule (4')} \\
&\Rightarrow (1 - 1 = 0 \rightarrow f_3(1 - 1, 0), f_1(1 - 1 - 1)) && \text{by rule (4')} \\
&\Rightarrow f_3(1 - 1, 0) && \text{by rule (2)} \\
&\Rightarrow (1 - 1 = 0 \rightarrow 0, f_1(1 - 1 - 1)) \\
&\Rightarrow 0,
\end{aligned}
$$

and so

$$f_1(1) = 0$$

Although the value associated with $f_1(1)$ is the same under either rule, the process by which this value is obtained is quite different.

As the reader may have noticed, the definitions of the *eaf*-rule and *eal*-rule are themselves examples of recursive definitions of functions, and can be expressed within the formalism. It is instructive to see how this is done. To avoid the technical complication of evaluating lists of expressions when many-place functions are present, we shall give recursive definitions of the *eaf* and *eal*-rule only as they apply to a single definition of the form

$$f(x) \text{ is } E,$$

where the expression E refers to at most one 1-place constant function g.

In order to construct the definitions, we need the following constant functions of free expressions:

(a) *gapp* and *gapply*, where $gapp(e)$ is *true* just in the case that e is an expression of the form $g(e')$, and $gapply(e)$ gives the constant expression which results when the function g is actually applied to the constant expression e. Similar functions can be defined in the general case, when E refers to more than one constant function; restricting our attention to a single constant function g serves only to shorten the definitions that follow.

(b) *fapp* and *fsub*, where $fapp(e)$ is *true* just in the case that e is an expression of the form $f(e')$, and $fsub(e)$ gives the expression which results when the free expression e is substituted for x throughout E. Once again, similar functions are easily defined in the more general case of a list of simultaneous recursive definitions.

(c) *rand*, where $rand(e) = e'$ if e is an expression of the form $f(e')$ or $g(e')$, i.e. $rand(e)$ is the operand of the applicative expression e.

(d) *cond*, *test*, *left* and *right*, where $cond(e)$ is *true* just in the case that e is a conditional expression of the form $(p \rightarrow e_1, e_2)$ in which case

$$test(e) = p, left(e) = e_1, \text{and } right(e) = e_2.$$

With these constant functions, we can define the functions *eaf* and *eal*, both acting on free expressions, as follows:

$$eaf(e) \text{ is } (cond(e) \rightarrow (eaf(test(e)) \rightarrow eaf(left(e)), eaf(right(e))),$$
$$gapp(e) \rightarrow gapply(eaf(rand(e))),$$
$$fapp(e) \rightarrow eaf(fsub(eaf(rand(e)))),$$
$$e),$$

and $\quad eal(e) \text{ is } (cond(e) \rightarrow (eal(test(e)) \rightarrow eal(left(e)), eal(right(e))),$
$$gapp(e) \rightarrow gapply(eal(rand(e))),$$
$$fapp(e) \rightarrow eal(fsub(rand(e))),$$
$$e).$$

These definitions are simple transcriptions of the previously described rules. Notice that the essential difference between *eaf* and *eal* occurs only in the case that $fapp(e)$ is *true*. In the general situation, when functions of more than one argument are present, $rand(e)$ will be a list of operands, and so some simple list processing functions will be needed to evaluate lists of expressions. This generalization is discussed in the exercises at the end of the chapter.

If we had given the above recursive definitions as the original definitions of the *eaf* and *eal*-rule, then a paradoxical situation would have been apparent. How can we possibly understand the meaning of a formalism if the meaning is expressed within the formalism itself? This situation is a common one with formalisms powerful and natural enough to express their own semantics. Indeed, the problem of circularity can never be avoided if we wish to define the meaning of a formalism completely precisely. Suppose F_1 is a formalism whose meaning we wish to specify exactly. This can be done by using a second formalism F_2 to express the meaning of F_1. But how can we be sure that we understand what we have written in F_2? Only by giving a third formalism F_3 to express the meaning of F_2 and so on. To avoid this infinite sequence of meta-formalisms, we have at some point to resort to informality. This is exactly the case with the definitions of *eaf* and *eal* above. We have only to understand the recursive definitions of *eaf* and *eal* on an informal and intuitive basis, in order to be able to describe precisely the evaluation of every other recursive definition.

Having defined the *eaf* and *eal* modes of evaluation, we can now describe the nature of the functions f_F and f_L induced by the recursive definition

$$f(x) \text{ is } E.$$

Supposing x is of type U and E is of type V, we need two further functions

$$code: U \rightarrow C(U)$$
$$decode: C(V) \rightarrow V,$$

for passing from constant expressions to the values they denote, and vice-versa. We define $f_F: U \rightarrow V$ by the equation

$$f_F(x) = decode(eaf(fsub(code(x))))$$

for all $x \in U$, and $f_L: U \rightarrow V$ by the equation

$$f_L(x) = decode(eal(fsub(code(x)))).$$

The important question now arises as to the nature of the relationship between f_F and f_L, or what is the same thing, the relationship between the function *eaf* and *eal*. To answer this question, let us write $f \subseteq g$ to mean that for all x, if $f(x)$ is defined, then $g(x)$ is defined and $f(x) = g(x)$. In other words, $f \subseteq g$ just in the case that the function g is a possibly trivial *extension* of the function f. The following theorems are stated in the case of a single recursive definition of a 1-place function, but are easily generalized to the case of simultaneous recursive definitions of not necessarily 1-place functions.

Theorem 1.   Let $f(x)$ *is* E be a given recursive definition. Then $f_F \subseteq f_L$.

Theorem 2.   Let $f(x)$ *is* E be a given recursive definition, and let

$$g(x) \text{ is } (p(x) \rightarrow E', E')$$

be a recursive definition, constructed by taking p to be any total constant predicate, and E' to be the expression which results when the letter g is substituted for the letter f throughout E. Then $f_F \subseteq g_L$.

Theorem 3.   Let $f(x)$ *is* $(p(x) \rightarrow E_1, E_2)$ be a recursive definition, where p is any constant predicate. Then $f_F = f_L$.

These theorems will not be proved until Section 8.2. The reason is that, since in the last analysis the definitions of the *eaf* and *eal*-rules of evaluation are recursively described, the three theorems are statements about the recursively defined functions *eaf* and *eal*. Consequently, to develop and justify the particular induction arguments necessary for proving the theorems at the present time, would anticipate the very purpose of our later work concerning the description and justification of proof techniques for statements about recursively defined functions. Nevertheless, some general remarks may hopefully help to make the intuitive basis of the theorems clear. The essential difference between the *eaf* and *eal*-rules is that, in the *eal*-rule, the evaluation of certain subexpressions is delayed until the values of these subexpressions are actually required to continue the evaluation. Thus, subexpressions which do not possess defined values may never be evaluated. The *eaf*-rule of evaluation, on the other hand, demands the evaluation of all subexpressions, and may fail to terminate because one of these subexpressions fails to have a defined value. It follows that the *eaf*-rule and *eal*-rule never return conflicting values, but the *eal*-rule may return a value when the *eaf*-rule does not. This is the substance of Theorem 1. On the other hand, the presence of the predicate expression $p(x)$ in the recursive definitions in Theorems 2 and 3 forces the evaluation of all arguments, whether or not the *eaf*-rule or *eal*-rule is specified. In the *eal*-rule, this evaluation takes one stage later than in the *eaf*-rule, but nevertheless it must take place. It follows that in such recursive definitions the difference between the *eaf* and *eal*-rules disappears, and this is the substance of Theorems 2 and 3. Theorem 2 is important because it says that we can pass from the *eaf*-mode of evaluation to the *eal*-mode and still specify the same function, provided only we make a slight change to the defining expression.

The next question concerns the extent of the formalism: how big is the class of functions that we can define recursively using one or other of the two evaluation rules? To fix upon a particular context, consider the number-theoretic formalism, defined in Section 6.3, and let $C(eaf)$ and $C(eal)$ denote the class of functions definable in the formalism using the *eaf*-rule and *eal*-rule respectively.

Theorem 4.   Both $C(eaf)$ and $C(eal)$ is the class of computable number-theoretic partial functions. More precisely, the (1-place) functions of $C(eaf)$ and $C(eal)$ are just the NORMA-computable functions.

Half of Theorem 4 will be proved in Section 6.5, where it is shown that every NORMA-computable function is recursively definable using either of the rules of evaluation. The proof of the other half of the theorem, namely that every function in $C(eaf)$ or $C(eal)$ is computable, is intuitively obvious. Given a recursive definition, or set of mutually recursive definitions, the application of either the *eaf*-rule or *eal*-rule can be carried out in an effective manner for any given arguments. Since function values are undefined if this process of evaluation fails to terminate, the recursively defined functions are computable, although possibly partial, number theoretic functions. The formal version of the proof, whereby each recursive definition of a 1-place function f is translated into a NORMA flowchart program for computing either f_F or f_L as the case may be, is however quite complicated. Either we have to provide a formally described and provably correct compiler for recursive definitions in terms of NORMA programs, or describe a suitable expression-processing machine on which the *eaf* and *eal*-rules can be implemented, and then show that this machine can be simulated by NORMA. Both these approaches involve some fairly substantial programming and would detract from our main purpose.

To see the formalism for number theoretic functions at work, let us consider the problem of expressing the function *prime* recursively, where

$$prime(x) = \text{ the } (x + 1)\text{st prime number in order of magnitude.}$$

Thus, $prime(0) = 2$, $prime(1) = 3$, etc. The example is instructive in that it demonstrates the use of predicates in the construction of number theoretic functions.

As a first step, we can define prime by

$prime(x)$ *is* $(x = 0 \rightarrow 2$, *the least* $y > prime(x - 1)$ *such that* y *is prime).*

This is certainly a natural recursive definition of the prime function, but requires that we give a recursive definition of the function

λx. *the least* $y > prime(x - 1)$ *such that* y *is prime.*

In general, the function f, where

$$f(z) = \text{ the least } y \geqslant z \text{ such that } p(y)$$

can be defined recursively by

$$f(z) \text{ is } (p(z) \rightarrow z, f(z + 1)).$$

It follows that we can define prime by

$$prime(x) \text{ is } (x = 0 \rightarrow 2, \text{ next } (prime(x - 1) + 1))$$
$$next(x) \text{ is } (x \text{ is prime} \rightarrow x, next(x + 1)),$$

which leaves only the problem of expressing the predicate $\lambda x . x$ *is prime.* Before doing this, it is worth pausing to consider the effect of the choice of evaluation rule on the interpretation of the above definitions. Euclid's famous theorem, asserting that the number of primes is infinite, shows that both *prime* and *next* are total functions; consequently, Theorem 1 can be used to conclude that the *eaf* and *eal* rules of evaluation describe the same functions. However, this result holds even if we did not know whether *prime* and *next* were total functions. The form of the recursive definitions means that Theorem 3 is applicable, and again shows that for this case the *eaf* and *eal* rules are equivalent.

Recall from Section 5.2 that the symbolic rendering of the predicate $\lambda x . x$ *is prime* is as follows:

$$\lambda x . (x > 1) \wedge \forall y . [\exists z . (y \times z = x) \supset y = 1 \vee y = x].$$

In order to give a recursive definition of the predicate $\lambda x \,.\, x$ *is prime*, consider first the problem of defining the predicate r, where

$$r(x) = p(x) \wedge q(x).$$

In normal propositional logic, the values of r are given by the entries in the following table:

$q(x)$ \ $p(x)$	true	false
true	true	false
false	false	false

However the normal definition of r is not sufficient in the present situation, since the values of $p(x)$ and $q(x)$ may be undefined. There are four logical ways in which the table can be extended to incorporate the value *undef*:

(a) natural

$q(x)$ \ $p(x)$	true	false	undef
true	true	false	undef
false	false	false	undef
undef	undef	undef	undef

Here, if either $p(x)$ or $q(x)$ is undefined, then so is $r(x)$.

(b) symmetric

$q(x)$ \ $p(x)$	true	false	undef
true	true	false	undef
false	false	false	false
undef	undef	false	undef

Here, provided at least one of $p(x)$ or $q(x)$ is *false*, then the value of $r(x)$ is *false*.

(c) *p*-ordered.

$q(x)$ \ $p(x)$	true	false	undef
true	true	false	undef
false	false	false	undef
undef	undef	false	undef

Here, $r(x)$ is *false* provided that $p(x)$ is *false*, whether or not $q(x)$ is defined.

(d) q-ordered.

$q(x)$ \ $p(x)$	true	false	undef
true	true	false	undef
false	false	false	false
undef	undef	undef	undef

Here, $r(x)$ is *false* provided that $q(x)$ is *false*, whether or not $p(x)$ is defined. It is instructive to see how these four possible ways of defining r can be expressed within the recursive formalism. The p-ordered and q-ordered extensions are captured by defining

$$r(x) \text{ is } (p(x) \to q(x), false)$$

and

$$r(x) \text{ is } (q(x) \to p(x), false),$$

respectively. These definitions can be interpreted by either the *eaf* or *eal*-rule, since both give the same result. The natural extension of r is given by defining

$$r(x) \text{ is } and(p(x), q(x))$$

$$and(x, y) \text{ is } (x \to y, false),$$

and using only the *eaf*-rule of evaluation. Alternatively, we can suppose *and* is a given constant function, and use either mode of evaluation. However, there is no way we can express the symmetric definition of r within the formalism. The definition

$$r(x) \text{ is } and(p(x), q(x)),$$

where *and* is the constant symmetric function given by table (b), will not work because, with either rule of evaluation, constant functions are only applied to evaluated arguments. Consequently, $r(x)$ will be undefined if either $p(x)$ or $q(x)$ is undefined, and this is not what is intended. The basic trouble is that the rules of evaluation are conceived of as sequential processes where the value of one argument is determined before the evaluation of another argument starts. It is possible to describe a more general evaluation process in which the arguments are evaluated in parallel. With this more general process, the definition of the symmetric *and* can be given: the evaluation of $p(x)$ and $q(x)$ proceeds step by step in parallel until either both evaluations are complete, or one results in returning the value *false*; in either case, the appropriate value of $r(x)$ can then be determined. To incorporate this possibility an extensive reformulation of the rules of evaluation would have to be given.

In the case of the predicate $\lambda x . x$ *is prime*, the distinctions disappear, since we know that both $p(x)$ and $q(x)$ will always have a defined value. This means that we can replace

$$r(x) = p(x) \wedge q(x),$$

by

$$r(x) \text{ is } (p(x) \to q(x), false).$$

Similarly, $r(x) = p(x) \vee q(x)$

can be replaced by

$$r(x) \, is \, (p(x) \rightarrow true, q(x)),$$

and $r(x) = p(x) \supset q(x)$

can be replaced by

$$r(x) \, is \, (p(x) \rightarrow q(x), true).$$

This leaves the problem of giving recursive definitions for the predicates of the form

$$p(x) = \forall y . r(x, y),$$

and $q(x) = \exists y . r(x, y),$

The trouble here is that, in general, neither p nor q are intuitively computable predicates, and so cannot be recursively defined. The best we can do is construct recursive definitions for

$$p(x, z) = \forall y \leqslant z . r(x, y)$$

and

$$q(x, z) = \exists y \leqslant z . r(x, y).$$

These are as follows:

$$p(x, z) \, is \, (z = 0 \rightarrow r(x, 0), r(x, z) \rightarrow p(x, z - 1), false)$$
$$q(x, z) \, is \, (z = 0 \rightarrow r(x, 0), r(x, z) \rightarrow true, q(x, z - 1)).$$

Since we can restate the definition of $\lambda x . x \, is \, prime$ in the form

$$\lambda x . (x > 1) \wedge \forall y \leqslant x . [\exists z \leqslant x . (y \times z = x) \supset y = 1 \vee y = x],$$

the recursive definition can now be given. We have

$isprime(x) \, is \, (x > 1 \rightarrow a(x), false)$

$a(x) \, is \, b(x, x)$

$b(x, y) \, is \, (y = 0 \rightarrow c(x, 0), c(x, y) \rightarrow b(x, y - 1), false)$

$c(x, y) \, is \, (d(x, y) \rightarrow e(x, y), true)$

$d(x, y) \, is \, f(x, y, x)$

$f(x, y, z) \, is \, (z = 0 \rightarrow x = 0, y \times z = x \rightarrow true, f(x, y, z - 1))$

$e(x, y) \, is \, (y = 1 \rightarrow true, y = x).$

6.5   The translation of programs into recursive definitions

We turn now to the problem of constructing a recursive definition for the function computed by a given program. We first describe the general method of translation, and then show with a number of examples how the translations work out in practice.

Flowchart programs

Suppose P is a flowchart program written as a set of labelled instructions with label identifiers $\{1, 2, \ldots, n\}$, where 1 is the initial label, and n is the unique terminal label. Suppose M is a machine with input set X and memory set V. Consider the set of simultaneous recursive definitions

$$f_1(v) \text{ is } E_1$$
$$f_2(v) \text{ is } E_2$$

$$\cdots \cdots \cdots$$

$$f_n(v) \text{ is } E_n,$$

where v is a variable of type V, and $E_1, E_2, \ldots, E_n$ are defined as follows:

(a) $E_j = f_k(F(v))$ if j: **do** F **then goto** k is in P

(b) $E_j = (T(v) \to f_k(v), f_l(v))$ if j: **if** T **then goto** k **else goto** l is in P

(c) $E_n = v$.

If we adjoin to this set a further definition

$$f_0(x) \text{ is } O(f_1(I(x))),$$

where x is a variable of type X, and interpret the identifiers O, I, F, T, etc., as the constant functions O_M, I_M, F_M, T_M, etc., defined by M, then we have

$$mP(x) = f_0(x)$$

for all $x \in X$, using either evaluation rule. When the *eaf*-rule is used, the step by step evaluation of $f_0(x)$ exactly matches the computation sequence of P on M with input x; when the *eal*-rule is used, the evaluation of $f_0(x)$ will proceed in a different order, but the form of the definitions guarantees that the final outcome will be the same.

while programs

For each **while** program W we can construct a recursive definition of a function f_W by applying the following rules:

(1) if $W = F; U$ then define

$$f_W(v) \text{ is } f_U(F(v));$$

(2) if $W = (\textbf{if } T \textbf{ then } X_1 \textbf{ else } X_2); U$, then define

$$f_W(v) \text{ is } f_U(f_X(v))$$
$$f_X(v) \text{ is } (T(v) \to f_{X_1}(v), f_{X_2}(v));$$

(3) if $W = $ **while** T **do** (X_1); U, then define

$$f_W(v) \, is \, f_U(f_X(v))$$
$$f_X(v) \, is \, (T(v) \rightarrow f_X(f_{X_1}(v)), v);$$

(4) if $W = $ **until** T **do** (X_1); U, then define

$$f_W(v) \, is \, f_U(f_X(v))$$
$$f_X(v) \, is \, (T(v) \rightarrow v, f_X(f_{X_1}(v)));$$

(5) if W is the null program, then construct

$$f_W(v) \, is \, v.$$

If we adjoin to the resulting set of definitions a further definition of the form

$$f_0(x) \, is \, O(f_W(I(x)),$$

and again interpret the constant identifiers as functions defined by M, then we have

$$mW(x) = f_0(x)$$

for all $x \in X$, using either rule of evaluation.

The above translations have been given for a general machine; in practice it is possible to simplify the recursive definitions in various ways. To illustrate this, let us consider the NORMA program

1: **if** $X = 0$ **then goto** *4* **else goto** *2*

2: **do** $X: = X - 1$ **then goto** *3*

3: **do** $Y: = Y + 1$ **then goto** *1*

Applying the general translation to this program we obtain the definitions

$$f_1(x, y) \, is \, (x = 0 \rightarrow f_4(x, y), f_2(x, y))$$
$$f_2(x, y) \, is \, f_3(x - 1, y)$$
$$f_3(x, y) \, is \, f_1(x, y + 1)$$
$$f_4(x, y) \, is \, (x, y)$$

together with

$$f_0(x) \, is \, O(f_1(I(x)),$$

where O is the constant function $\lambda(x, y) . y$. We can replace $I(x)$ by its value $(x, 0)$ in the definition of f_0 and obtain the simpler definition

$$f_0(x) \, is \, O(f_1(x, 0)).$$

We can also remove the output function O. Notice that the function variables $f_1, \ldots, f_4$ are each of type $N^2 \rightarrow N^2$ since they describe functions of the memory set into itself. However, as only the final value of Y is needed for the output, we can redefine $f_1, \ldots, f_4$ as functions of the memory set into Y, i.e. of type $N^2 \rightarrow N$. We thus obtain the following set of definitions:

$$f_0(x) \text{ is } f_1(x, 0)$$
$$f_1(x, y) \text{ is } (x = 0 \rightarrow f_4(x, y), f_2(x, y))$$
$$f_2(x, y) \text{ is } f_3(x - 1, y)$$
$$f_3(x, y) \text{ is } f_1(x, y + 1)$$
$$f_4(x, y) \text{ is } y.$$

Either evaluation rule can be used to evaluate these definitions, since both specify the same function for f_0. To see this, observe that each argument to a call of a recursively defined function is built up of constant functions applied to variables of type N. Since NORMA, like all other machines, defines total constant functions, each function argument always possesses a defined value, whether or not this value is evaluated before the function call, as in the *eaf*-rule, or at some later stage, as in the *eal*-rule. Hence both rules specify the same function for f_0.

This point about total constant functions is actually quite important. Suppose, for the sake of example, that the operation $X := X - 1$ does in fact give an undefined result when the contents of X is zero, and consider the following NORMA program:

1: **do** $X := X - 1$ **then goto** 2
2: **do** $Y := Y + 1$ **then goto** 3.

In this case we obtain the following definition for f_0:

$$f_0(x) \text{ is } f_1(x, 0)$$
$$f_1(x, y) \text{ is } f_2(x - 1, y)$$
$$f_2(x, y) \text{ is } f_3(x, y + 1)$$
$$f_3(x, y) \text{ is } y$$

Now, if we evaluate $f_0(0)$ by the *eaf*-rule we obtain

$$f_0(0) \Rightarrow f_1(0, 0) \Rightarrow f_2(0 - 1, 0) \Rightarrow undefined,$$

since we are supposing $0 - 1 =$ undefined. On the other hand, evaluating $f_0(0)$ by the *eal*-rule gives

$$f_0(0) \Rightarrow f_1(0, 0) \Rightarrow f_2(0 - 1, 0) \Rightarrow f_3(0 - 1, 0 + 1) \Rightarrow 0 + 1 \Rightarrow 1.$$

This situation cannot arise with our definition of machines, since operation identifiers are always interpreted as total functions.

To return to the first example, we can make further simplifications by judicious substitutions, in order to eliminate some of the definitions. For instance, we can eliminate f_2, f_3 and f_4 by substituting their defining expressions into the remaining definitions to obtain

$$f_0(x) \text{ is } f_1(x, 0)$$
$$f_1(x, y) \text{ is } (x = 0 \rightarrow y, f_1(x - 1, y + 1)).$$

Once again, the use of these substitutions can be justified only because both evaluation rules give the same results. In general, such substitutions are *not* valid with the *eaf*-evaluation rule, since the resulting definitions may describe an extension of the original function (see Exercise 6.15).

This discussion of NORMA programs shows how every NORMA-computable function can be defined recursively in the number-theoretic formalism, and so completes the proof of Theorem 4 as promised in Section 6.4.

We shall now consider a number of further examples.

Example 1:   computing powers

The following program P computes the value x^n into register y:

$$y: = 1;$$

while $n \neq 0$ **do**

> **begin if** *even*(n) **then** $n: = n/2$
>
> > **else begin** $n: = (n - 1)/2; \ y: = y \times x$ **end**;
>
> $x: = x^2$

end

The inputs to P are integers $x \geqslant 0$ and $n \geqslant 0$, and the output integer is taken from y. The function f computed by P can be recursively defined as follows:

$$f(x, n) \text{ is } g(x, n, 1)$$
$$g(x, n, y) \text{ is } (n = 0 \to y, even(n) \to g(x^2, n/2, y),$$
$$g(x^2, (n - 1)/2, y \times x)).$$

Here, the translation of the **while** program P has been simplified in an obvious way. The correctness of P can be established by proving that

$$f(x, n) = x^n \quad \text{for all integers } n \geqslant 0.$$

To do this, one must prove the more general assertion

$$g(x, n, y) = y \times x^n \quad \text{for all integers } n \geqslant 0.$$

For this example, the necessary induction argument is straightforward, and we might as well give it. As the basis for the induction on n, we have

$$g(x, 0, y) = y = y \times x^0,$$

by the definition of g. The induction step is to assume that

$$g(x, m, y) = y \times x^m \quad \text{for all } m, \qquad 0 \leqslant m \leqslant n,$$

and then prove that this equation also holds in the case $m = n + 1$. Now $n + 1 \neq 0$, so only two cases arise:

(a) $(n + 1)$ is even, in which case

$$g(x, n + 1, y) = g(x^2, (n + 1)/2, y) = y \times (x^2)^{(n + 1)/2} = y \times x^{(n + 1)}$$

(b) $(n + 1)$ is odd, in which case

$$g(x, n + 1, y) = g(x^2, n/2, y \times x) = y \times x \times (x^2)^{n/2} = y \times x^{(n+1)}.$$

The induction is thus established, and we have

$$f(x, n) = g(x, n, 1) = 1 \times x^n = x^n.$$

The reader should compare this proof, which establishes the *total* correctness of P, with a proof of partial correctness using the axiomatic method of Chapter 5.

Example 2: square root

The following program Q computes $\lfloor \sqrt{a} \rfloor$ in x:

$$x: = 0; y: = 1; z: = 1;$$
$$\textbf{while } y \leqslant a \textbf{ do}$$
$$\textbf{begin } x: = x + 1;$$
$$z: = z + 2;$$
$$y: = y + z$$
$$\textbf{end}$$

The translation of Q into a set of recursive definitions uses another simplifying device: since a is never changed by the program, we can interpret it as a constant identifier in the resulting definitions. Thus we can construct

$$f(x, y, z) \text{ is } (y \leqslant a \rightarrow f(x + 1, y + z + 2, z + 2), x),$$

and take

$$f(0, 1, 1) = \lfloor \sqrt{a} \rfloor$$

as the correctness condition of Q. In this case we have to prove the more general assertion

$$f(x, y, z) = x + n, \quad \text{where}$$
$$n = \text{the least } n \geqslant 0 \text{ such that } y + nz + n(n + 1) > a,$$

for all x, y, and z. It then follows that

$$f(0, 1, 1) = \text{the least } n \geqslant 0 \text{ such that } (n + 1)^2 > a$$
$$= \lfloor \sqrt{a} \rfloor.$$

Example 3: binary search

Given inputs A, x, and $n \geqslant 1$, where A is an array whose elements satisfy

$$A(0) < A(1) < \cdots < A(n) \quad \text{and} \quad A(0) < x,$$

the following program B will exit at label *true* if there is a j such that $A(j) = x$, and at label *false* otherwise:

$$i: = \lceil n/2 \rceil; \quad n: = \lfloor n/2 \rfloor;$$

$F:$ **if** $x < A(i)$ **then goto** G **else**

      if $x > A(i)$ **then goto** H **else**

      goto *true*;

$G:$ **if** $n = 0$ **then goto** *false* **else**

            begin $i: = i - \lceil n/2 \rceil; n: = \lfloor n/2 \rfloor;$ **goto** F **end**;

$H:$ **if** $n = 0$ **then goto** *false* **else**

            begin $i: = i + \lceil n/2 \rceil; n: = \lfloor n/2 \rfloor;$ **goto** F **end**.

Suppose we define

$$tn = \lceil n/2 \rceil = \text{the least integer} \geqslant n/2$$
$$bn = \lfloor n/2 \rfloor = \text{the greatest integer} \leqslant n/2.$$

The predicate b computed by B can then be defined recursively as follows:

$$b(n) \text{ is } f(tn, bn)$$
$$f(i, n) \text{ is } (x < A(i) \rightarrow g(i, n),$$
$$x > A(i) \rightarrow h(i, n),$$
$$true)$$
$$g(i, n) \text{ is } (n = 0 \rightarrow false, f(i - tn, bn))$$
$$h(i, n) \text{ is } (n = 0 \rightarrow false, f(i + tn, bn))$$

As in the previous example, we treat the inputs x and A as constants in the recursive definition since they are not changed by the program. The correctness condition of B is that under the input assumption

$$n \geqslant 1 \wedge A(0) < x \wedge \forall i, j . [i < j \supset A(i) < A(j)],$$

we have

$$b(n) = \exists j . [A(j) = x \wedge 1 \leqslant j \leqslant n].$$

This can be proved as a special case of the equation

$$f(i, n) = \exists j . [A(j) = x \wedge i - n \leqslant j \leqslant i + n].$$

Example 4:   *in situ permutation*

Finally, let us translate the program P for *in situ* permutation discussed in Section 5.5. P was given by the following instructions:

1                            $j: = 1;$

2   **while** $j \leqslant n$ **do**

3   **begin** $k: = f(j);$

```
4                    while j < k do k: = f(k);
5                    if k = j then
6                      begin y: = X(j);
7                        while j ≠ f(k) do
8                          begin X(k): = X(f(k)); k: = f(k) end;
9                        X(k): = y
10                     end;
11                   j: = j + 1
12                 end
```

Suppose $L(X)$ denotes the transformation effected by P on the array X (treating n as a constant). Since P takes the form

$$j: = 1; \textbf{while } j \leqslant n \textbf{ do } (X: = F(j, X); j: = j + 1),$$

we can define $L(X)$ recursively as follows:

$$L(X) \text{ is } A(1, X)$$
$$A(j, X) \text{ is } (j \leqslant n \to A(j + 1, F(j, X)), X).$$

We must now provide a definition for the function F.
Lines 3–10 of P have the form

$$k: = B(j);$$
$$\textbf{if } k = j \textbf{ then } X: = D(j, X);$$

We can define B as follows:

$$B(j) \text{ is } C(j, f(j))$$
$$C(j, k) \text{ is } (j < k \to C(j, f(k)), k).$$

Thus F can be defined by

$$F(j, X) \text{ is } (j = B(j) \to D(j, X), X).$$

This leaves us with the definition of D, which can be given as follows:

$$D(j, X) \text{ is } E(j, j, X(j), X)$$
$$E(j, k, y, X) \text{ is } (j \neq f(k) \to E(j, f(k), y, G(k, X(f(k)), X), G(k, y, X))$$
$$G(k, z, X) \text{ is } \lambda x . (x = k \to z, X(x)).$$

Here, we have used a slightly different way of translating **while** statements. The standard way of translating

$$\textbf{while } T \textbf{ do } (U); V$$

is to define

$$f(x) \text{ is } f_V(f_L(x))$$
$$f_L(x) \text{ is } (T(x) \to f_L(f_U(x)), x).$$

However, an equivalent way is to define

$$f(x) \text{ is } (T(x) \to f(f_U(x)), f_V(x)).$$

The second alternative has been used in the present case, since it avoids the necessity of defining the effect of lines 7 and 8 on the variable k. The function G represents the effect on X of the single assignment

$$X(k): = z.$$

G is thus a functional taking a function X into a new function X', identical to X except for argument k.

Exercises

1. Assuming $x, y, z: N$ and $g: N^2 \to N$, determine the type of f in each of the following cases:

    (i) $f(g, x) = g(g(x, x), x)$,

    (ii) $f(x)(g) = g(g(x, x), x)$,

    (iii) $f(x)(y)(z) = g(x, g(y, z))$.

2. Write down the exponential function and the simple composition operator . in λ-notation.

3. Give a recursive definition for the following functions in terms of the functions $\lambda x . x + 1$, $\lambda x . x - 1$, the predicate $\lambda x . x = 0$:

    (i) exp, where $exp(x, y) = x^y$,

    (ii) lcm, where $lcm(x, y) =$ the lowest common multiple of x and y.

    (iii) $\lambda x \in N .\lfloor \log_2 (x + 1) \rfloor$.

    (iv) min, where $min (x, y) =$ the smaller of x and y.

4. Give recursive definitions for the function f in terms of the function g in each of the following cases:

    (i) $f(x) = \prod_{y=0}^{x} g(y)$,

    (ii) $f(x) = \max \{g(y): 0 \leqslant y \leqslant x\}$.

5. Supposing x and p are variables of type N and $N \to T$ respectively, and f and g are variables of type $N \to N$, determine whether the following sequences of symbols are expressions as defined in Section 3:

    (i) $(p \to f, f)(x)$

    (ii) $(p(x) \to f(x), g(x))$

    (iii) $(f(x) \to p(x), p(x))$

    (iv) $(p(x) \to p(x), p(x))$

(v) $f(p(x) \to x, x)$

(vi) $f((p(x) \to f, g))$.

6. Under what conditions would

$$f(x_1, x_2, \ldots, x_n)(y) \text{ is } e$$

constitute a well formed recursive definition?

7. In a similar manner to the number theoretic formalism, construct a list theoretic formalism based on the concept of a linear list L of abstract quantities, and the following constants of lists:

(i) *head*, where *head*$(L) =$ the first element of L, e.g.

$head([x, y, z]) = x$.

(ii) *tail*, where *tail*$(L) =$ the list that remains when *head*(L) is removed from L, e.g.

$tail([x, y, z]) = [y, z]$.

(iii) *null*, where *null* is a constant that denotes the empty list.

(iv) *cons*, where *cons*$(x, L) =$ the list which results when the element x is inserted at the head of L, e.g.

$cons\ (x, null) = [x]$.

(Notice the difference between x and $[x]$).

(v) *nullist*, where *nullist*$(L) = true$ if $L = null$, and *false* otherwise.

Within this formalism, give recursive definitions for the following functions:

(vi)   *join*, where *join* $(L_1, L_2) =$ the list which results when L_1 is joined with L_2, e.g.

$join\ ([x, y], [z, u]) = [x, y, z, u]$.

(vii)   *reverse*, where *reverse*$(L) =$ the list L in reverse order.

(viii)   *equal*, where *equal* $(L_1, L_2) = true$ if $L_1 = L_2$, and *false* otherwise.

8. Modify the descriptions of rules (1), (4) and (4′) in the definitions of the *eaf* and *eal*-rules of evaluation, to deal with the case of a set of simultaneous recursive definitions.

9. Determine whether or not the *eaf* and *eal*-rules of evaluation describe the same function for the definition

$f(x, y) \text{ is } (x = 0 \to 1, y = 0 \to f(x, 1) + 1, f(y - 1, f(x, y - 1)))$.

10. Verify formally that the definitions

$$f_1(x) \text{ is } f_2(f_3, x)$$

$$f_2(g, x) \text{ is } g(x, g(x, 0))$$

$$f_3(x, y) \text{ is } (x = 0 \to y, f_1(x - 1))$$

is a properly formed set of simultaneous recursive definitions.

11. Using the list processing machinery described in Question (7), give recursive definitions of *eaf* and *eal* when many place functions are present, i.e. when *rand*(*e*) may be a list of operands.

12. A confusion can arise when writing down expressions involving expression-processing functions; e.g. does

$$eaf(f(e))$$

mean: (1) apply f to e and then apply *eaf* to the resulting value, or (2) apply *eaf* to the expression $f(e)$ itself? By modifying the syntax of the class of formal expressions, or otherwise, show how this confusion can be avoided.

13. A number $n > 1$ is said to be *perfect* if the sum of its divisors (including 1, but excluding n) adds up to n. Construct a recursive definition in the number theoretic formalism for the function perfect, where

$$perfect(x) = \text{the } (x + 1)\text{st perfect number.}$$

Comment on the effect of the choice of evaluation rule for this definition. (No one knows whether perfect is a total function or not).

14. In the translation of **while** programs, justify the alternative constructions:

(2′) if $W = (\textbf{if } T \textbf{ then } X_1 \textbf{ else } X_2); U$ then construct

$$f_W(v) \text{ is } (T(v) \to f_U(f_{X_1}(v)), f_U(f_{X_2}(v)),$$

(3′) if $W = \textbf{while } T \textbf{ do } (X_1); U$, then construct

$$f_W(v) \text{ is } (T(v) \to f_W(f_{X_1}(v)), f_U(v)).$$

What is the alternative construction for the case (4)?

15. Consider the following two recursive definitions of a function f:

(a) $f(x, y) \text{ is } (x = 0 \to 0, h(x - 1, f(x, y))$
    $h(x, y) \text{ is } (x = 0 \to 0, y)$

(b) $f(x, y) \text{ is } (x = 0 \to 0, (x - 1) = 0 \to 0, f(x, y))$

In definition (b), the function h has been eliminated by substituting its definition into the definition of f. Comment on the effect of choice of evaluation rules on these two definitions.

16. Construct recursive definitions for the functions computed by the following two programs:

(i) **input** x; **output** y;

$z: = x; y: = 0; t: = 0;$

until $x = 0$ **do**

begin $x: = x - 1;$

       until $z = 0$ **do begin** $z: = z - 1; y: = y + 1; t: = t + 1;$ **end**

       $z: = t$

end

(ii) **input** X, n; **output** X;

$k: = 1$;

while $k \leqslant n$ **do begin** $X(k): = -X(k); k: = k + 1$ **end**;

$m: = n$;

while $m > 0$ **do**

    begin $j: = m; i: = X(j)$;

        while $i > 0$ **do**

            begin $j: = i; i: = X(j)$ **end**;

        $X(j): = X(-i); X(-i): = m$;

        $m: = m - 1$

    end.

Chapter 7

The Fixed Point Theory
of Recursion

We turn now to a different view of recursion, one based on a mathematical rather than computational interpretation of recursive definitions. The essential idea is to regard recursive definitions as straightforward mathematical equations, replacing the separator *is* by the usual sign ($=$) for equality. This leads us to think of recursively defined functions as fixed points of functions of higher type. As we shall see, the theory of fixed points provides an elegant treatment of recursion. What is of greater practical importance, it also leads to the discovery and exploitation of a powerful induction rule for proving facts about recursively defined functions.

7.1   Fixed points

There are two closely related problems that have to be overcome in a mathematical treatment of recursion; both were raised briefly in Chapter 6. The first is to develop a theory of partial functions which allows functions to have defined values for undefined or partially defined arguments. Such a theory is necessary to resolve the differences between our usual notion of function and the concept of a conditional expression. Consider, for example, the equation

$$f(x, y) = (x = 0 \rightarrow 0, y),$$

where x and y are non-negative integers. Apparently, this is a straightforward definition of a function f, but if it is, then what is the value of $f(0, h(0))$, where h is a partial function which is undefined for argument 0? As we have seen, the computational answer is that this question is meaningless because a rule of evaluation has not been specified; when it is, then the question can be answered by inspecting the order of evaluation implied by the rule. To avoid appealing to evaluation rules, we have to regard the above equation as defining values for f, not only for well defined arguments x and y, but also when x and y may be undefined, and this involves generalizing the usual notion of function.

The second problem concerns the interpretation of recursive definitions. Consider, for example, the recursive definition

$$f(x, y) = (x = y \rightarrow y + 1, f(x, f(x - 1, y + 1))),$$

where we have replaced *is* by =. This is an equation, and so asserts identity between the left and right hand sides. The equation can be put in the form $f = F(f)$, where F is a certain functional. Using λ-notation we can even say what F is:

$$F = \lambda g \cdot \lambda x, y \cdot (x = y \to y + 1, g(x, g(x - 1, y + 1))).$$

The definition of f thus amounts to saying that f is a *fixed point* of F. (By definition, a fixed point of a function h is any value x for which $h(x) = x$). Since f is supposed to be uniquely defined by the equation $f = F(f)$, the problems we must solve are these:

(1) What general conditions ensure that functionals such as F do indeed have fixed points?

(2) If F has more than one fixed point, how do we select the one which defines f?

In fact, if we suppose that x and y range over all integer values, positive or negative, then the functional F given above does in fact have more than one fixed point. Consider the functions f_1 and f_2, where

$$f_1(x, y) = x + 1$$

and
$$f_2(x, y) = (x \geqslant y \to x + 1, y - 1).$$

We have

$$
\begin{aligned}
F(f_1)(x, y) &= (x = y \to y + 1, f_1(x, f_1(x - 1, y + 1))) \\
&= (x = y \to y + 1, f_1(x, x)) \\
&= (x = y \to y + 1, x + 1) \\
&= f_1(x, y),
\end{aligned}
$$

and

$$
\begin{aligned}
F(f_2)(x, y) &= (x = y \to y + 1, f_2(x, f_2(x - 1, y + 1))) \\
&= (x = y \to y + 1, f_2(x, x - 1 \geqslant y + 1 \to x, y)) \\
&= (x = y \to y + 1, x \geqslant y + 2 \to f_2(x, x), f_2(x, y)) \\
&= (x = y \to y + 1, x \geqslant y + 2 \to x + 1, x \geqslant y \to x + 1, y - 1) \\
&= (x \geqslant y \to x + 1, y - 1) \\
&= f_2(x, y).
\end{aligned}
$$

Thus both f_1 and f_2 are fixed points of F.

As another example, consider the definition

$$f(x) = (x = 0 \to 1, f(x + 1))$$

where $x \in N$. This definition has the form $f = G(f)$, where G is the functional $\lambda g \cdot \lambda x \cdot (x = 0 \to 1, g(x + 1))$. Now G has an infinite number of fixed points, in fact each of the functions $f_0, f_1, \ldots$, where $f_n = \lambda x \cdot (x = 0 \to 1, n)$, is a fixed point of G. There is one further fixed point of G, namely the function $\lambda x \cdot (x = 0 \to 1,$

undefined). This last function is important since it is just the function specified by the definition

$$f(x) \ is \ (x = 0 \to 1, f(x + 1))$$

according to the evaluation rules of the last chapter.

It is clearly important to examine the relationship between fixed points and recursively defined functions specified by evaluation rules. A further problem to be resolved is therefore:

(3) What is the connection between the fixed point approach and the computational approach?

The next section deals with the general problem of partial functions. As will be seen, the resulting theory provides a framework for the study of fixed points.

7.2   A theory of partial functions

Since total functions are easier to deal with than partial functions, we would like to construct a theory of partial functions using total functions only. The basic idea is to represent partial functions by total functions over extended sets of arguments and values. We can model a partial function $f: D_1 \to D_2$ by a total function in the following way. Introduce two new elements ω_1 and ω_2 into D_1 and D_2 respectively, each of which denote the *undefined value*. If we let

$$D_1^+ = D_1 \cup \{\omega_1\} \quad \text{and} \quad D_2^+ = D_2 \cup \{\omega_2\},$$

then we can represent the partial function $f: D_1 \to D_2$ by the *total* function $f^+: D_1^+ \to D_2^+$, where

$$f^+(x) = f(x) \quad \text{if } f(x) \text{ is defined}$$
$$= \omega_2 \quad \text{if } f(x) \text{ is not defined,}$$
$$\text{or if } x = \omega_1.$$

We shall refer to f^+ as the *natural extension* of f. The reasoning behind the introduction of ω_2 into D_2 is clear: every undefined value of f gets mapped into ω_2 by the natural extension of f. The introduction of ω_1 into D_1 at first sight seems unnecessary; however, its existence is important when we consider the composition of partial functions. Thus, the natural extension of the function $f \cdot g$, where

$$(f \cdot g)(x) = f(g(x)),$$

is now easily seen to be $f^+ \cdot g^+$.

As will appear in due course, the idea of having different undefined elements for each type D, rather than just one undefined element for every type, is also an important one.

Notice it does not follow that f^+ is a computable total function if f is a computable partial function. The reason is that ω_1 and ω_2 are not like any other elements of D_1 and D_2, and cannot be treated in the same fashion. The way to make this feeling about the subordinate status of the undefined elements precise, is to introduce the idea of a *partial ordering* on the elements of D^+.

Partial ordering on D^+

Suppose D^+ is a set with the adjoined element ω. We define the relation $\subseteq$ on D^+ by the condition

$$x \subseteq y \quad \text{if } x = \omega \text{ or if } x = y.$$

We read $x \subseteq y$ as 'x *approximates* y'. Thus in D^+, x approximates y if x is either ω or y itself. The relation $\subseteq$ is called a partial ordering because the following three conditions are satisfied:

(1) the reflexive law: $x \subseteq x$,

(2) the antisymmetric law: $x \subseteq y$ and $y \subseteq x$ implies $x = y$,

(3) the transitive law: $x \subseteq y$ and $y \subseteq z$ implies $x \subseteq z$.

We can represent the partial ordering succinctly by drawing a picture; for example, if $D = \{0, 1\}$, then the partial ordering $\subseteq$ on D^+ is given by the picture

where the line $x \longrightarrow y$ signifies that $x \subseteq y$. When drawing pictures, we shall not put in the lines implied by reflexivity or transitivity.

So far, of course, the partial ordering is very simple. However, once the concept of partial orderings to separate the undefined elements from the defined elements has been established, it can be used with much greater impact, as we shall now show.

Partial ordering on $(D \times D)^+$

The obvious way to define $(D \times D)^+$ is to adjoin a single new undefined element to $(D \times D)$, just as we did in the case of D. However, a moment's reflection shows that a more sensible way of defining $(D \times D)^+$ is to let

$$(D \times D)^+ = D^+ \times D^+.$$

In other words, in $(D \times D)^+$ we have both the *very* undefined element (ω, ω), where ω is the undefined element of D^+, and also the *not so* undefined elements (x, ω) and (ω, x) for each $x \in D$. More precisely, we can define the partial ordering $\subseteq$ on $(D \times D)^+$ by the conditions

$$(x, y) \subseteq (x', y') \quad \text{if } x \subseteq x' \text{ and } y \subseteq y'.$$

Of course, we should have used a different symbol to denote this new partial ordering, but the ambiguity is not damaging, and avoids a proliferation of new symbols. As an example, if $D = \{0, 1\}$, then the partial ordering on $(D \times D)^+$ can be pictured as follows:

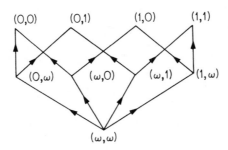

Clearly, this partial ordering is not so trivial as in the case of D^+.

In general, we define $(D_1 \times D_2 \times \cdots \times D_n)^+$ by

$$(D_1 \times D_2 \times \cdots \times D_n)^+ = (D_1^+ \times D_2^+ \times \cdots \times D_n^+),$$

and associate with $(D_1 \times D_2 \times \cdots \times D_n)^+$ the partial ordering $\subseteq$ defined by the condition

$$(x_1, x_2, \ldots, x_n) \subseteq (y_1, y_2, \ldots, y_n) \quad \text{if } x_k \subseteq y_k \text{ for } 1 \leq k \leq n.$$

To emphasize the difference between D^+ and $(D \times D)^+$, we shall sometimes refer to D^+ as a *basic* domain, and $(D \times D)^+$ as a *derived* domain. Another sort of derived domain arises when we consider functions.

Partial ordering on $(D \to D)^+$

It is also useful to consider a partial ordering on function spaces. The first thing to note is that we are now dealing exclusively with total functions. The obvious but not very interesting way of defining $(D \to D)^+$ is to take it to be the set of all (total!) functions from D^+ to D^+, and define the partial ordering $\subseteq$ by

$$f \subseteq g \quad \text{if } f = g \text{ or } f = \Omega,$$

where Ω is the everywhere undefined function, i.e. $\Omega(x) = \omega$ for all $x \in D^+$, and ω is the undefined element of D^+. A more sensible way to define the partial ordering has already made its appearance in Section 6.4, namely to define

$$f \subseteq g \quad \text{if } f(x) \subseteq g(x) \text{ for all } x \in D^+.$$

In other words, function f approximates function g if each value of f approximates the corresponding value of g. This settles the question of which partial ordering to take, but still leaves the problem of determining which functions should be in $(D \to D)^+$. Let us consider some of the alternatives.

(1) We could take $(D \to D)^+ = (D^+ \to D^+)$, i.e. the set of all possible functions from D^+ to D^+. However, this proposal means that we allow for consideration functions like

$$f(x) = a \quad \text{for all } x \neq \omega$$
$$f(\omega) = b,$$

where ω is the undefined element of D^+, and a and b are distinct elements of D^+. Such functions are in no sense models of the partial functions we started out to consider. There is no way we can think of f as being computable; it gives a well defined value for argument ω, but one that is different from the value for all other arguments. Therefore f is 'ignoring' the special status of ω. Consequently, this proposed definition of $(D \to D)^+$ is too general since it takes in functions that we cannot regard as computable.

(2) As a second possibility, we could take

$$(D \to D)^+ = \{f : f \in (D^+ \to D^+) \text{ and } f(\omega) = \omega\}.$$

This proposal is in line with our original intentions: each function in $(D \to D)^+$ is a natural extension of a partial function. The defect of this proposal is that it is too restrictive; we would like to consider functions that are not natural extensions of ordinary partial functions. Consider the function θ given by

$$\theta(x, y, z) = (x = 0 \to y, z), \quad \text{where } x, y, z \in N^+.$$

According to the natural interpretation of conditional expressions, we have

$$\theta(0, y, z) = y$$

for all y and z, *including* $z = \omega$; for example,

$$\theta(0, 2, \omega) = 2.$$

However θ cannot be admitted as a function under this proposal, since it returns a defined value for some 'partially undefined' arguments. As another example, consider f where

$$f(x) = 7 \quad \text{for all } x \in N^+.$$

In particular, $f(\omega) = 7$. This function can be regarded as computable; the algorithm which computes f simply returns the value 7 without ever evaluating the argument. But again, f is not admitted under this definition of $(D \to D)^+$.

The solution to these difficulties lies in a third alternative. We say a function $f : D^+ \to D^+$ is *monotonic* if for all x and $y \in D^+$ we have

$$x \subseteq y \quad \text{implies } f(x) \subseteq f(y).$$

In other words, we consider just those functions that conform to the natural computability requirement: the more an argument is defined, the more defined is the value. The third proposal is to take

$$(D \to D)^+ = \{f : f \in (D^+ \to D^+), f \text{ is monotonic}\}.$$

This definition of $(D \to D)^+$ is natural and avoids the extremes of proposals (1) and (2). The example function in (1) is not monotonic and is therefore excluded, while both the functions in (2) are monotonic and are therefore included.

In a moment, we shall consider yet a fourth way of defining $(D \to D)^+$, but let us first consider some examples of partial orderings on monotonic functions.

Examples

We consider three examples. If $D = \{0, 1\}$, then there are 11 monotonic functions in $(D^+ \to D^+)$

	ω	0	1			ω	0	1
Ω	ω	ω	ω		f_5	ω	0	1
f_1	ω	ω	0		f_6	ω	1	ω
f_2	ω	ω	1		f_7	ω	1	0
f_3	ω	0	ω		f_8	ω	1	1
f_4	ω	0	0		f_9	0	0	0
					f_{10}	1	1	1

The partial ordering of $(D \to D)^+$ can be pictured as follows:

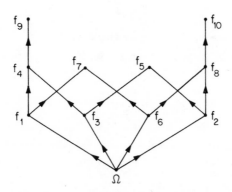

If we take $D = \{0\}$, then there are just 3 monotonic functions in $(D^+ \to D^+)$:

	ω	0
Ω	ω	ω
f	ω	0
g	0	0

The partial ordering of $(D \to D)^+$ is just

Finally, let us consider $((D \to D) \to (D \to D))^+$ when $D = \{0\}$. There are 10 monotonic functionals in $(D \to D)^+ \to (D \to D)^+$:

	Ω	f	g		Ω	f	g
F_1	Ω	Ω	Ω	F_6	Ω	g	g
F_2	Ω	Ω	f	F_7	f	f	f
F_3	Ω	Ω	g	F_8	f	f	g
F_4	Ω	f	f	F_9	f	g	g
F_5	Ω	f	g	F_{10}	g	g	g

The partial ordering of $((D \to D) \to (D \to D))^+$ can be pictured as follows:

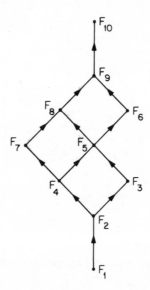

It should not be thought that monotonic functions are necessarily computable functions; the condition of monotonicity simply serves to exclude from our consideration some obviously non-computable functions. The function $f : N^+ \to N^+$, where

$f(x) = 1$ if the xth NORMA flowchart program

halts on input x

$= 0$ if the xth NORMA flowchart program
does not halt on input x

$= \omega$ if $x = \omega$,

is clearly monotonic, but just as clearly non-computable from the results of Chapter 4. It is natural to consider whether or not one can formulate a stronger requirement than monotonicity for excluding intuitively non-computable functions. It is difficult to imagine what more could be said for functions of the lowest order, but as soon as we consider functionals, another source of non-computability becomes apparent. Consider, for example, the functional $F:(N \to N)^+ \to N^+$, where

$$F(f) = (total(f) \to 1, \omega),$$

where

$$total(f) = true \ \ \text{if } f(x) \neq \omega \ \ \text{for all } x \neq \omega$$
$$= false \ \text{otherwise.}$$

F is an example of a function each of whose arguments contain an infinite amount of information, being themselves functions. In order to be considered computable, such functionals should return a value only on the basis of a finite amount of the information 'contained' in their arguments; in the present example, only on the basis of a finite number of values of the argument f. If F needs to know the value of f for an infinite number of arguments, then the process of obtaining these values will take infinitely long, and the computation of F with argument f cannot be regarded as taking place in a finite amount of time. This is just the case with the present example. In order to return a value, F needs to know whether its argument f represents a total function with no undefined values. In general, this information can only be gathered by looking at the values of f for each of its arguments, but since f has an infinite domain this involves an infinite process. Consequently, we cannot regard F as a computable functional. F is, however, monotonic as can be seen as follows. Suppose $f \subseteq g$; either $total(f) = true$, in which case $total(g) = true$ also, and

$$F(f) = 1 = F(g), \quad \text{i.e. } F(f) \subseteq F(g),$$

or $total(f) = false$, in which case

$$F(f) = \omega \subseteq F(g).$$

The insight necessary to formulate a condition which excludes functions like F comes from the observation that, unlike the basic domain N^+, the partial ordering on $(N \to N)^+$ is quite complicated; in particular, infinitely long sequences of approximations exist in $(N \to N)^+$. For example, given f, let $f_0, f_1, \dots$ etc., be defined by the condition

$$f_n(x) = f(x) \quad \text{for all } x \leqslant n, \text{ including } x = \omega$$
$$= \omega \text{ otherwise.}$$

Then we have

$$f_0 \subseteq f_1 \subseteq f_2 \subseteq \cdots.$$

Such a sequence is called a *chain* of *approximations*, or simply a *chain*. Each element in the chain represents a certain finite approximation to the 'limit' function f. Now the requirement that the functional F should make use only of a finite amount of information about its argument f can be expressed by the following condition: for all f there exists an n such that

$$F(f) = F(f_n).$$

To simplify this condition, notice that if F is monotonic, then we have

$$F(f_0) \subseteq F(f_1) \subseteq \cdots,$$

which is another chain. It seems reasonable to suppose that this chain also possess a 'limit', which we can denote by $\lim_{n \to \infty} F(f_n)$. Moreover, by the natural properties of limits we have

$$F(f_n) \subseteq \lim_{n \to \infty} F(f_n) \quad \text{for each } n \geqslant 0,$$

so that the above condition on F implies

$$F(f) = F(\lim_{n \to \infty} f_n) \subseteq \lim_{n \to \infty} F(f_n).$$

We can actually go one stage further: since

$$f_n \subseteq \lim_{n \to \infty} f_n,$$

and F is monotonic by supposition, it follows that

$$F(f_n) \subseteq F(\lim_{n \to \infty} f_n).$$

Hence $F(\lim_{n \to \infty} f_n)$ is an upper bound of the chain

$$F(f_0) \subseteq F(f_1) \subseteq \cdots.$$

Now the natural definition of limits is in terms of least upper bounds, as we shall see in a moment when we make this whole discussion more rigorous. This means that

$$\lim_{n \to \infty} F(f_n) \subseteq F(\lim_{n \to \infty} f_n).$$

Consequently, we can state the new condition on F as

$$F(\lim_{n \to \infty} f_n) = \lim_{n \to \infty} F(f_n).$$

In other words, F must be *continuous* in an appropriate sense.

Before placing the argument on a firmer footing, let us check that this new condition of continuity confirms our intuition about the non-computable function F. Recall that

$$F(f) = (total(f) \to 1, \omega).$$

Suppose f is a function such that $total(f) = true$, whence

$$F(f) = 1.$$

Construct the chain $f_0 \subseteq f_1 \subseteq \cdots$ as described above, i.e.

$$f_n(x) = (x \leqslant n \to f(x), \omega) \quad \text{for } n \geqslant 0.$$

Clearly $total(f_n) = false$ for every n, and so

$$F(f_n) = \omega \quad \text{for all } n.$$

We therefore have

$$\lim_{n \to \infty} F(f_n) = \omega \neq F(\lim_{n \to \infty} f_n) = 1.$$

Hence F is not continuous, as we had hoped.

The fourth proposal concerning $(D \to D)^+$ is that we should take

$$(D \to D)^+ = \{f : f \in (D^+ \to D^+) \text{ and } f \text{ is continuous}\}.$$

In order to see how this proposal differs from the third proposal, in which every monotonic function is allowed, it is necessary to be more precise about the concepts of chain, limit, and continuous function.

Definitions 1

(1) Suppose X is some set partially ordered by a relation $\subseteq$. A sequence $x_0, x_1, \ldots$ of elements of X is called a *chain* if $x_n \subseteq x_{n+1}$ for all $n \geqslant 0$.

(2) A chain $x_0 \subseteq x_1 \subseteq \cdots$ of elements of X is said to have a *unique limit* x *in* X if $x \in X$ is such that

  (i) $x_n \subseteq x$ for all $n \geqslant 0$

  (ii) if $x_n \subseteq y$ for all $n \geqslant 0$, then $x \subseteq y$.

In other words, x is the unique least upper bound of the set $\{x_0, x_1, \ldots\}$ under the relation $\subseteq$. We also denote x by $\lim_{n \to \infty} x_n$.

(3) We say that D is a *domain*, if

  (i) D is partially ordered by some relation $\subseteq$,

  (ii) D contains a least element under $\subseteq$, i.e. an element $\omega \in D$ such that $\omega \subseteq x$ for all $x \in D$,

  (iii) each chain in D has a unique limit in D.

Definitions 2

(1) A function $f : D_1 \to D_2$, where D_1 and D_2 are domains, is *monotonic* if for all $x, y \in D_1$,

$$x \subseteq y \quad \text{implies } f(x) \subseteq f(y).$$

(2) A function $f: D_1 \to D_2$ is *continuous* if it is monotonic and for every chain $x_0 \subseteq x_1 \subseteq \cdots$ of D_1, we have

$$f(\lim_{n \to \infty} x_n) = \lim_{n \to \infty} f(x_n).$$

Lemma 1

Let $D^+ = D \cup \{\omega\}$ with the partial ordering

$$x \subseteq y \quad \text{if } x = \omega \text{ or } x = y$$

for all $x, y \in D^+$. Then D^+ is a domain.

Proof. Conditions (i) and (ii) on the definition of domains are immediately satisfied. The only chains $x_0 \subseteq x_1 \subseteq \cdots$ of D^+ are ones for which either

(a) $x_n = \omega$ for all $n \geqslant 0$, or

(b) for some $k > 0, x_n = \omega$ for all $n < k$, and $x_n = x \neq \omega$ for all $n \geqslant k$.

Clearly, in case (a) we have

$$\lim_{n \to \infty} x_n = \omega,$$

and in case (b)

$$\lim_{n \to \infty} x_n = x.$$

Basic domains thus have the property that every chain is essentially finite.

Lemma 2. If D_1 and D_2 are domains, then so is $D_1 \times D_2$ under the partial ordering

$$(x, y) \subseteq (x', y') \quad \text{if } x \subseteq x' \text{ and } y \subseteq y'$$

for all $x, x' \in D_1$ and $y, y' \in D_2$.

Proof. Again conditions (i) and (ii) are immediate, the least element of $D_1 \times D_2$ being (ω_1, ω_2), where ω_1 and ω_2 are the least elements of D_1 and D_2 respectively.

Suppose $(x_0, y_0) \subseteq (x_1, y_1) \subseteq \cdots$ is a chain of $D_1 \times D_2$. Let $\lim_{n \to \infty} x_n = x$ and $\lim_{n \to \infty} y_n = y$. Clearly

$$(x_n, y_n) \subseteq (x, y) \quad \text{for all } n \geqslant 0,$$

whence (x, y) is an upper bound of the set $\{(x_n, y_n): n \geqslant 0\}$. Moreover, by the defining properties of limits in D_1 and D_2, (x, y) is in fact the least upper bound of this set. Hence we can define limits of chains in $D_1 \times D_2$ by taking

$$\lim_{n \to \infty} (x_n, y_n) = (\lim_{n \to \infty} x_n, \lim_{n \to \infty} y_n).$$

Lemma 2 shows, for example, that $(D_1 \times D_2)^+$ is a domain, where

$$(D_1 \times D_2)^+ = D_1^+ \times D_2^+.$$

Lemma 3. Suppose D_1 and D_2 are domains, and let

$$D_M = \{f : f \in (D_1 \to D_2), f \text{ monotonic}\},$$
$$D_C = \{f : f \in (D_1 \to D_2), f \text{ continuous}\}.$$

Then both D_M and D_C are domains under the partial ordering

$$f \subseteq g \quad \text{if } f(x) \subseteq g(x) \text{ for all } x \in D_1,$$

for all f and g.

Proof. Condition (i) is immediate. For condition (ii), it is easy to see that the least element Ω, where

$$\Omega(x) = \omega_2 \quad \text{for all } x \in D_1,$$

and ω_2 is the least element of D_2, is both monotonic and continuous.

To show that condition (iii) is satisfied for D_M, let $f_0 \subseteq f_1 \subseteq \cdots$ be a chain in D_M. From the given partial ordering on D_M it follows that

$$f_0(x) \subseteq f_1(x) \subseteq \cdots$$

is a chain for each $x \in D_1$. Hence we can define $\lim_{n \to \infty} f_n$ by the equation

$$(\lim_{n \to \infty} f_n)(x) = \lim_{n \to \infty} f_n(x).$$

We must also show that $\lim_{n \to \infty} f_n$ is in D_M, i.e. is a monotonic function. Suppose $x \subseteq y$, where $x, y \in D_1$. Since each f_n is monotonic, we have

$$f_n(x) \subseteq f_n(y) \quad \text{for all } n \geqslant 0.$$

Hence

$$(\lim_{n \to \infty} f_n)(x) = \lim_{n \to \infty} f_n(x) \subseteq \lim_{n \to \infty} f_n(y) = (\lim_{n \to \infty} f_n)(y),$$

and so the limit is indeed monotonic.

To show that condition (iii) is satisfied for D_C, let $f_0 \subseteq f_1 \subseteq \cdots$ be a chain of continuous functions in D_C. We again define the limit by the equation

$$(\lim_{n \to \infty} f_n)(x) = \lim_{n \to \infty} f_n(x),$$

but this time we have to show that $\lim_{n \to \infty} f_n$ is continuous as well as monotonic. Since each f_n is continuous, and hence monotonic by definition, the monotonicity of $\lim_{n \to \infty} f_n$ follows as before. To show that the limit is continuous, let $x_0 \subseteq x_1 \subseteq \cdots$ be a chain in D_1. Then

$$(\lim_{n \to \infty} f_n)(\lim_{m \to \infty} x_m) = \lim_{n \to \infty} f_n(\lim_{m \to \infty} x_m)$$
$$= \lim_{n \to \infty} \lim_{m \to \infty} f_n(x_m),$$

using the definition of the limit, and the continuity of each f_n. Since

$$f_n(x_m) \subseteq f_n(x_{m+1})$$

and $f_n(x_m) \subseteq f_{n+1}(x_m)$,

it can be shown (see Exercise 7.10) that

$$\lim_{n \to \infty} \lim_{m \to \infty} f_n(x_m) = \lim_{m \to \infty} \lim_{n \to \infty} f_n(x_m),$$

i.e. the order in which the limits are taken is immaterial. It follows that

$$(\lim_{n \to \infty} f_n)(\lim_{m \to \infty} x_m) = \lim_{m \to \infty} (\lim_{n \to \infty} f_n)(x_m),$$

which establishes the continuity of $\lim_{n \to \infty} f_n$.

Notice that $D_C \subseteq D_M$. When the domain D_1 is sufficiently simple in structure, the domains D_C and D_M coincide.

Lemma 4.   Let D_1 be a basic domain D^+ (as described in Lemma 1). Then $D_C = D_M$.

Proof.   The lemma is proved by showing that every monotonic function over D_1 is continuous. Let $x_0 \subseteq x_1 \subseteq \cdots$ be a chain of D_1. Since D is a basic domain in which only finite chains exist, we must have

$$\lim_{n \to \infty} x_n = x_k$$

for some $k \geqslant 0$. In other words, in a basic domain limits of chains are themselves elements of the chain. Suppose f is monotonic, whence

$$f(x_0) \subseteq f(x_1) \subseteq \cdots.$$

Moreover,

$$\lim_{n \to \infty} f(x_n) = f(x_k) = f(\lim_{n \to \infty} x_n)$$

whence f is continuous.

Lemma 4 shows why it was impossible to distinguish between the conditions of monotonicity and continuity for functions of the lowest order; the difference only becomes apparent for functions at the level of functionals and above. Lemma 3 indicates that either condition will lead to a consistent theory; the choice of continuous functions is motivated partly by computability considerations, but also because it turns out that continuity is just what we need to establish the existence of fixed points. We henceforth take

$$(D_1 \to D_2)^+ = \{f : f \in (D_1^+ \to D_2^+), f \text{ is continuous}\}$$

7.3   The fixed point theorem

The concepts of continuous function, domain, and fixed point come together in the following important theorem, due to Kleene.

Theorem 1.   (*The fixed point theorem*)

Suppose D is a domain and $f: D \to D$ is a continuous function. Then f possesses a fixed point x given by

$$x = \lim_{n \to \infty} f^n(\omega)$$

where ω is the least element of D, and $f^n(\omega) = f(f \ldots (f(\omega)) \ldots)(n$ times$)$. Moreover, x is the least fixed point of f under the partial ordering of D.

Proof. We must show that

$$\omega \subseteq f(\omega) \subseteq f^2(\omega) \subseteq \cdots$$

is indeed a chain, so that the limit x is well defined. As a basis for the simple induction argument, we have $\omega \subseteq f(\omega)$ since ω is the least element of D. Assuming $f^n(\omega) \subseteq f^{n+1}(\omega)$ as the induction step, we have

$$f^{n+1}(\omega) = f(f^n(\omega)) \subseteq f(f^{n+1}(\omega)) = f^{n+2}(\omega),$$

since f is continuous and thus monotonic. This completes the induction and shows that

$$x = \lim_{n \to \infty} f^n(\omega)$$

is a well defined element of D.

Next, we have

$$f(\lim_{n \to \infty} f^n(\omega)) = \lim_{n \to \infty} f^{n+1}(\omega) = \lim_{n \to \infty} f^n(\omega),$$

since f is continuous. Hence x is a fixed point of f.

Finally, we show that x is the least fixed point of f. Let y be any fixed point of f; we show that $f^n(\omega) \subseteq y$ for all $n \geq 0$. Clearly $\omega \subseteq y$, and assuming $f^n(\omega) \subseteq y$, we have

$$f^{n+1}(\omega) = f(f^n(\omega)) \subseteq f(y) = y,$$

by the monotonicity of f. By the properties of limits, it therefore follows that

$$x = \lim_{n \to \infty} f^n(\omega) \subseteq y,$$

which completes the proof of the theorem.

The fact that the fixed point theorem is applicable when D is a function domain suggests a way to interpret recursive definitions in terms of fixed points. Recall from Section 1 that a single recursive definition can be stated in the form

$$f = F(f),$$

where F is an appropriately chosen functional. The questions we posed about such definitions, and the answers we can now give, are as follows:

(1) What general conditions ensure that functionals like F have fixed points? Answer: the condition that F is continuous.

(2) How do we select, among the possibly many fixed points of F, the one which defines f? Answer: take f to be the *least* fixed point of F under the partial ordering $\subseteq$ on functions defined by

$$f \subseteq g \quad \text{if } f(x) \subseteq g(x) \text{ for all } x.$$

To complete the interpretation of recursive definitions as fixed points, it is of course necessary to show that the functionals that arise from recursive definitions are continuous. We can have some confidence that this is indeed the case; such functionals are intuitively computable, and intuitively computable functions are both monotonic and continuous. The only point to watch is that the constant functions appearing in the definitions of the functionals must themselves be continuous. When these constant functions are functions over a basic domain, it is sufficient by Lemma 4 to ensure that they are monotonic. The most important way to obtain monotonic functions is to use natural extensions.

Definition. A functional F is *normal* if each constant function appearing in the definition of F is understood to be naturally extended, and the conditional connective $(p \to x, y)$, where $p \in \{true, false\}^+$ and $x, y \in V^+$ for some V, is understood to be defined by the rules

$$(true \to x, y) = x$$
$$(false \to x, y) = y$$
$$(undefined \to x, y) = \omega$$

for all $x, y \in V^+$, where *undefined* and ω are the undefined elements of $\{true, false\}^+$ and V^+ respectively.

Notice that $\lambda p, x, y \,.\, (p \to x, y)$ is *not* the natural extension of any partial function, even though it is monotonic. When simplifying functional expressions, we shall often make implicit use of the following two important properties of conditionals:

(1) $(p \to f(x), f(y)) \subseteq f(p \to x, y)$

(2) if $f(\omega) = \omega'$, then $f(p \to x, y) = (p \to f(x), f(y))$.

Both properties can be proved by straightforward case analysis. For (2) the critical case is when $p = undefined$; since $(undefined \to x, y) = \omega$, the value of the left hand side is $f(\omega)$, and the value of the right hand side is ω'. However, $f(\omega) = \omega'$ by assumption. This result can be regarded as a warning that the simplification of expressions of the form $f(e_1 \to e_2, e_3)$ to $(e_1 \to f(e_2), f(e_3))$ is only valid when $f(\omega) = \omega'$, i.e. when f is a natural extension. In the more general case, we can simplify expressions of the form

$$f(e, e_1 \to e_2, e_3),$$

to obtain

$$(e_1 \to f(e, e_2), f(e, e_3)),$$

only when $f(x, \omega) = \omega'$.

A warning of a different sort arises with naturally extended predicates. Consider, for example, the predicate *equals*, where $equals = \lambda x, y \in N . (x = y)$ The monotonic natural extension $equals^+ : (N \times N)^+ \to \{true, false\}^+$ of *equals* is given by

$$equals^+ (x, y) = true \text{ if } x \neq \omega, y \neq \omega, \text{ and } x = y$$
$$= false \text{ if } x \neq \omega, y \neq \omega, \text{ and } x \neq y$$
$$= undefined \text{ if } x = \omega \text{ or } y = \omega.$$

In particular, notice that

$$equals^+ (\omega, \omega,) = undefined$$

and not *true* as one might expect. The 'strong' equality predicate *sequels*, which satisfies

$$sequels (\omega, \omega) = true$$

is *not* monotonic; consequently functionals involving *sequels* will not in general be continuous. It is essential to be clear about the two roles of the sign '=' when talking about functions and functionals: within (normal) functional expressions it signifies the predicate $equals^+$; outside these formal expressions it signifies ordinary mathematical equality.

Of course, constant functions do not have to be naturally extended in order to be monotonic. One example was the function $\bar{\lambda} p, x, y . (p \to x, y)$; another is given by extending the multiplication function $mult : N^2 \to N$ to a monotonic function $mult'$ by defining

$$mult'(x, 0) = mult'(0, x) = 0$$

for all $x \in N^+$, including the undefined value ω. Other values of $mult'$ coincide with $mult^+$, the natural extension of *mult*. Any functional involving $mult'$ will still be continuous and possess a least fixed point. We shall, however, be primarily concerned with normal functionals.

In Section 7·4 we shall prove formally that normal functionals are continuous. For the present, let us assume that the continuity condition is satisfied, and turn to some examples of fixed points.

Examples of fixed points

(1) Consider the definition

$$f(x) = (x = 0 \to 0, (2x - 1) + f(x - 1))$$

where $x \in N$. The normal functional involved here is

$$F : ((N \to N) \to (N \to N))^+$$

given by

$$F = \lambda f \in (N \to N)^+ . \lambda x \in N^+ . (x = 0 \to 0, (2x - 1) + f(x - 1)).$$

We are therefore assuming that the constant functions

$$\lambda x \,.\, (x = 0): N^+ \to \{true, false\}^+$$
$$\lambda x \,.\, 2x: N^+ \to N^+$$
$$\lambda x \,.\, (x - 1): N^+ \to N^+$$
$$\lambda xy \,.\, (x + y): (N \times N)^+ \to N^+,$$

are the naturally extended versions of the appropriate number theoretic functions. This still leaves the choice of taking either $0 - 1 = \omega$ or $0 = 1 = 0$ in the case of the predecessor function, but this decision does not affect the calculation that follows.

In order to find the least fixed point of F, we have to construct the limit of the chain

$$f_0 \subseteq f_1 \subseteq f_2 \subseteq \cdots,$$

where $f_0 = \lambda x \in N^+ \,.\, \omega$ (the least element of $(N \to N)^+$), and $f_{n+1} = F(f_n)$ for all $n \geqslant 0$. To start off, we have

$$f_1 = \lambda x \,.\, (x = 0 \to 0, (2x - 1) + f_0(x - 1))$$
$$= \lambda x \,.\, (x = 0 \to 0, \omega),$$

since $(2x - 1) + \omega = \omega$ in the natural extension of addition. Next,

$$f_2 = \lambda x \,.\, (x = 0 \to 0, (2x - 1) + f_1(x - 1))$$
$$= \lambda x \,.\, (x = 0 \to 0, (2x - 1) + (x - 1 = 0 \to 0, \omega))$$
$$= \lambda x \,.\, (x = 0 \to 0, x = 1 \to 1, \omega).$$

Continuing in this way, we arrive at the following functions, whose values are arranged in a table:

	ω	0	1	2	3	4	5	...
f_0	ω	ω	ω	ω	ω	ω	ω	...
f_1	ω	0	ω	ω	ω	ω	ω	
f_2	ω	0	1	ω	ω	ω	ω	
f_3	ω	0	1	4	ω	ω	ω	
f_4	ω	0	1	4	9	ω	ω	
f_5	ω	0	1	4	9	16	ω	

Clearly

$$(\lim_{n \to \infty} f_n)(x) = x^2,$$

so that the least fixed point of F is the function

$$\lambda x \in N^+ \,.\, x^2,$$

which should cause no surprise.

(2) Consider the definition

$$f(x, y) = (x = 0 \to 1, y \times f(x + 1, y)),$$

where $x, y \in N$. The normal functional here is

$$F : ((N^2 \to N) \to (N^2 \to N))^+$$

given by

$$F = \lambda f \in (N^2 \to N)^+ . \lambda x, y \in N^+ . (x = 0 \to 1, y \times f(x + 1, y)),$$

where we assume the natural extension of multiplication. To calculate the least fixed point of F, we take

$$f_0(x, y) = \omega$$

for all $x, y \in N^+$, and then compute $f_1, f_2, \ldots$ as follows:

$$f_1(x, y) = (x = 0 \to 1, y \times f_0(x + 1, y))$$
$$= (x = 0 \to 1, \omega),$$

since $y \times \omega = \omega$ in the natural extension of multiplication,

$$f_2(x, y) = (x = 0 \to 1, y \times f_1(x + 1, y))$$
$$= (x = 0 \to 1, y \times (x + 1 = 0 \to 1, \omega))$$
$$= (x = 0 \to 1, \omega).$$

Since $f_1 = f_2$, it follows that the limit of the sequence of functions, and the least fixed point of F, is the function

$$f = \lambda x, y \in N^+ . (x = 0 \to 1, \omega).$$

The first few values of f are given by the entries in the following table:

x	ω	0	1	2	$\ldots$
y ω	ω	1	ω	ω	
0	ω	1	ω	ω	
1	ω	1	ω	ω	
2	ω	1	ω	ω	

Now, suppose that in the definition of F we assume, not the natural extension of multiplication, but the extension for which

$$0 \times \omega = \omega \times 0 = 0.$$

This is a monotonic extension of multiplication, and so F is still continuous, but in this case F has a slightly different least fixed point. We have

$$f_1(x, y) = (x = 0 \to 1, y \times f_0(x + 1, y))$$
$$= (x = 0 \to 1, y \times \omega),$$

and this f_1 differs from the previous f_1 in that

$$f_1(x,0) = (x = 0 \rightarrow 1, 0).$$

The least fixed point of F in this case turns out to be

$$f = \lambda x, y \in N^+ . (x = 0 \rightarrow 1, y = 0 \rightarrow 0, \omega),$$

the first few values of f being given by the entries in the following table:

x	ω	0	1	2	...
y ω	ω	1	ω	ω	
0	ω	1	0	0	
1	ω	1	ω	ω	
2	ω	1	ω	ω	

This example demonstrates how the least fixed point of a functional critically depends on the manner in which the constant functions are extended to continuous functions over an augmented domain.

(3) Consider the definition

$$f(x, y) = (x = y \rightarrow y + 1, f(x, f(x - 1, y + 1))),$$

where $x, y \in Z$, the set of all integers. This example was discussed in Section 1, where it was claimed that both $\lambda x, y . (x + 1)$ and $\lambda x, y . (x \geqslant y \rightarrow x + 1, y - 1)$ satisfied the above equation. Let us first reconsider this claim in the light of the present theory. Here, the normal functional F is given by

$$F = \lambda f \in (Z^2 \rightarrow Z)^+ . \lambda x, y \in Z^+ . (x = y \rightarrow y + 1, f(x, f(x - 1, y + 1))).$$

Notice that the natural extension $equal^+$ of $\lambda x, y . (x = y)$ satisfies

$$equal^+(x, \omega) = equal^+(\omega, x) = \omega$$

for all $x \in Z^+$, and in particular, $equal^+(\omega, \omega) = \omega$.

We calculate $F(g)$, where $g = \lambda x, y \in Z^+ . (x \geqslant y \rightarrow x + 1, y - 1)$, as follows:

$$F(g) = \lambda x, y \in Z^+ . (x = y \rightarrow y + 1, g(x, g(x - 1, y + 1)))$$
$$= \lambda x, y \in Z^+ . (x = y \rightarrow y + 1, g(x, x - 1 \geqslant y + 1 \rightarrow x - 1 + 1, y + 1 - 1))$$
$$= \lambda x, y \in Z^+ . (x = y \rightarrow y + 1, x - 1 \geqslant y + 1 \rightarrow g(x, x), g(x, y)).$$

This last step is justified by distributive property of conditionals since $g(x, \omega) = \omega$, for all $x \in Z^+$. It follows that

$$F(g) = \lambda x, y \in Z^+ . (x = y \rightarrow y + 1, x \geqslant y + 2 \rightarrow x + 1, x \geqslant y \rightarrow x + 1, y - 1)$$
$$= \lambda x, y \in Z^+ (x \geqslant y \rightarrow x + 1, y - 1),$$
$$= g,$$

and so g is indeed a fixed point.

Next, let us calculate $F(h)$, where $h = \lambda x, y \in Z^+ . (x + 1)$:

$$F(h) = \lambda x, y \in Z^+ . (x = y \to y + 1, h(x, h(x - 1, y + 1)))$$
$$= \lambda x, y \in Z^+ . (x = y \to y + 1, h(x, x))$$
$$= \lambda x, y \in Z^+ . (x = y \to y + 1, x + 1)$$
$$= k, \text{ say.}$$

Now, $k \neq h$, since $k(x, \omega) = \omega$ and $h(x, \omega) = x + 1$. Thus h is *not* a fixed point of F. It can be shown, however, that k is a fixed point of F.

To determine the least fixed point of F, we compute the functions $f_0, f_1, \ldots$ as follows:

$$f_0(x, y) = \omega,$$
$$f_1(x, y) = (x = y \to y + 1, f_0(x, f_0(x - 1, y + 1)))$$
$$= (x = y \to y + 1, \omega),$$
$$f_2(x, y) = (x = y \to y + 1, f_1(x, f_1(x - 1, y + 1))).$$

Now

$$f_1(x - 1, y + 1) = (x = y + 2 \to y + 2, \omega),$$

so that

$$f_1(x, f_1(x - 1, y + 1)) = (x = y + 2 \to f_1(x, y + 2), f_1(x, \omega))$$
$$= (x = y + 2 \to y + 3, \omega).$$

Hence

$$f_2(x, y) = (x = y \to y + 1, x = y + 2 \to y + 3, \omega).$$

In general, we can show

$$f_n(x, y) = (x = y \to y + 1, x = y + 2 \to y + 3, \ldots$$
$$x = y + 2(n - 1) \to y + 2n - 1, \omega).$$

Hence the least fixed point of F is the function

$$\lambda x, y \in Z^+ . (x \geqslant y \wedge (x - y)even \to x + 1, \omega).$$

(4) Finally, let us consider another recursive definition discussed in Section 1:

$$f(x) = (x = 0 \to 1, f(x + 1)),$$

where $x \in N$. The normal functional in this case is

$$F = \lambda f \in (N \to N)^+ . \lambda x \in N^+ . (x = 0 \to 1, f(x + 1)).$$

The least fixed point of F is given as the limit of the sequence $f_0, f_1, \ldots,$ where

$$f_0(x) = \omega,$$
$$f_1(x) = (x = 0 \to 1, f_0(x + 1))$$
$$= (x = 0 \to 1, \omega)$$

$$f_2(x) = (x = 0 \rightarrow 1, f_1(x + 1))$$
$$= (x = 0 \rightarrow 1, x + 1 = 0 \rightarrow 1, \omega)$$
$$= (x = 0 \rightarrow 1, \omega), \quad \text{etc.}$$

Since $f_2 = f_1$, the limit is

$$\lambda x \in N^+ .(x = 0 \rightarrow 1, \omega).$$

Simultaneous recursive definitions

So far we have considered only single recursive definitions, but the theory is easily extended to the case of two or more simultaneous definitions. Suppose, for example, we are given two recursive definitions in the form

$$f = F(f, g)$$
$$g = G(f, g),$$

where F and G are continuous. Here we need to find two fixed points at one go. The trick is to construct the functional H, where

$$H(f, g) = (F(f, g), G(f, g)),$$

so that if $F: D_1 \times D_2 \rightarrow D_1$ and $G: D_1 \times D_2 \rightarrow D_2$, then $H: D_1 \times D_2 \rightarrow D_1 \times D_2$. Now $D_1 \times D_2$ is a domain if D_1 and D_2 are, and H is continuous if F and G are, so that Theorem 1 applies and shows that the least fixed point of H is

$$\lim_{n \rightarrow \infty} H^n(\omega_1, \omega_2),$$

where ω_1 and ω_2 are the least elements of the domains D_1 and D_2 respectively. The first few terms in the chain are

$$(\omega_1, \omega_2),$$
$$(F(\omega_1, \omega_2), G(\omega_1, \omega_2)),$$
$$(F(F(\omega_1, \omega_2), G(\omega_1, \omega_2)), G(F(\omega_1, \omega_2), G(\omega_1, \omega_2)))$$

If we write this chain in the form

$$(f_0, g_0) \subseteq (f_1, g_1) \subseteq \cdots,$$

then

$$f = \lim_{n \rightarrow \infty} f_n \quad \text{and} \quad g = \lim_{n \rightarrow \infty} g_n$$

by the property of limits.

As a simple example, consider the definitions

$$f(x) = (x = 0 \rightarrow 1, f(x - 1) + g(x)),$$
$$g(x) = (x = 0 \rightarrow 0, f(x - 1) + g(x - 1)),$$

where $x \in N$. The normal functionals are

$$F = \lambda f, g \in (N \rightarrow N)^+ . \lambda x \in N^+ .(x = 0 \rightarrow 1, f(x - 1) + g(x))$$
$$G = \lambda f, g \in (N \rightarrow N)^+ . \lambda x \in N^+ .(x = 0 \rightarrow 0, f(x - 1) + g(x - 1)).$$

The simultaneous fixed points are

$$\lim_{n \to \infty} f_n \quad \text{and} \quad \lim_{n \to \infty} g_n,$$

where $f_0 = g_0 = \lambda x . \in N^+ . \omega$, and

$$f_{n+1} = F(f_n, g_n)$$
$$g_{n+1} = G(f_n, g_n)$$

for all $n \geqslant 0$. The first few functions are given in the following two tables:

	ω	0	1	2	3	4	5	...
f_0	ω	ω	ω	ω	ω	ω	ω	...
f_1	ω	1	ω	ω	ω	ω	ω	...
f_2	ω	1	ω	ω	ω	ω	ω	...
f_3	ω	1	2	ω	ω	ω	ω	...
f_4	ω	1	2	5	ω	ω	ω	...
f_5	ω	1	2	5	13	ω	ω	...

	ω	0	1	2	3	4	5	...
g_0	ω	ω	ω	ω	ω	ω	ω	...
g_1	ω	0	ω	ω	ω	ω	ω	...
g_2	ω	0	1	ω	ω	ω	ω	...
g_3	ω	0	1	3	ω	ω	ω	...
g_4	ω	0	1	3	8	ω	ω	...
g_5	ω	0	1	3	8	21	ω	...

7.4 Continuous functionals

This section is devoted to a formal proof that the functionals associated with recursive definitions are indeed continuous. To see what has to be done, consider the simple definition

$$f(x) = E,$$

where x is a variable of type V, E is an expression of type U—as defined in Section 6.3—and f is a variable of type $(V \to U)$. We have to show that the functional F defined by

$$F = \lambda f \in (V \to U)^+ . \lambda x \in V^+ . E$$

is an element of the domain

$$((V \to U) \to (V \to U))^+,$$

when every constant function (i.e. every function apart from f) appearing in E is extended to a continuous function over the appropriate domain. Now, $((V \to U)$

$\rightarrow (V \rightarrow U))^+$ is the collection of all continuous functions from $(V \rightarrow U)^+$ to $(V \rightarrow U)^+$, and $(V \rightarrow U)^+$ is, in turn, the collection of all continuous functions from V^+ to U^+. Thus, we have to prove that

(a) $F(f)$ is a continuous function for each fixed continuous f, i.e. $\lambda x \in V^+ . E$ is a continuous function of x;

(b) F is a continuous function of f.

Putting it another way, we have to show that the expression

$$F(f)(x)$$

is a continuous function of both x and f.

More generally, in the case of a set of simultaneous definitions

$$f_1(x_1, x_2, \ldots, x_n) = E_1$$

$$. \quad . \quad . \quad . \quad . \quad . \quad . \quad . \quad . \quad . \quad . \quad . \quad .$$

$$f_k(x_1, x_2, \ldots, x_n) = E_k$$

we have to show that the functionals

$$F_j = \lambda(f_1, \ldots, f_k) . \lambda(x_1, \ldots, x_n) . E_j$$

for $1 \leqslant j \leqslant k$, are continuous in both $(f_1, \ldots, f_k)$ and $(x_1, \ldots, x_n)$. We can, however, restrict our attention to functions of a single argument by using the following lemma.

Lemma 5. A many-place function is continuous if and only if it is continuous in each argument considered separately; that is,

$$\lambda(x_1, \ldots, x_n) . f(x_1, \ldots, x_n)$$

is continuous if and only if

$$\lambda x_j . f(x_1, \ldots, x_n)$$

is continuous for each j, the values of x_i for $i \neq j$ being assumed fixed.

Proof. For simplicity, we consider only the case $n = 2$. Suppose first that

$$f = \lambda xy . f(x, y)$$

is continuous. Keep y fixed, and suppose $x \subseteq x'$. It follows that

$$(x, y) \subseteq (x', y)$$

by the partial ordering on cross-product domains, and so

$$f(x, y) \subseteq f(x', y)$$

by the monotonicity of f. Hence f is monotonic in its first argument. Next, let $x_0 \subseteq x_1 \subseteq x_2 \ldots$ be a chain, so that for each fixed $y, (x_0, y) \subseteq (x_1, y) \subseteq \ldots$ is a chain over the product domain. Since f is continuous, we have

$$f(\lim_{n\to\infty}(x_n, y)) = \lim_{n\to\infty} f(x_n, y),$$

and since

$$f(\lim_{n\to\infty} x_n, y) = f(\lim_{n\to\infty}(x_n, y))$$

by the definition of limit in product domains, it therefore follows that f is continuous in its first argument. A similar proof can be given for continuity in the second argument.

Conversely, suppose f is monotonic and continuous in each argument. If $(x, y) \subseteq (x', y')$, then

$$f(x, y) \subseteq f(x', y) \quad \text{since } x \subseteq x',$$
$$\subseteq f(x', y') \quad \text{since } y \subseteq y',$$

and so f is monotonic. Let $(x_0, y_0) \subseteq (x_1, y_1)\ldots$ be a chain. We have

$$f(\lim_{n\to\infty}(x_n, y_n)) = f(\lim_{n\to\infty} x_n, \lim_{m\to\infty} y_m)$$

$$= \lim_{n\to\infty} f(x_n, \lim_{m\to\infty} y_m) \quad \text{by continuity in } x,$$

$$= \lim_{n\to\infty} \lim_{m\to\infty} f(x_n, y_m) \quad \text{by continuity in } y.$$

Let $k = \max(n, m)$, whence $f(x_n, y_m) \subseteq f(x_k, y_k)$ by monotonicity. It follows that the last expression is equal to

$$\lim_{k\to\infty} f(x_k, y_k),$$

and so f is continuous.

Lemma 5 enables the following theorem to be generalized to the case of simultaneous definitions of not necessarily 1-place functions.

Theorem 2. Suppose $f(x) = E$ is a recursive definition, where x is of type V, E is of type U, and f is of type $(V \to U)$. If the constant functions appearing in the expression E are extended to continuous functions over the appropriate domains, then the functional

$$\lambda f \in (V \to U)^+ . \lambda x \in V^+ . E$$

is of an element of the domain

$$((V \to U) \to (V \to U))^+$$

Proof. The proof is by induction on the structure of E. To simplify the analysis, we can introduce the conditional function $\theta : (T \times W^2 \to W)^+$ for each type W, where $T = \{true, false\}$ and

$$\theta(p, x, y) = (p \to x, y).$$

Although θ is not the natural extension of any partial function, it is monotonic and continuous (see Exercise 7.15). By introducing θ as an extra constant function, we can treat the formation of conditional expressions as a special case of function application, and so simplify the definition of the class of expressions.

Suppose now that χ_E denotes the functional associated with expression E, so that $\chi_E(f)(x) = E$. We can analyse the structure of χ_E as follows:

(1) If E is the variable x or a constant c standing by itself, then

$$\chi_E(f)(x) = x$$

or $$\chi_E(f)(x) = c.$$

(2) If E is of the form $h(E_1, E_2, \ldots, E_n)$, then

   (a) $\chi_E(f)(x) = g(\chi_{E_1}(f)(x), \ldots, \chi_{E_n}(f)(x))$, in the case that h is a constant function g;
   (b) $\chi_E(f)(x) = f(\chi_{E_1}(f)(x), \ldots, \chi_{E_n}(f)(x))$, in the case that h is the variable f;
   (c) $\chi_E(f)(x) = x(\chi_{E_1}(f)(x), \ldots, \chi_{E_n}(f)(x))$, in the case that x is a function variable, and h is x.

The first stage of the proof is to show by induction on the structure of E, that

$$\chi_E(f)(x)$$

is a continuous function of x when f is a given fixed continuous function. This is obviously true for case (1). For case (2) we suppose for simplicity that $n = 2$, the generalization being straightforward. To establish the induction in case (2a), let $x_0 \subseteq x_1 \subseteq \cdots$ be a chain of V^+; we have

$$\chi_E(f)(\lim_{n \to \infty} x_n) = g(\chi_1(f)(\lim_{n \to \infty} x_n), \chi_2(f)(\lim_{n \to \infty} x_n))$$
$$= g(\lim_{n \to \infty} \chi_1(f)(x_n), \lim_{m \to \infty} \chi_2(f)(x_m)),$$

using the induction hypothesis for χ_1 and χ_2. This last expression is just

$$\lim_{n \to \infty} \lim_{m \to \infty} g(\chi_1(f)(x_n), \chi_2(f)(x_m))$$

since by supposition g is continuous. By monotonicity we have

$$g(\chi_1(f)(x_n), \chi_2(f)(x_m)) \subseteq g(\chi_1(f)(x_k), \chi_2(f)(x_k)),$$

where $k = \max(n, m)$, and so

$$\chi_E(f)(\lim_{n \to \infty} x_n) = \lim_{k \to \infty} \chi_E(f)(x_k).$$

Case (2b) is similar to case (2a). For case (2c) we have

$$\chi_E(f)(\lim_{n \to \infty} x_n) = (\lim_{n \to \infty} x_n)(\chi_1(f)(\lim_{n \to \infty} x_n), \chi_2(f)(\lim_{n \to \infty} x_n))$$
$$= \lim_{n \to \infty} \lim_{m \to \infty} \lim_{r \to \infty} x_n(\chi_1(f)(x_m), \chi_2(f)(x_r))$$

Using the induction hypothesis for χ_1 and χ_2, and the fact that if V is a function space, then each $x_n \in V^+$ is continuous. Once again, we can use the monotonicity of x_n, $\chi_1(f)$, and $\chi_2(f)$ to obtain

$$x_n(\chi_1(f)(x_m)(\chi_2(f)(x_r)) \subseteq x_k(\chi_1(f)(x_k), \chi_2(f)(x_k))$$

for $k = \max(n, m, r)$, and so establish the induction step.

The second stage of the proof is to show that χ_E is a continuous function of f, i.e.

$$\chi_E(\lim_{n \to \infty} f_n)(x) = \lim_{n \to \infty} \chi_E(f_n)(x)$$

for all $x \in V^+$. The proof is very similar to the first induction argument, and can safely be left to the reader.

7.5   Relationship between the two approaches to recursion

Suppose $f(x) = E$ is a given recursive definition, and $F = \lambda f . \lambda x . E$ is the functional associated with E when every constant function appearing in E is naturally extended. Let f denote the least fixed point of F, and let f_F and f_L denote the functions described by the recursive definition $f(x)$ is E using the *eaf* and *eal* rules of evaluation respectively. The third question to be asked about the fixed point approach to recursion is: what is the relationship between f, f_F, and f_L? The answer is given by the following theorem.

Theorem 3. $f = f_L$.

The proof of Theorem 3 will not be given until Section 8.3, since it makes use of the induction technique to be developed in the next section.

Recall, from Section 6.4, that the function defined by using the *eal* rule may be a non-trivial extension of the function defined by using the *eaf* rule i.e. $f_F \subseteq f_L$. It follows from Theorem 3 that the *eaf* mode of evaluation does not in general lead to the least fixed point. Now, all the techniques we are about to develop for proving properties of recursively defined functions is based on the assumption that the function given by a recursive definition is exactly the least fixed point. Apparently then, the techniques do not apply to functions defined by the *eaf* rule. However, they can be made to apply by using Theorem 6.2 as follows.

Suppose we are given a recursive definition

$$f(x) \text{ is } E,$$

and we wish to prove something about the function f_F given by this definition using the *eaf* rule. Theorem 6.2 says that $f_F = g_L$, where g_L is the function given by applying the *eal* rule to the definition

$$g(x) \text{ is } (p(x) \to E', E'),$$

where p is any constant predicate, and E' is identical to E except that g is substituted everywhere for f. Theorem 3 says that g_L is identical to the least fixed point of the normal functional associated with the expression

$$(p(x) \to E', E').$$

In this way, we can prove facts about *eaf*-defined functions by proving facts about the least fixed points of slightly modified functionals.

7.6 Fixed point induction

Having successfully interpreted recursive definitions in terms of fixed points, we can now use the theory in the practical task of proving assertions about recursively defined functions. In this section we consider a particular induction technique, called *fixed point induction*, and show how it can be used to prove statements about the least fixed points of functions. Substantial examples of its use in the proof of program properties will be given in Chapter 8.

Consider a functional

$$F: ((D_1 \rightarrow D_2) \rightarrow (D_1 \rightarrow D_2))^+,$$

associated with a typical recursive definition. The least fixed point of F is given by the limit of the chain

$$\Omega \subseteq F(\Omega) \subseteq F^2(\Omega) \subseteq \cdots,$$

where Ω denotes the least element of $(D_1 \rightarrow D_2)^+$. We shall denote the least fixed point of F by $\phi(F)$; thus

$$\phi(F) = \lim_{n \to \infty} F^n(\Omega).$$

The notation $\phi(F)$ is perfectly acceptable because it is possible to consider ϕ as the well defined function

$$\phi = \lambda F . \lim_{n \to \infty} F^n(\Omega).$$

It even turns out (see Exercise 7.18) that

$$\phi: (((D_1 \rightarrow D_2) \rightarrow (D_1 \rightarrow D_2)) \rightarrow (D_1 \rightarrow D_2))^+,$$

so that ϕ is monotonic and continuous. To avoid too many parentheses, we shall often write functional application by juxtaposition, e.g. fx for $f(x)$ and ϕF for $\phi(F)$.

Suppose we wish to prove that some mathematical statement Π holds for ϕF. One way of doing this immediately suggests itself from the way that ϕF is defined:

(1) show that Π holds for each element in the chain $\Omega \subseteq F(\Omega) \subseteq F^2(\Omega) \subseteq \cdots$, and

(2) show that Π remains true in the limit.

To make this idea more precise, suppose $\Pi[f]$ is a statement which involves the function f.

Definition A statement $\Pi[f]$ is *admissible* if for every chain $f_0 \subseteq f_1 \subseteq \cdots$, we have

$$\Pi[f_n] \quad \text{for all } n \geqslant 0 \text{ implies } \Pi[\lim_{n \to \infty} f_n].$$

Thus, in effect, a statement is admissible if it remains true in the limit. It is tempting to try and think of admissibility as some sort of continuity condition on Π, but this idea does not work. We can, if we wish, regard a mathematical statement Π, involving functions from the domain $(D_1 \rightarrow D_2)^+$, as a predicate

$$\Pi : (D_1 \rightarrow D_2)^+ \rightarrow \{true, false\}^+,$$

although Π differs from general predicates in one very important respect, namely that $\Pi[f]$ takes only the values *true* and *false*, and never the value *undefined* of $\{true, false\}^+$. The continuity of Π is expressed by the condition:

$$\Pi[\lim_{n \rightarrow \infty} f_n] = \lim_{n \rightarrow \infty} \Pi[f_n],$$

for every chain $f_0 \subseteq f_1 \subseteq \cdots$ of $(D_1 \rightarrow D_2)^+$. However, in order for the limit on the right hand side of this equation to be well defined, Π must satisfy the additional requirement that

$$\Pi[f] = \Pi[g] \quad \text{whenever } f \subseteq g.$$

In particular, it follows that $\Pi[f] = \Pi[\Omega]$ for every function f, and so any meaningful notion of continuity collapses. The problem can be avoided, and the concept of continuity re-established, by taking a different domain from $\{true, false\}^+$ in the definition of Π (see Exercise 7.19), but this idea will not be developed in the text. Alternatively, one can get at the spirit of continuity, by saying that Π should not only remain true in the limit, but also remain false in the limit. This is equivalent to the condition that both Π and $\overline{\Pi}$, the negation of Π, should be admissible.

In order to show that Π holds for each element in the chain $\Omega \subseteq F(\Omega) \subseteq F^2(\Omega) \subseteq \cdots$, it is clearly sufficient to prove

(a) $\Pi[\Omega]$, and

(b) $\Pi[f]$ implies $\Pi[F(f)]$, for all f in $(D_1 \rightarrow D_2)^+$.

Provided Π is an admissible statement, proving (a) and (b) establishes the truth of $\Pi[\phi F]$. This is the method of fixed point induction.

Fixed point induction

To show that $\Pi[\phi F]$ holds, where Π is an admissible statement and $F : ((D_1 \rightarrow D_2) \rightarrow (D_1 \rightarrow D_2))^+$ for some domains D_1 and D_2, it is sufficient to show

(a) $\Pi[\Omega]$ holds, where Ω is the least element of $(D_1 \rightarrow D_2)^+$, and

(b) $\Pi[f]$ implies $\Pi[F(f)]$, for all $f \in (D_1 \rightarrow D_2)^+$.

More generally, the statement Π may involve two or more fixed points. In such a case, $\Pi[f, g, \ldots]$ is admissible if $\Pi[h]$ is admissible, where $h = (f, g, \ldots)$. Effectively, this means that a statement is admissible if and only if it is admissible in each dependent function considered separately. For example, to show that $\Pi[\phi F, \phi G]$ holds, where Π is admissible, it is sufficient to prove:

(a) $\Pi[\Omega_1,\Omega_2]$, where Ω_1 and Ω_2 are the least elements of the appropriate domains, and

(b) $\Pi[f,g]$ implies $\Pi[F(f), G(g)]$ for all f and g over the appropriate domains.

Before we can apply fixed point induction to particular examples, it is necessary to determine what sort of statements are admissible.

Lemma 6. Suppose G and H are functionals of type $((D_1 \to D_2) \to (D_1 \to D_2))^+$ for some domains D_1 and D_2. Then the statement

$$G(f) \subseteq H(f)$$

is admissible.

Proof. Suppose $f_0 \subseteq f_1 \subseteq \cdots$ is some chain of $(D_1 \to D_2)^+$, and $G(f_n) \subseteq H(f_n)$ for all $n \geqslant 0$. Since H is monotonic, we have

$$G(f_n) \subseteq H(\lim_{n \to \infty} f_n) \quad \text{for } n \geqslant 0.$$

Since G is continuous, we have

$$G(\lim_{n \to \infty} f_n) = \lim_{n \to \infty} G(f_n) \subseteq H(\lim_{n \to \infty} f_n),$$

which gives the desired result. Notice that the proof does not make use of the continuity of H.

Corollary. Let Π be a statement of the form

$$\forall x, y \ldots E_1[f, g, \ldots, x, y, \ldots] \subseteq E_2[f, g, \ldots, x, y, \ldots],$$

where E_1 and E_2 are arbitrary expressions involving the variables $f, g, \ldots, x, y, \ldots$. Then Π is admissible.

Proof. From Theorem 2, the functionals F_1 and F_2, where

$$F_j = \lambda fg \ldots \ . \ \lambda xy \ldots E_j[f, g, \ldots, x, y, \ldots],$$

are monotonic and continuous when the constant functions appearing in E_i are extended to continuous functions over the appropriate domain. Statement Π thus has the form

$$F_1(f, g, \ldots) \subseteq F_2(f, g, \ldots),$$

and Lemma 6 shows that such statements are admissible.

Lemma 7. (i) if Π_1 and Π_2 are admissible, then so are

$$\Pi_1 \wedge \Pi_2 \quad \text{and} \quad \Pi_1 \vee \Pi_2,$$

(ii) if Π_2 and $\overline{\Pi}_1$, the negation of Π, are admissible, then so is $\Pi_1 \supset \Pi_2$.

Proof. (i) To show that $\Pi_1 \wedge \Pi_2$ is admissible, let $f_0 \subseteq f_1 \subseteq \cdots$ be any chain such that $(\Pi_1 \wedge \Pi_2)[f_n]$ holds for all $n \geqslant 0$. It follows, from the definition of conjunction, that $\Pi_1[f_n]$ holds for all $n \geqslant 0$, and also $\Pi_2[f_n]$ holds for all $n \geqslant 0$. By the admissibility of Π_1 and Π_2, it follows that both $\Pi_1[\lim_{n\to\infty} f_n]$ and $\Pi_2[\lim_{n\to\infty} f_n]$ hold, whence $\Pi_1 \wedge \Pi_2$ is admissible.

To show the admissibility of $\Pi_1 \vee \Pi_2$, let $f_0 \subseteq f_1 \subseteq \cdots$ be any chain such that $(\Pi_1 \vee \Pi_2)[f_n]$ holds for all $n \geqslant 0$. This means that there exists two chains $g_0 \subseteq g_1 \subseteq \cdots$ and $h_0 \subseteq h, \subseteq \cdots$, where each f_j is either g_n or h_m for some n and m, such that

$$\Pi_1[g_n] \quad \text{holds for } n \geqslant 0 \quad \text{and}$$
$$\Pi_2[h_n] \quad \text{holds for } n \geqslant 0.$$

Now, either $\lim_{n\to\infty} g_n = \lim_{n\to\infty} f_n$ or $\lim_{n\to\infty} h_n = \lim_{n\to\infty} f_n$ (see Exercise 7.20), so that by the admissibility of Π_1 and Π_2, at least one of $\Pi_1[\lim_{n\to\infty} f_n]$ and $\Pi_2[\lim_{n\to\infty} f_n]$ is true. Hence $\Pi_1 \vee \Pi_2$ is admissible.

(ii) Immediate from above, since $\Pi_1 \supset \Pi_2$ is just $\overline{\Pi}_1 \vee \Pi_2$.

Lemma 8. If $\Pi[f, x, y, \ldots]$ is admissible (for f), then

$$\forall x, y, \ldots \Pi[f, x, y, \ldots] \quad \text{is admissible.}$$

Proof. Immediate.

Corollary. If Π is admissible, then so is

$$\forall x, y, \ldots \Sigma[x, y \ldots] \supset \Pi[f, x, y, \ldots],$$

where Σ is any statement not involving f.

Proof. Immediate from Lemma 8 and Lemma 7(ii), since $\overline{\Sigma}$ is admissible.

We now consider a number of simple examples in the use of fixed point induction; more complicated examples will be given in Chapter 8.

Example 1

Suppose we wish to prove that the function f given by the recursive definition

$$f(x) = (x = 0 \to 0, (2x - 1) + f(x - 1))$$

satisfies the relation $f(x) \subseteq x^2$ for all $x \geqslant 0$. We have to show that

$$\phi F \subseteq \lambda x . x^2,$$

where F is the normal functional $\lambda f . \lambda x . (x = 0 \to 0, (2x - 1) + f(x - 1))$. We take $\Pi[f]$ to be the statement

$$f \subseteq \lambda x . x^2.$$

$\Pi[f]$ is admissible by Lemma 6.

(a) Clearly $\Pi[\Omega]$ holds, since $\Omega \subseteq \lambda x . x^2$ by definition of Ω.

(b) Suppose $\Pi[f]$ holds, i.e. $f \subseteq \lambda x . x^2$. We have

$$F(f) = \lambda x . (x = 0 \to 0, (2x - 1) + f(x - 1))$$
$$\subseteq \lambda x . (x = 0 \to 0, (2x - 1) + (x - 1)^2)$$
$$= \lambda x . x^2.$$

Thus $\Pi[F(f)]$ holds, and the induction is complete. Notice that the stronger assertion $\Pi[f]: f = \lambda x . x^2$ cannot be used, since $\Pi[\Omega]$ in this case is false. Nevertheless, the proof that $\phi F(x) = x^2$ for all $x \geqslant 0$ is quite straightforward, provided we use normal mathematical induction instead of fixed point induction. We consider this further in the next section.

Example 2

Suppose we wish to show that $\phi F \cdot \phi F = \phi F$ where

$$F = \lambda f . \lambda x . (p(x) \to x, f(f(h(x)))),$$

p and h being given naturally extended monotonic and continuous functions. The obvious induction hypothesis is to take

$$\Pi[f]: f \cdot f = f.$$

However, it turns out that a better choice is to take

$$\Pi[f]: (\phi F \cdot f = f), \quad \text{i.e. } (\phi F \cdot f \subseteq f) \wedge (f \subseteq \phi F \cdot f).$$

Now ϕF is monotonic and continuous, so that $\lambda f . \phi F \cdot f$ is continuous. Hence Π is admissible by Lemma 7(i).

(a) To show that $\Pi[\Omega]$ holds, i.e. $\phi F \cdot \Omega = \Omega$, we compute as follows:

$$\phi F \cdot \Omega(x) = \phi F(\omega)$$
$$= (p(\omega) \to \omega, \phi F(\phi F(h\omega)))$$
$$= \omega = \Omega(x),$$

by the definition of ϕF and the fact that p is naturally extended.

(b) To show that $\phi F \cdot F(f) = F(f)$ follows from $\phi F \cdot f = f$, we compute as follows:

$$\phi F \cdot F(f)(x) = \phi F(px \to x, f \cdot f \cdot (hx))$$
$$= (px \to \phi F(x), \phi F \cdot f \cdot f \cdot (hx))$$
$$= (px \to x, f \cdot f \cdot (hx)),$$

using the induction hypothesis, and the fact that $\phi F(x) = x$ if $p(x) = true$. Since the last expression is just $F(f)(x)$, the induction is established.

Example 3

Consider the two definitions

$$f(x, y) = (p(x) \to y, h(f(k(x), y)))$$
$$g(x, y) = (p(x) \to y, g(k(x), h(y))).$$

We wish to show that $\phi F = \phi G$, where

$$F = \lambda f . \lambda x y . (p(x) \to y, h(f(k(x), y)))$$
$$G = \lambda f . \lambda x y . (p(x) \to y, g(k(x), h(y))),$$

p, k, and h being naturally extended functions. We take the admissible induction hypothesis to be

$$\Pi[f, g] : \forall x, y . (f(x, y) = g(x, y)) \wedge (g(x, h(y)) = h(g(x, y))).$$

(a) $\Pi[\Omega, \Omega]$ holds because $\Omega(x, h(y)) = \omega = h(\Omega(x, y))$, since $h(\omega) = \omega$.

(b) To show $\Pi[F(f), G(g)]$ follows from $\Pi[f, g]$, we proceed as follows:

(i) $F(f)(x, y) = (p(x) \to y, h(f(kx, y)))$
$\qquad = (p(x) \to y, h(g(kx, y)))$
$\qquad = (p(x) \to y, g(kx, hy)))$
$\qquad = G(f)(x, y),$

using the two parts of the induction hypothesis;

(ii) $G(g)(x, hy) = (p(x) \to hy, g(kx, h^2 y))$
$\qquad = (p(x) \to hy, h(g(kx, hy))$
$\qquad = h(G(g)(x, y)).$

This completes the induction and shows, in particular, that $\phi F = \phi G$.

7.7 Other proof techniques

Fixed point induction is not the only method for proving properties of recursively defined functions. In suitable cases, the following lemma can be applied directly.

Lemma 9. To show that $\phi F \subseteq g$, it is sufficient to prove that $F(g) \subseteq g$.

Proof. Suppose $F(g) \subseteq g$. We prove that $F^n(\Omega) \subseteq g$ for all $n \geqslant 0$ by induction. For $n = 0$, we have $\Omega \subseteq g$; the induction step is

$$F^{n+1}(\Omega) \subseteq F(g) \subseteq g,$$

using the induction hypothesis and the monotonicity of F. It follows that

$$\phi F = \lim_{n \to \infty} F^n(\Omega) \subseteq g.$$

Lemma 9 can sometimes be employed to show that $g(x) = h(x)$ for each x in some set A, where g and h are given recursively defined functions. It is sufficient to find a continuous functional F such that (i) $F(g) \subseteq g$; (ii) $F(h) \subseteq h$; and (iii) $\phi F(x) \neq \omega$ for all $x \in A$. By Lemma 9,

$$\phi F(x) \subseteq g(x) \quad \text{and} \quad \phi F(x) \subseteq h(x),$$

so that if $\phi F(x) \neq \omega$, then we have $g(x) = h(x)$ by the properties of the partial ordering $\subseteq$. Historically, this technique, called *recursion-induction*, was the first to be used in proofs about recursively defined functions.

While the proofs of (i) and (ii) are usually straightforward, the proof of (iii) can cause trouble. Consider, for example, the statement

$$\Pi[f]\colon \forall x \in N \cdot f(x) \neq \omega,$$

where $f\colon (N \to N)^+$, and ω is the least element of N^+. Although Π is an admissible statement, it cannot be used in any fixed point induction proof, since $\Pi[\Omega]$ is always false. The way round this problem is to introduce the functional $D\colon ((N \to T) \to (N \to T))^+$, where $T = \{true, false\}$, given by

$$D = \lambda d \cdot \lambda x \cdot (x = 0 \to true, d(x - 1)).$$

The least fixed point ϕD of D is a predicate such that

$$\phi D(x) = true \text{ if } x \in N,$$
$$= undefined, \text{ otherwise,}$$

where *undefined* is the least element of T^+. Fixed point induction, with the hypothesis

$$\Pi[d, f]\colon \forall x \in N \cdot d(x) \subseteq (f(x) \neq \omega),$$

can be used to show that $\Pi[\phi D, \phi F]$ and this gives the desired result. The basis $\Pi[\Omega_1, \Omega_2]$ holds, since

$$\Omega_1(x) \subseteq (\Omega_2(x) \neq \omega)$$

is always true. We must, of course, show that Π is admissible. It is sufficient to show that Π is admissible in each argument considered separately. Suppose $d_0 \subseteq d_1 \subseteq \ldots$ is a chain of predicates and f is a fixed function such that $\Pi[d_n, f]$ holds, i.e.

$$d_n(x) \subseteq (f(x) \neq \omega) \text{ for all } x \in N.$$

It follows that $\lim_{n \to \infty} d_n(x) \subseteq (f(x) \neq \omega)$, and so $\Pi[\lim_{n \to \infty} d_n, f]$. On the other hand, suppose $f_0 \subseteq f_1 \subseteq \ldots$ is a chain and d is fixed such that $\Pi[d, f_n]$ holds for $n \geq 0$. There are three cases to be considered:

(i) $d(x) = true$; in this case $f_n(x) \neq \omega$ for $n \geq 0$ implies $\lim_{n \to \infty} f_n(x) \neq \omega$.

(ii) $d(x) = false$; in this case $f_n(x) = \omega$ for $n \geq 0$ implies $\lim_{n \to \infty} f_n(x) = \omega$.

(iii) $d(x) = undefined$; in this case $d(x) \subseteq (f(x) \neq \omega)$ is true for any f.

Hence Π is admissible.

As an example of the use of the above technique, consider the problem of proving that the function defined by

$$f(x) = (x = 0 \to 0, (2x - 1) + f(x - 1))$$

terminates for every $x \in N$. This example was considered in the last section, where it was shown that $\phi F(x) \subseteq x^2$ for $x \in N$ by a simple fixed point induction. Here,

$$F = \lambda f \cdot \lambda x \cdot (x = 0 \to 0, (2x - 1) + f(x - 1)).$$

Let $\Pi[d, f]$: $\forall x \in N \,.\, d(x) \subseteq (f(x) \neq \omega)$.

(a) $\Pi[\Omega_1, \Omega_2]$; obvious.

(b) suppose $\Pi[d, f]$. Then

$$D(d)(x) = (x = 0 \to true, d(x - 1)).$$

Now $true \subseteq (F(f)(0) \neq \omega)$, and $d(x - 1) \subseteq (f(x - 1) \neq \omega)$ by assumption, so that

$$F(f)(x) = (x = 0 \to 0, (2x - 1) + f(x - 1))$$
$$\neq \omega$$

Hence

$$D(d)(x) \subseteq (F(f)(x) \neq \omega),$$

which establishes

$$\Pi[D(d), F(f)].$$

By taking the admissible statement

$$\Pi[d, f]: \forall x \in N \,.\, d(x) \subseteq (f(x) = x^2),$$

one can, of course, prove that $\phi F(x) = x^2$ directly. In fact, there is a much simpler way to prove that $\phi F(x) = x^2$ for $x \geq 0$, namely by normal mathematical induction on the natural numbers. In its simplest form, this induction method says that to show $\Pi[x]$ holds for all integers $x \geq 0$, it is sufficient to show:

(a) $\Pi[0]$ holds, and

(b) $\Pi[x]$ implies $\Pi[x + 1]$ for all $x \in N$.

Taking $\Pi[x]$: $\phi F(x) = x^2$ in our example, we have

$$\phi F(0) = (0 = 0 \to 0, (2 \times 0 - 1) + \phi F(0 - 1))$$
$$= 0,$$

using the fact that $\phi F = F(\phi F)$, and this establishes $\Pi[0]$. As the induction step, we have

$$\phi F(x + 1) = (x + 1 = 0 \to 0, (2x + 1) + \phi F(x))$$
$$= (2x + 1) + x^2 = (x + 1)^2,$$

and the induction is complete. The simple form of F makes the induction easy in this case.

Mathematical induction is more appropriately called *structural induction*, because it depends on the fact that the natural numbers have the structural property of being *well-ordered*, i.e. every subset of N contains a least element. Structural induction can be applied to other well-ordered structures. Consider, for example, the set Σ^* of all finite strings over some finite alphabet Σ, including the null string λ. Let $t(x)$ give the string which remains when the first symbol of the non-null string x is removed. To show that $\Pi[x]$ holds for all strings $x \in \Sigma^*$ it is sufficient to show:

(a) $\Pi[\lambda]$ holds

(b) $\Pi[t(x)]$ implies $\Pi[x]$ for all $x \neq \lambda$.

An example of the use of this induction rule is given in Exercise 7.23.

Exercises

1. Let f^+ denote the natural extension of the number theoretic function f. Prove that

$$(f \cdot g)^+ = (f^+ \cdot g^+).$$

2. Construct two possible definitions for $(D_1 \cup D_2)^+$, indicating the partial ordering in each case.

3. In how many ways can the multiplication function $\lambda x, y \in N . x \times y$ be extended to a monotonic function in $(N \times N)^+ \to N^+$?

4. Assuming $A = \{0, 1\}$ and $B = \{0\}$, draw the partial orderings of each of the following domains:

(i) $(A \times B)^+$

(ii) $(A \to B)^+$

(iii) $(A^2 \to B)^+$

(iv) $((B \to B) \to A^2)^+$

5. Verify that $(D \to D)^+$ is a domain, where

(a) $(D \to D)^+ = (D^+ \to D^+)$

(b) $(D \to D)^+ = \{f : (D^+ \to D^+), f(\omega) = \omega\}$.

6. Determine whether the following predicates, taking values in $\{true, false\}^+$, are monotonic:

(i) $\lambda x, y \in D^+ . x \subseteq y$

(ii) $\lambda x, y \in D^+ . (x \subseteq y) \wedge (y \subseteq x)$

(iii) $\lambda x, y \in D^+ . p(x) \vee p(y)$, where p is monotonic, and v is the symmetrical extension of disjunction.

7. Suppose $F = \lambda f . \lambda x \in D^+ . (\forall y . (fy = y) \to fx, \omega)$. Which of the following assertions are true?

(i) $F : (D \to D)^+ \to (D \to D)^+$

(ii) $F : ((D \to D) \to (D \to D))^+$

(iii) $F : (D^+ \to D^+) \to (D \to D)^+$

8. Show that the least upper bound of a set X is unique if it exists.

9. Let $D = \{x : 0 \leqslant x < 1\}$. Is D a domain under the partial ordering $<$?

10. Let $\{x_{n,m}: n \geqslant 0, m \geqslant 0\}$ be a set of elements of a domain such that

$$x_{n,m} \subseteq x_{(n+1),m}$$
$$x_{n,m} \subseteq x_{n,(m+1)}$$

for all $n, m \geqslant 0$. Show that

$$\lim_{n \to \infty} \lim_{m \to \infty} x_{n,m} = \lim_{m \to \infty} \lim_{n \to \infty} x_{n,m} = \lim_{n \to \infty} x_{n,n}.$$

11. Show that every monotonic function of $(N \times N)^+ \to N^+$ is continuous.

12. Generalize Theorem 7.1 by showing that if $f: D \to D$ is continuous, and x_0 is any element of domain D such that $x_0 \subseteq f(x_0)$, then $\lim_{n \to \infty} x_n$, where $x_{n+1} = f(x_n)$ for $n \geqslant 0$, is a fixed point of f.

13. Let $F = \lambda f. \lambda x \in N^+ . g(f(x))$, where $g: N^+ \to N^+$. Show that $F: ((N \to N) \to (N \to N))^+$ if and only if $g: (N \to N)^+$.

14. Let $F = \lambda f. \lambda x \in N^+ . f(f(x))$. Which of the following statements are true?

   (i) $F: (N^+ \to N^+) \to (N^+ \to N^+)$

   (ii) $F: ((N \to N) \to (N \to N))^+$

   (iii) $F: (N^+ \to N^+) \to (N^+ \to N^+)$ and F is continuous.

15. Prove that $\theta: (T \times V^2 \to V)^+$ where $\theta(p, x, y) = (p \to x, y)$.

16. Suppose

$$F_1 = \lambda f \in (U \to V)^+ . g$$

and $$F_2 = \lambda f \in (U \to V)^+ . (total(f) \to f, h),$$

where g is *not* an element of $(U \to V)^+$, h *is* an element of $(U \to V)^+$, and $total(f)$ is given by

$$total(f) = true \text{ if } f(x) \neq \omega \text{ for all } x \neq \omega$$
$$= false \text{ otherwise.}$$

Show that F_1 is continuous but is not an element of $(U \to V)^+ \to (U \to V)^+$, and F_2 is an element of $(U \to V)^+ \to (U \to V)^+$ but is not continuous.

17. Let $S = \lambda f, g . \lambda x . f(x)(g(x))$.
Show that $S \in ((V \to (U \to W)) \times (V \to U) \to (V \to W))^+$ for appropriate U, V, and W.

18. Show that $\phi: ((D \to D) \to D)^+$, where $\phi = \lambda f. \lim_{n \to \infty} f^n(\omega)$.

19. We can regard a mathematical statement Π, involving functions from the domain $(D_1 \to D_2)^+$ as a predicate

$$\Pi: (D_1 \to D_2)^+ \to T,$$

where T is the two element domain

Show that, under this interpretation Π is continuous if and only if both Π and $\overline{\Pi}$ are admissible.

20. Suppose $\Pi[f]: \forall x \in D^{+} . x \neq \omega \supset f(x) \neq \omega$, where $f:(D \to D)^{+}$. Show that Π is admissible, but $\overline{\Pi}$ is not admissible.

21. Say that Π is *weakly admissible,* if for each chain of the form $\Omega \subseteq F(\Omega) \subseteq F^{2}(\Omega) \subseteq \ldots$, we have

$$\Pi[F^{n}(\Omega)] \quad \text{for all } n \geq 0 \text{ implies } \Pi[\phi F].$$

   (i) Show that $\Pi_{1} \wedge \Pi_{2}$ is weakly admissible if both Π_{1} and Π_{2} are.

   (ii) By taking $\Pi_{1}[f]: \forall x \in D^{+} . f(x) = \omega$, and $\Pi_{2}[f]: \exists x, y, \in D^{+} . (f(x) \neq f(y))$, or otherwise, show that $\Pi_{1} \vee \Pi_{2}$ is not necessarily weakly admissible even if both Π_{1} and Π_{2} are.

22. Complete the proof of Lemma 7.7 (i) by showing that if $g_{0} \subseteq g_{1} \subseteq \cdots$ and $h_{0} \subseteq h_{1} \subseteq \cdots$ are two chains which partition the chain $f_{0} \subseteq f_{1} \subseteq f_{2} \subseteq \ldots$, then either $\lim_{n \to \infty} g_{n} = \lim_{n \to \infty} f_{n}$ or $\lim_{n \to \infty} h_{n} = \lim_{n \to \infty} f_{n}$.

23. Let Σ^{*} be the set of strings over a finite alphabet Σ, including the null string λ. Let the constant functions

$$h: \Sigma^{*} \to \Sigma, \quad t: \Sigma^{*} \to \Sigma^{*}, \quad \text{and} \quad c: \Sigma^{*} \times \Sigma^{*} \to \Sigma^{*},$$

be given by

$h(x)$ = the first letter of the non-null string x,
$t(x)$ = the string which remains when the first letter of the non-null string x is removed,

$c(a, x)$ = the concatenation of the symbol a with the string x.

By structural induction on Σ^{*}, prove that $r(x)$ is defined for all $x \in \Sigma^{*}$, where

$$r(x) = f(x, \lambda)$$
$$f(x, y) = (x = \lambda \to y, f(t(x), c(h(x), y))).$$

Chapter 8

Applications of the Fixea
Point Theory

This chapter contains a number of examples of the use of fixed point induction in proofs about programs and recursively defined functions. In particular, Section 2 contains the proofs of the three theorems stated in Chapter 6 concerning the relationship between the *eaf* and *eal* rules of evaluation. Section 3 contains the proof of Theorem 7.3, relating the fixed point interpretation of recursive definitions to the interpretation by evaluation rules. Section 6 is devoted to a second proof of the partial correctness of *in situ* permutation, which was discussed in Chapter 5.

Each proof involves, to a greater or lesser extent, algebraic manipulation of functions, conditional expressions, and the partial ordering $\subseteq$. Section 1 describes some general rules governing such manipulations.

8.1 Preliminaries

We shall now describe some simple results concerning the manipulation and simplification of functional expressions. These results will be used without explicit mention in subsequent sections; indeed, some have already been used in the previous chapter.

(1) *if $f \subseteq f'$ and $g \subseteq g'$, then $(p \to f, g) \subseteq (p \to f', g')$ for any p.*

(2) $(p \to f, f) \subseteq f$.

(3) *if $f \subseteq f'$, then $f \cdot g \subseteq f' \cdot g$ for any g.*

(4) *if f is monotonic and $g \subseteq g'$, then $f \cdot g \subseteq f \cdot g'$.*

(5) $(p \to f, g) \cdot h = (p \cdot h \to f \cdot h, g \cdot h)$

(6) $(p \to f \cdot g, f \cdot h) \subseteq f \cdot (p \to g, h)$; *in addition, if $f\omega = \omega$ then $f \cdot (p \to g, h)$* $= (p \to f \cdot g, f \cdot h)$

(7) $(p \to (p \to a, b), c) = (p \to a, c)$

(8) $(p \to a, (p \to b, c)) = (p \to a, c)$

(9) $(p \to (q \to a, b), (q \to c, d)) = (q \to (p \to a, c), (p \to b, d))$

(10) *if $p \supset q$, then $(p \to (q \to a, b), c) = (p \to a, c)$*

(11) *if $f = (p \to g, h)$, then $f = (p \to g, f)$*

183

Most of these results are self-evident. To prove (11), observe that

$$(p \to g, f) = (p \to g, (p \to g, h)) = (p \to g, h) = f,$$

using (8). As a simple application of (11), we can prove

(12) *if* $f\omega = \omega$ *and* $f = (p \to f \cdot g, h)$, *then* $f = f \cdot (p \to g, 1)$, *where* 1 *denotes the identity function.*

Since $f = (p \to f \cdot g, h)$, we have $f = (p \to f \cdot g, f)$ by (11). Thus, from (6) we have $f = f \cdot (p \to g, 1)$.

8.2   Relationship between *eaf* and *eal*

In this section we use fixed point induction to prove Theorems 6.1, 6.2, and 6.3, the statements of which can be found in Section 6.4. Recall that, for a simple recursive definition of the form $f(x)$ *is* E, where E is an expression referring to at most one 1-place constant function g, the *eaf* and *eal* rules of evaluation can be defined recursively as follows:

$$eaf(e) \text{ is } (cond(e) \to (eaf \cdot test(e) \to eaf \cdot left(e), eal \cdot right(e)),$$

$$gapp(e) \to gapply \cdot eaf \cdot rand(e)$$

$$fapp(e) \to eaf \cdot fsub \cdot eaf \cdot rand(e),$$

$$e)$$

and

$$eal(e) \text{ is } (cond(e) \to (eal \cdot test(e) \to eal \cdot left(e), eal \cdot right(e)),$$

$$gapp(e) \to gapply \cdot eal \cdot rand(e),$$

$$fapp(e) \to eal \cdot fsub \cdot rand(e),$$

$$e).$$

In these definitions, e is an arbitrary free expression, i.e. an expression in which only constants and the variable f may appear. The functions f_F and f_L, associated with the definition $f(x)$ *is* E under the *eaf* and *eal* rules of evaluation respectively, are given by

$$f_F = decode \cdot eaf \cdot fsub \cdot code$$

and $$f_L = decode \cdot eal \cdot fsub \cdot code,$$

where *decode* and *code* are functions for passing to and from abstract values to their identifying constant expressions. Theorem 6.1 says that $f_F(x) = f_L(x)$ whenever $f_F(x)$ is defined.

   The first important step in the construction of a proof of Theorem 6.1 is to realize that the definitions of *eaf* and *eal*, although given recursively, stand outside the formal framework of recursive definitions and evaluation rules. Any attempt to attach formal meaning to the definitions, through the use of one or other of the evaluation rules, leads immediately into a semantic paradox, since the definitions are themselves supposed to define the very evaluation rule with which they are trying to be understood. This apparent dilemma can be used to our advantage however; one further interpretation of the definitions, not based on evaluation rules, is available to us, namely in terms of least fixed points. In the fixed point approach, the definitions take the form

$$eaf(e) = F(eaf)(e)$$

and
$$eal(e) = L(eal)(e),$$

where F and L are the obvious normal functionals; for example,

$$L = \lambda f . (cond \rightarrow (f \cdot test \rightarrow f \cdot left, f \cdot right),$$
$$gapp \rightarrow gapply \cdot f \cdot rand,$$
$$fapp \rightarrow f \cdot fsub \cdot rand,$$
$$iden),$$

where *iden* is the identity function on the domain D of free expressions augmented with an undefined element ω, and *cond*, *test*, etc. are monotonically extended functions over D. Note, especially, that *gapply* must be naturally extended, i.e. $gapply(\omega) = \omega$, in order to conform to the requirements of the evaluation process.

The functions f_F and f_L are now given by

$$f_F = decode \cdot \phi F \cdot fsub \cdot code$$

and
$$f_L = decode \cdot \phi L \cdot fsub \cdot code$$

Hence a formal statement of Theorem 6.1 is just that

$$\phi F \subseteq \phi L.$$

This result is an easy consequence of the following lemma.

Lemma 1 $\phi L \cdot fsub \cdot \phi L \subseteq \phi L \cdot fsub.$

Proof of Theorem 6.1

Using Lemma 1, we have

$$F(\phi L) \subseteq L(\phi L) = \phi L,$$

whence $\phi F \subseteq \phi L$ by Lemma 7.9.

Lemma 1 is proved as a particular case of a more general result. To state this generalization, we need the idea of a substitution function.

Suppose E is any expression in which the variable x appears. We write $E[x/e]$ to denote the expression which results when the expression e is substituted for x throughout E. We say that θ is a *substitution function* if

$$\theta = \lambda e . E[x/e]$$

for some expression E. We shall sometimes write $\theta = \theta_E$ to emphasize the dependence of θ on E. Notice that for the definition $f(x)$ *is* E, *fsub* is just the function θ_E. If the only variable appearing in E, apart from f, is x, then θ is a function from free expressions to free expressions. Other necessary facts about substitution functions are given in the following lemma.

Lemma 2   (i) *iden* and *fsub* are substitution functions.

(ii) if θ_E is a substitution function and $cond(E) = true$, then $test \cdot \theta_E$, $left \cdot \theta_E$, and $right \cdot \theta_E$ are substitution functions.

(iii) if θ_E is a substitution function and $gapp(E) = true$, or $fapp(E) = true$, then $rand \cdot \theta_E$ is a substitution function.

(iv) if θ and θ' are substitution functions, then so is $\theta \cdot \theta'$.

Proof   (i), (ii), and (iii) are straightforward. To prove (iv), suppose

$$\theta = \lambda e . E[x/e] \quad \text{and} \quad \theta' = \lambda e . E'[x/e].$$

Then $\theta \cdot \theta' = \lambda e . E[x/E'[x/e]] = \lambda e . E[x/E'][x/e]$.

Proof of Lemma 1

We prove the more general result that

$$\phi L \cdot \theta \cdot \phi L \subseteq \phi L \cdot \theta$$

for any substitution function θ; Lemma 1 then follows by taking $\theta = fsub$. The proof is by fixed point induction with the admissible hypothesis

$$\Pi[\alpha]: \alpha \cdot \theta \cdot \phi L \subseteq \phi L \cdot \theta,$$

where α is a function from free expressions to free expressions.

(a) $\Pi[\Omega]$; obvious.

(b) Assuming $\alpha \cdot \theta \cdot \phi L \subseteq \phi L \cdot \theta$, we have to show that

$$L(\alpha) \cdot \theta \cdot \phi L \subseteq \phi L \cdot \theta.$$

Now,

$$
\begin{aligned}
L(\alpha) \cdot \theta \cdot \phi L(e) = (cond \cdot \theta \cdot \phi L &\to (\alpha \cdot test \cdot \theta \cdot \phi L \to \alpha \cdot left \cdot \theta \cdot \phi L, \\
&\qquad\qquad \alpha \cdot right \cdot \theta \cdot \phi L), \\
gapp \cdot \theta \cdot \phi L &\to gapply \cdot \alpha \cdot rand \cdot \theta \cdot \phi L, \\
fapp \cdot \theta \cdot \phi L &\to \alpha \cdot fsub \cdot rand \cdot \theta \cdot \phi L, \\
\theta \cdot \phi L)(e).&
\end{aligned}
$$

To simplify this equation, we make repeated use of the fact that, if $p \supset q$, then

$$(p \to a, c) = (p \to (q \to a, b), c)$$

for any choice of b.

(1) Take $p = cond \cdot \theta \cdot \phi L(e)$,

$\qquad q = cond \cdot \theta(e)$,

$\qquad b = \phi L \cdot \theta(e)$.

$$a = (\alpha \cdot test \cdot \theta \cdot \phi L \rightarrow \alpha \cdot left \cdot \theta \cdot \phi L, \ \alpha \cdot right \cdot \theta \cdot \phi L)(e)$$
$$\subseteq (\phi L \cdot test \cdot \theta \rightarrow \phi L \cdot left \cdot \theta, \ \phi L \cdot right \cdot \theta)(e),$$

using the induction hypothesis and Lemma 2.

We have $(q \rightarrow a, b) \subseteq \phi L \cdot \theta(e)$, and also $p \supset q$, since θ is a substitution function and $\phi L(e)$ is a constant expression whenever it is defined.

(2) Similarly, we can take

$$p = gapp \cdot \theta \cdot \phi L(e)$$
$$q = gapp \cdot \theta(e)$$
$$b = \phi L \cdot \theta(e)$$
$$a = gapply \cdot \alpha \cdot rand \cdot \theta \cdot \phi L(e)$$
$$\subseteq gapply \cdot \phi L \cdot rand \cdot \theta(e)$$

using the induction hypothesis, Lemma 2, and the fact that *gapply* is monotonically extended in the definition of L. We again have $p \supset q$ and $(q \rightarrow a, b) \subseteq \phi L \cdot \theta(e)$.

(3) Similarly, we can take

$$p = fapp \cdot \theta \cdot \phi L(e)$$
$$q = fapp \cdot \theta(e)$$
$$a = \alpha \cdot fsub \cdot rand \cdot \theta \cdot \phi L(e)$$
$$\subseteq \phi L \cdot fsub \cdot rand \cdot \theta(e),$$

and $$b = \phi L \cdot \theta(e)$$

It follows that

$$L(\alpha) \cdot \theta \cdot \phi L(e) \subseteq (cond \cdot \theta \cdot \phi L \rightarrow \phi L \cdot \theta,$$
$$gapp \cdot \theta \cdot \phi L \rightarrow \phi L \cdot \theta,$$
$$fapp \cdot \theta \cdot \phi L \rightarrow \phi L \cdot \theta,$$
$$\theta \cdot \phi L)(e).$$

Now, if $cond \cdot \theta \cdot \phi L(e)$, $gapp \cdot \theta \cdot \phi L(e)$, and $fapp \cdot \theta \cdot \phi L(e)$ are all *false*, then either $\theta(e) = e$, or $\theta(e) = c$ for some constant c. In the first case, we have

$$\theta \cdot \phi L(e) = \phi L(e) = \phi L \cdot \theta(e),$$

and, in the second case,

$$\theta \cdot \phi L(e) \subseteq c = \phi L(c) = \phi L \cdot \theta(e).$$

Thus

$$L(\alpha) \cdot \theta \cdot \phi L(e) \subseteq \phi L \cdot \theta(e)$$

and the induction is established. This completes the proof of Lemma 1, and also the proof of Theorem 6.1.

In order to prove Theorems 6.2 and 6.3, we shall need the following lemma, which is similar to Lemma 1.

Lemma 3.   Suppose θ is a given substitution function. Then

$$\phi F(e) \neq \omega \supset \phi F \cdot \theta(e) \subseteq \phi F \cdot \theta \cdot \phi F(e),$$

for all free expressions e, where ω is the undefined element of the domain of free expressions.

Proof.   The proof is by fixed point induction, using the admissible hypothesis

$$\Pi[\alpha]: (\forall e \, . \, \phi F(e) \neq \omega \supset \alpha \cdot \theta(e) \subseteq \phi F \cdot \theta \cdot \phi F(e)) \wedge (\alpha \subseteq \phi F).$$

(a) $\Pi[\Omega]$; obvious.

(b) Assume $\Pi[\alpha]$. To prove $\Pi[F(\alpha)]$, we have firstly that

$$F(\alpha) \subseteq F(\phi F) = \phi F,$$

by the monotonicity of F and the assumption $\alpha \subseteq \phi F$.
Next, suppose $\phi F(e) \neq \omega$; then

$$
\begin{aligned}
F(\alpha) \cdot \theta(e) = (cond \cdot \theta &\rightarrow (\alpha \cdot test \cdot \theta \rightarrow \alpha \cdot left \cdot \theta, \alpha \cdot right \cdot \theta), \\
gapp \cdot \theta &\rightarrow gapply \cdot \alpha \cdot rand \cdot \theta, \\
fapp \cdot \theta &\rightarrow \alpha \cdot fsub \cdot \alpha \cdot rand \cdot \theta, \\
\theta&)(e).
\end{aligned}
$$

Since $\phi F(e) \neq \omega$, each of the propositions $cond \cdot \theta \cdot \phi F(e)$, $gapp \cdot \theta \cdot \phi F(e)$, and $fapp \cdot \theta \cdot \phi F(e)$ take defined values; moreover

$$cond \cdot \theta \cdot \phi F(e) \supset cond \cdot \theta(e),$$
$$gapp \cdot \theta \cdot \phi F(e) \supset gapp \cdot \theta(e),$$
and $\qquad\qquad fapp \cdot \theta \cdot \phi F(e) \supset fapp \cdot \theta(e),$

since θ is a substitution function. Using these facts together with the induction hypothesis, we have

$$
\begin{aligned}
F(\alpha) \cdot \theta(e) \subseteq (cond \cdot \theta \cdot \phi F &\rightarrow (\phi F \cdot test \cdot \theta \cdot \phi F \rightarrow \phi F \cdot left \cdot \theta \cdot \phi F, \phi F \cdot right \cdot \theta \cdot \phi F), \\
gapp \cdot \theta \cdot \phi F &\rightarrow gapply \cdot \phi F \cdot rand \cdot \theta \cdot \phi F, \\
fapp \cdot \theta \cdot \phi F &\rightarrow \phi F \cdot fsub \cdot \phi F \cdot rand \cdot \theta \cdot \phi F, \\
F(\alpha) \cdot \theta&)(e).
\end{aligned}
$$

Now,

$$F(\alpha) \cdot \theta(e) \subseteq F(\phi F) \cdot \theta(e) = \phi F \cdot \theta(e),$$

by the second clause of the induction hypothesis. Furthermore, if $cond \cdot \theta \cdot \phi F(e)$,

$gapp \cdot \theta \cdot \phi F(e)$, and $fapp \cdot \theta \cdot \phi F(e)$ are all *false*, then either:

(i) $\theta(e) = e$, in which case

$$\phi F \cdot \theta(e) = \theta \cdot \phi F(e),$$

or (ii) $\theta(e) = c$ for some constant c, in which case

$$\phi F \cdot \theta(e) = c = \theta \cdot \phi F(e)$$

since $\phi F(e) \neq \omega$ by supposition.

Putting all this together, we have

$$F(\alpha) \cdot \theta(e) \subseteq F(\phi F) \cdot \theta \cdot \phi F(e) = \phi F \cdot \theta \cdot \phi F(e),$$

and the induction is complete.

Now let us turn to the statement and proof of Theorem 6.2. Suppose

$$f(x) \text{ is } E$$

and $$f(x) \text{ is } (p(x) \to E, E)$$

are two recursive definitions, where p is some (total) constant predicate. Roughly speaking, Theorem 6.2 says that using *eaf* on the first definition gives the same result as using *eal* on the second. To formulate the theorem more precisely, let $\theta = \theta_E$ and $\theta' = \theta_{E'}$, where $E' = (p(x) \to E, E)$. Then Theorem 6.2 states that

$$\phi F \cdot \theta(c) = \phi L' \cdot \theta'(c),$$

for all constants c, where L' is identical to L except that θ' replaces θ as the definition of *fsub*.

Proof of Theorem 6.2

Since $\theta'(c)$ is a conditional expression, we have

$$\phi L' \cdot \theta'(c) = (papply \cdot \phi L' \to \phi L' \cdot \theta, \phi L' \cdot \theta)(c),$$

where *papply* is the function which applies the constant predicate p. It follows that

$$\phi L' \cdot \theta'(c) = \phi L' \cdot \theta(c),$$

since $\phi L'(c) \neq \omega$ for any constant c. Therefore, in order to prove the theorem, it is sufficient to show that $\phi F = \phi L'$. This is done in two steps:

(1) $\phi F \subseteq \phi L'$. Since

$$\phi L' \cdot \theta' \cdot \phi L' = \phi L' \cdot \theta \cdot \phi L',$$

and

$$\phi L' \cdot \theta' \cdot \phi L' \subseteq \phi L' \cdot \theta'$$

by Lemma 1, we have

$$F(\phi L') \subseteq L'(\phi L') = \phi L'.$$

Thus $\phi F \subseteq \phi L'$ by Lemma 7.9.

(2) $\phi L' \subseteq \phi F$. Since

$$\phi F \cdot \theta'(e) = (papply \cdot \phi F \to \phi F \cdot \theta, \ \phi F \cdot \theta)(e),$$

and

$$\phi F(e) \neq \omega \supset \phi F \cdot \theta(e) \subseteq \phi F \cdot \theta \cdot \phi F(e)$$

by Lemma 3, it follows that

$$\phi F \cdot \theta' \subseteq \phi F \cdot \theta \cdot \phi F.$$

Thus

$$L'(\phi F) \subseteq F(\phi F) = \phi F,$$

whence $\phi L' \subseteq \phi F$ using Lemma 7.9.

This completes the proof of Theorem 6.2

Finally, let us deal with Theorem 6.3. Suppose

$$f(x) \ is \ (p(x) \to E_1, E_2)$$

is a given recursive definition. Theorem 6.3 says that, for this definition, both the *eaf* and *eal* rules of evaluation lead to the same function. In other words,

$$\phi F = \phi L,$$

provided that the function *fsub*, which appears in F and L, has the definition

$$\theta = \lambda e \,.\, (p(x) \to E_1, E_2)[x/e].$$

Proof of Theorem 6.3

Since $\theta(e)$ is a conditional expression for any expression e, we have

$$\phi F \cdot \theta(e) = (papply \cdot \phi F \to \phi F \cdot \theta_{E_1}, \phi F \cdot \theta_{E_2})(e).$$

This equation shows that $\phi F \cdot \theta(e) = \omega$ if $\phi F(e) = \omega$. On the other hand, if $\phi F(e) \neq \omega$, then

$$\phi F \cdot \theta(e) \subseteq \phi F \cdot \theta \cdot \phi F(e)$$

by Lemma 3. Thus

$$\phi F \cdot \theta \subseteq \phi F \cdot \theta \cdot \phi F.$$

It follows that $L(\phi F) \subseteq F(\phi F) = \phi F$, whence $\phi L \subseteq \phi F$ by Lemma 7.9. But we already know that $\phi F \subseteq \phi L$ from Theorem 6.1. Thus $\phi F = \phi L$ and the proof is complete.

8.3   Relationship between *eal* and least fixed point

We turn now to a proof of Theorem 7.3 stated in Section 7.5. Informally, this theorem says that the function described by the recursive definition $f(x) \ is \ E$, using the *eal* rule of evaluation, is exactly the least fixed point of the normal functional $\lambda f . \lambda x . E$. We can give a more precise statement of the theorem using the notation of the last section. Let

$$\theta = \lambda e . E[x/e]$$

be the substitution function associated with the expression E,

$$L(\theta) = \lambda f . (cond \to (f \cdot test \to f \cdot left, f \cdot right),$$
$$gapp \to gapply \cdot f \cdot rand,$$
$$fapp \to f \cdot \theta \cdot rand,$$
$$iden)$$

be the functional associated with the *eal* rule of evaluation (taking θ as the definition of *fsub*), and

$$F(\theta) = \lambda f . \lambda x . \theta(x) \equiv \lambda f . \lambda x . E$$

be the normal functional associated with the expression E. Theorem 7.3 then asserts that

$$decode \cdot \phi(L(\theta)) \cdot \theta \cdot code = \phi(F(\theta)),$$

where *decode* is a function from constant expressions to the associated abstract values, and *code* is a function from abstract values to the identifying constant expressions. Since it is possible to interpret $\phi(F(\theta))$ directly as a function from constant expressions to constant expressions, we can avoid the necessity for the functions *code* and *decode*, and omit them altogether from the discussion.

The proof of Theorem 7.3 depends upon two lemmas, the first of which uses, not fixed point induction, but structural induction on the complexity of expressions in its proof. To see what is involved in this particular induction technique, suppose $\Pi[e]$ is some assertion concerning the expression e. To prove that $\Pi[e]$ holds for all expressions e, it is sufficient to carry out the following steps:

(a) prove that $\Pi[e]$ holds for all variable or constant expressions e:
(b) prove that $\Pi[e]$ follows from $\Pi[test(e)]$, $\Pi[left(e)]$, and $\Pi[right(e)]$ in the case $cond(e) = true$; or prove that $\Pi[e]$ follows from $\Pi[rand(e)]$ in the case

$$gapp(e) = true \text{ or } fapp(e) = true.$$

Since every expression is built up from variable or constant expressions by forming conditionals, or using function application, steps (a) and (b) clearly suffice to establish the truth of $\Pi[e]$ for any expression e.

Lemma 4. Suppose $\psi = \psi_{E'}$ is a substitution function, where E' is any expression except the identifier f standing by itself. Then

$$F(\psi)(\phi L \cdot \theta)(x) \subseteq \phi L \cdot \psi(x)$$

for all constants x, where $L = L(\theta)$.

Proof. The proof is by structural induction on the complexity of the expression E', or, in other words, on the complexity of the function ψ. Let $\phi L \cdot \theta$ be denoted by α for short.

(a) Suppose first that $\psi = \lambda e . e$ corresponding to the case that E' is a variable identifier. In this case

$$F(\psi)(\alpha)(x) = x = \phi L \cdot \psi(x)$$

for all constants x. On the other hand, if $\psi = \lambda e . c$, where c is constant, then

$$F(\psi)(\alpha)(x) = c = \phi L \cdot \psi(x)$$

for all x.

(b) Suppose first that E' is a conditional expression, i.e. $cond \cdot \psi(x) = true$ for each constant x. In this case, we have

$$
\begin{aligned}
F(\psi)(\alpha)(x) &= (F(test \cdot \psi) \to F(left \cdot \psi), F(right \cdot \psi))(\alpha)(x) \\
&\subseteq (\phi L \cdot test \cdot \psi \to \phi L \cdot left \cdot \psi, \phi L \cdot right \cdot \psi)(x) \\
&= \phi L \cdot \psi(x),
\end{aligned}
$$

using the induction hypothesis. Next, if $gapp \cdot \psi(x) = true$, then

$$
\begin{aligned}
F(\psi)(\alpha)(x) &= gapply(F(rand \cdot \psi)(\alpha)(x)) \\
&\subseteq gapply \cdot \phi L \cdot rand \cdot \psi(x) \\
&= \phi L \cdot \psi(x),
\end{aligned}
$$

using the induction hypothesis and the fact that $gapply$ is just the monotonic constant function g in the normal functional F.
Finally, if $fapp \cdot \psi(x) = true$, then

$$
\begin{aligned}
F(\psi)(\alpha)(x) &= \alpha(F(rand \cdot \psi)(\alpha)(x)) \\
&\subseteq \phi L \cdot \theta \cdot \phi L \cdot rand \cdot \psi(x),
\end{aligned}
$$

using the induction hypothesis and the fact that $\alpha = \phi L \cdot \theta$. Now Lemma 1 of the last section asserts that $\phi L \cdot \theta \cdot \phi L \subseteq \phi L \cdot \theta$, so we have

$$F(\psi)(\alpha)(x) \subseteq \phi L \cdot \theta \cdot rand \cdot \psi(x) = \phi L \cdot \psi(x).$$

This completes the induction and the proof of the lemma.

Lemma 5. Let ψ be an arbitrary substitution function. Then

$$\phi L \cdot \psi(x) \subseteq F(\psi)(\phi F)(x)$$

for all constants x, where ϕL and ϕF are short for $\phi(L(\theta))$ and $\phi(F(\theta))$ respectively.

Proof. The proof is by fixed point induction with the admissible induction hypothesis

$$\Pi[\alpha]: \forall x . \alpha \cdot \psi(x) \subseteq F(\psi)(\phi F)(x).$$

(a) $\Pi[\Omega]$; obvious.

(b) $\Pi[\alpha]$ implies $\Pi[L(\theta)(\alpha)]$; we have

$$L(\theta)(\alpha) \cdot \psi(x) = (cond \cdot \psi \to (\alpha \cdot test \cdot \psi \to \alpha \cdot left \cdot \psi, \; \alpha \cdot right \cdot \psi),$$
$$gapp \cdot \psi \to gapply \cdot \alpha \cdot rand \cdot \psi,$$
$$fapp \cdot \psi \to \alpha \cdot \theta \cdot rand \cdot \psi,$$
$$\psi)(x),$$
$$\subseteq (cond \cdot \psi \to (F(test \cdot \psi) \to F(left \cdot \psi), \; F(right \cdot \psi))(\phi F),$$
$$gapp \cdot \psi \to gapply \cdot F(rand \cdot \psi)(\phi F),$$
$$fapp \cdot \psi \to F(\theta \cdot rand \cdot \psi)(\phi F),$$
$$\psi)(x),$$

using the induction hypothesis and the monotonicity of *gapply*. Since

$$F(\theta \cdot \psi)(f) = F(\theta)(f) \cdot F(\psi)(f)$$

for all θ, ψ, and f, we have

$$F(\theta \cdot rand \cdot \psi)(\phi F) = F(\theta)(\phi F) \cdot F(rand \cdot \psi)(\phi F)$$
$$= \phi F \cdot F(rand \cdot \psi)(\phi F).$$

Now

$$F(\psi)(\phi F)(x) = (cond \cdot \psi \to (F(test \cdot \psi) \to F(left \cdot \psi) \; F(right \cdot \psi))(\phi F),$$
$$gapp \cdot \psi \to gapply \cdot F(rand \cdot \psi)(\phi F),$$
$$fapp \cdot \psi \to \phi F \cdot F(rand \cdot \psi)(\phi F),$$
$$\psi)(x),$$

so that

$$L(\theta)(\alpha) \cdot \psi(x) \subseteq F(\psi)(\phi F)(x)$$

for all x. This establishes the induction and completes the proof of the lemma.

Proof of Theorem 7.3

Note first that $f(x)$ *is* f is not a well formed recursive definition; this means we can take $\psi = \theta$ in Lemma 4, in which case

$$F(\theta)(\phi L \cdot \theta) \subseteq \phi L \cdot \theta,$$

regarding each side as a function from constant expressions to constant expressions. It follows from Lemma 7.9 that

$$\phi F \subseteq \phi L \cdot \theta.$$

Similarly, taking $\psi = \theta$ in Lemma 5, we have

$$\phi L \cdot \theta \subseteq F(\theta)(\phi F) = \phi F,$$

whence $\phi L \cdot \theta = \phi F$.

8.4   Two equivalence proofs

In this section we give two examples of the use of fixed point induction in the proof of program equivalence. Both examples illustrate the need for carefully chosen induction hypotheses.

Example 1

Let W be the **while** program

$$y: = x;$$
$$\textbf{while } p(x) \textbf{ do } x: = a(x);$$
$$\textbf{while } p(y) \textbf{ do}$$
$$(y: = a(y); \; x: = b(x)),$$

and R be the procedure

$$R \textbf{ is (if } p(x) \textbf{ then } x: = a(x); R; \; x: = b(x) \textbf{ else } y: = x).$$

We wish to prove that W is equivalent to R under all interpretations of the functions a, b, and p; i.e. equivalent on all register machines.

The first job is to obtain recursive definitions for the functions computed by W and R. To do this we need the following functions and predicates, which describe the effect of the basic assignment and tests on a given value of the memory set:

$$A = \lambda xy \,.\, (ax, y) \qquad I = \lambda xy \,.\, (x, y)$$
$$B = \lambda xy \,.\, (bx, y) \qquad P = \lambda xy \,.\, p(x)$$
$$C = \lambda xy \,.\, (x, ay) \qquad Q = \lambda xy \,.\, p(y).$$
$$D = \lambda xy \,.\, (x, x)$$

Program W then computes the function

$$\phi F \cdot \phi G \cdot D,$$

where

$$F = \lambda f \,.\, (Q \to f \cdot B \cdot C, I),$$

and

$$G = \lambda f \,.\, (P \to f \cdot A, I),$$

and procedure R computes the function ϕH, where

$$H = \lambda f \,.\, (P \to B \cdot f \cdot A, D).$$

Thus, we have to show that

$$\phi F \cdot \phi G \cdot D = \phi H.$$

Note that F, G, and H are normal functionals, which means that we assume the natural extensions of the constant functions $A, B, \ldots$, etc., over the augmented domain. Thus

$$A(\omega, \omega) = \omega, B(\omega, \omega) = \omega, \quad \text{etc.,}$$

where ω is the undefined element.

To simplify the notation as much as possible, we shall henceforth omit the composition symbol between functions. The proof is by fixed point induction, using the admissible induction hypothesis

$$\Pi[\alpha, \beta, \gamma] : (\alpha\beta D = \gamma)$$
$$\wedge\ (\alpha\beta = B\alpha)$$
$$\wedge\ (\beta C = C\beta)$$
$$\wedge\ (\forall\ X, Y.(Q \to X, Y)\beta = (Q \to X\beta, Y\beta)).$$

The first clause in Π gives the result we are after; the other clauses are necessary to enable the induction step for the first clause to be established. We shall need the following relationships between the various constant functions:

(a) $PC = P$ (d) $QB = Q$ (g) $BC = CB$
(b) $PD = P$ (e) $QA = Q$ (h) $DA = CAD$
(c) $QD = P$ (f) $AC = CA$

(1) $\Pi[\Omega, \Omega, \Omega]$; straightforward, using the fact that $X\Omega = \Omega$ for all naturally extended X.

(2) $\Pi[\alpha, \beta, \gamma]$ implies $\Pi[F(\alpha), G(\beta), H(\gamma)]$.
  (i) $F(\alpha)G(\beta)D = F(\alpha)(P \to \beta A, I)D$
$$= F(\alpha)(P \to \beta AD, D) \quad \text{by (b),}$$
$$= (P \to F(\alpha)\beta AD, F(\alpha)D).$$

Now

$$F(\alpha)\beta AD = (Q \to \alpha BC, I)\beta AD$$
$$= (Q \to \alpha BC\beta, \beta)AD \quad \text{by hypothesis,}$$
$$= (P \to \alpha BC\beta AD, \beta AD) \quad \text{by (e) and (c);}$$

and

$$F(\alpha)D = (Q \to \alpha BC, I)D$$
$$= (P \to \alpha BCD, D) \quad \text{by (c).}$$

Thus

$$F(\alpha)G(\beta)D = (P \to \alpha BC\beta AD, D)$$
$$= (P \to B\alpha\beta CAD, D) \quad \text{by hypothesis,}$$
$$= (P \to B\alpha\beta DA, D) \qquad \text{by (h),}$$
$$= (P \to B\gamma A, D) \qquad \text{by hypothesis,}$$
$$= H(\gamma).$$

  (ii) $F(\alpha)B = (Q \to \alpha BC, I)B$
$$= (Q \to \alpha BCB, B) \quad \text{by (d),}$$

$$= (Q \to \alpha BBC, B) \quad \text{by (g),}$$
$$= (Q \to B\alpha BC, B) \quad \text{by hypothesis,}$$
$$= B(Q \to \alpha BC, I)$$
$$= BF(\alpha).$$

(iii) $G(\beta)C = (P \to \beta A, I)C$
$$= (P \to \beta AC, C) \quad \text{by (a),}$$
$$= (P \to C\beta A, C) \quad \text{by (f) and hypothesis,}$$
$$= CG(\beta).$$

(iv) $(Q \to X, Y)G(\beta) = (P \to (Q \to X, Y)\beta A, (Q \to X, Y))$
$$= (P \to (Q \to X\beta A, Y\beta A), (Q \to X, Y))$$
$$\text{by (e) and hypothesis,}$$
$$= (Q \to (P \to X\beta A, X), (P \to Y\beta A, Y))$$
$$= (Q \to XG(\beta), YG(\beta)).$$

This establishes the induction and completes the proof.

Example 2

The second example is similar to the previous one. Let U be the program

$$x := a(x);$$
$$\textbf{while } p(x) \textbf{ do } x := a(x);$$
$$y := b(y);$$
$$\textbf{while } q(y) \textbf{ do } y := b(y),$$

and V be the program

$$x := a(x);$$
$$y := b(y);$$
$$\textbf{while } p(x) \textbf{ do}$$
$$(x := a(x);$$
$$\textbf{if } q(y) \textbf{ then } y := b(y));$$
$$\textbf{while } q(y) \textbf{ do } y := b(y).$$

We wish to show that U is equivalent to V on all register machines. The basic functions here are

$$A = \lambda xy . (ax, y) \qquad P = \lambda xy . p(x)$$
$$B = \lambda xy . (x, by) \qquad Q = \lambda xy . q(y).$$
$$I = \lambda xy . (x, y)$$

U computes the function

$$\phi F \cdot B \cdot \phi G \cdot A,$$

where
$$F = \lambda f.(Q \rightarrow fB, I)$$
and
$$G = \lambda f.(P \rightarrow fA, I),$$
and V computes the function
$$\phi F \cdot \phi H \cdot B \cdot A,$$
where
$$H = \lambda f.(P \rightarrow f(Q \rightarrow B, I)A, I).$$

The proof that $\phi F \cdot B \cdot \phi G \cdot A = \phi F \cdot \phi H \cdot B \cdot A$ uses fixed point induction with the hypothesis

$$\Pi[\alpha, \beta] : (\phi F \cdot \alpha = \phi F \cdot \beta)$$
$$\wedge (B\alpha = \alpha B)$$
$$\wedge (\forall X, Y.(Q \rightarrow X, Y)\alpha = (Q \rightarrow X\alpha, Y\alpha)).$$

We need the following relationships:

$$\text{(a)} \ \ AB = BA \quad \text{(b)} \ \ QA = Q \quad \text{(c)} \ \ PB = P$$

(1) $\Pi[\Omega, \Omega]$; straightforward using the fact that $X\Omega = \Omega$ for all naturally extended X.

(2) $\Pi[\alpha, \beta]$ implies $\Pi[G(\alpha), H(\beta)]$; there are three steps in the induction:

(i)
$$\phi F \cdot G(\alpha) = \phi F(P \rightarrow \alpha A, I)$$
$$= (P \rightarrow \phi F\alpha A, \phi F)$$

Now
$$\phi F = F(\phi F) = (Q \rightarrow \phi FB, I)$$
$$= (Q \rightarrow \phi FB, \phi F)$$
$$= \phi F(Q \rightarrow B, I).$$

Hence
$$\phi F \cdot G(\alpha) = (P \rightarrow \phi F(Q \rightarrow B, I)\alpha A, \phi F)$$
$$= (P \rightarrow \phi F(Q \rightarrow B\alpha, \alpha)A, \phi F) \quad \text{by hypothesis,}$$
$$= (P \rightarrow \phi F\alpha(Q \rightarrow B, I)A, \phi F) \quad \text{by hypothesis,}$$
$$= (P \rightarrow \phi F\beta(Q \rightarrow B, I)A, \phi F)$$
$$= \phi F \cdot H(\beta).$$

(ii)
$$B \cdot G(\alpha) = B(P \rightarrow \alpha A, I)$$
$$= (P \rightarrow B\alpha A, I)$$
$$= (P \rightarrow \alpha AB, B) \quad \text{by hypothesis and (a),}$$
$$= (P \rightarrow \alpha A, I)B \quad \text{by (c),}$$
$$= G(\alpha)B$$

(iii)
$$(Q \rightarrow X, Y)G(\alpha) = (P \rightarrow (Q \rightarrow X, Y)\alpha A, (Q \rightarrow X, Y))$$
$$= (P \rightarrow (Q \rightarrow X\alpha A, Y\alpha A), (Q \rightarrow X, Y))$$
$$\text{by hypothesis and (b)}$$
$$= (Q \rightarrow XG(\alpha), YG(\alpha)).$$

This completes the induction, and therefore show that

$$\phi F \cdot \phi G = \phi F \cdot \phi H \quad \text{and} \quad B \cdot \phi G = \phi G \cdot B.$$

From this it follows that

$$\phi F \cdot B \cdot \phi G \cdot A = \phi F \cdot \phi G \cdot B \cdot A = \phi F \cdot \phi H \cdot B \cdot A,$$

which is the desired result.

8.5   Partial correctness of binary search

In Example 3 of Section 6.5 we considered the problem of translating a program, which carried out a binary search on an array A, into a set of recursive definitions. We now take up this example again and prove its partial correctness. The program B (for Binary search) was the following:

$$i: = \lceil n/2 \rceil; \quad n: = \lfloor n/2 \rfloor;$$

F: **if** $x < A(i)$ **then goto** G **else**

     if $x > A(i)$ **then goto** H **else**

     goto $true$;

G: **if** $n = 0$ **then goto false else**

     $(i: = i - \lceil n/2 \rceil;$

     $n: = \lfloor n/2 \rfloor;$ **goto** F);

H: **if** $n = 0$ **then goto** $false$ **else**

     $(i: = i + \lceil n/2 \rceil;$

     $n: = \lfloor n/2 \rfloor;$ **goto** F).

The partial correctness of B can be expressed in the following way. Given inputs x, n, and A such that

  (i) x is a non-negative integer,

 (ii) n is a positive integer,

(iii) A is a 1-dimensional array, whose elements, $A(0), \ldots, A(n)$, are such that

$$A(0) < A(1) < \cdots < A(n) \quad \text{and} \quad A(0) < x,$$

then program B will, if it terminates, exit at label $true$ if there is a j, where $1 \leqslant j \leqslant n$, such that $A(j) = x$, and exit at label $false$ if there is no j such that $A(j) = x$. Since the inputs x and A are unchanged in any execution of B, we can regard B as computing a predicate p of the single argument n. This predicate can be defined recursively as follows:

$$p(n) = f(t(n), b(n))$$
$$f(i, n) = (x < A(i) \rightarrow g(i, n),$$
$$x > A(i) \rightarrow h(i, n),$$
$$true).$$

$$g(i, n) = (n = 0 \rightarrow false, f(i - t(n), b(n)))$$
$$h(i, n) = (n = 0 \rightarrow false, f(i + t(n), b(n))),$$

where t and b are the constant functions $\lambda x . \lceil x/2 \rceil$ and $\lambda x . \lfloor x/2 \rfloor$ respectively. Interpreting these definitions in the fixed point theory, we have

$$p(n) = \phi F(t(n), b(n)),$$

where F is the normal functional

$$\lambda f . \lambda i, n . (x < A(i) \rightarrow (n = 0 \rightarrow false, f(i - t(n), b(n))),$$
$$x > A(i) \rightarrow (n = 0 \rightarrow false, f(i + t(n), b(n))),$$
$$true).$$

The partial correctness of B can be expressed as

$$p(n) \subseteq \exists j . (A(j) = x \wedge 1 \leqslant j \leqslant n),$$

under the stated assumptions about the inputs. We shall use fixed point induction to prove the more general assertion

$$\phi F(i, n) \subseteq \exists j (A(j) = x \wedge i - n \leqslant j \leqslant i + n).$$

Since $t(n) + b(n) = n$, and

$$t(n) - b(n) = 0 \quad \text{if } n \text{ is even}$$
$$= 1 \quad \text{if } n \text{ is odd},$$

we have

$$p(n) = \phi F(t(n), b(n))$$
$$\subseteq \exists j . (A(j) = x \wedge 0 \leqslant j \leqslant n)$$
$$\subseteq \exists j . (A(j) = x \wedge 1 \leqslant j \leqslant n)$$

since $A(0) \neq x$. Thus the partial correctness of B follows as a special case of the more general assertion.

The admissible induction hypothesis is

$$\Pi[\alpha]: \forall i, n . \alpha(i, n) \subseteq \exists j . (A(j) = x \wedge i - n \leqslant j \leqslant i + n).$$

Since $\Pi[\Omega]$ is obvious, we need only show that $\Pi[\alpha]$ implies $\Pi[F(\alpha)]$. The argument is by cases:

(i) Suppose $x < A(i)$ and $n = 0$. Then

$$F(\alpha)(i, 0) = false \subseteq \exists j . (A(j) = x \wedge i \leqslant j \leqslant i)$$

(ii) Suppose $x < A(i)$ and $n \neq 0$. Then

$$F(\alpha)(i, n) = \alpha(i - tn, bn)$$
$$\subseteq \exists j . (A(j) = x \wedge i - tn - bn \leqslant j \leqslant i - tn + bn)$$
$$= \exists j . (A(j) = x \wedge i - n \leqslant j \leqslant i + n),$$

since $x \neq A(j)$ for $j \geq i$ by the ordering on A.

(iii) Suppose $x > A(i)$ and $n = 0$. Then

$$F(\alpha)(i, 0) = false \subseteq \exists j . (A(j) = x \wedge i \leq j \leq i)$$

(iv) Suppose $x > A(i)$ and $n \neq 0$. Then

$$F(\alpha)(i, n) = \alpha(i + tn, bn)$$
$$\subseteq \exists j . (A(j) = x \wedge i + tn - bn \leq j \leq i + tn + bn)$$
$$= \exists j . (A(j) = x \wedge i - n \leq j \leq i + n)$$

since $x \neq A(j)$ for $j \leq i$.

(v) Finally, if $x = A(i)$, then

$$F(\alpha)(i, n) = true = \exists j . (A(j) = x \wedge i - n \leq j \leq i + n).$$

Cases (i) to (v) establish the induction, and yield the final result.

To prove the total correctness of B, one must also show that ϕF is everywhere defined, i.e.

$$\phi F(i, n) \neq \omega \quad \text{for all } n \geq 0.$$

Informally, this is easy to see from the definition of F. Since $b(n) < n$ for all $n > 0$, each sequence of the form

$$n, b(n), b^2(n), \ldots$$

is monotone decreasing and must eventually reach 0, in fact, after at most n steps. This means that

$$F^n(\Omega)(i, n) \neq \omega$$

and since $F^n(\Omega) \subseteq \phi F$, the conclusion follows.

8.6   Partial correctness of *in situ* permutation

In Section 5.5 we used the axiomatic method to prove the partial correctness of a program P for permuting the elements of a given array. This program was considered again briefly in Section 6.5, where the following recursive definition of the function $L(X)$ computed by the program was constructed:

$$L(X) = A(1, X)$$
$$A(j, X) = (j \leq n \rightarrow A(j + 1, F(j, X)), X)$$
$$F(j, X) = (j = B(j) \rightarrow D(j, X), X)$$
$$B(j) = C(j . fj)$$
$$C(j, k) = (j < k \rightarrow C(j, fk), k)$$
$$D(j, X) = E(j, j, Xj, X)$$
$$E(j, k, y, X) = (j = fk \rightarrow G(k, y, X), E(j, fk, y, G(k, Xfk, X)))$$
$$G(k, z, X) = \lambda x . (x = k \rightarrow z, X(x)).$$

The object of this section is to give a second proof of the partial correctness of P, this time using fixed point induction. Thus our object is to prove that

$$L(X) \subseteq \lambda x \, . \, X(fx)$$

where f is a permutation on the set $S = \{1, 2, \ldots, n\}$, and x is a variable restricted to S. Rather than immediately give the complete induction hypothesis, with all its attendant clauses, we shall sketch the proof in stages, developing the necessary hypotheses as they arise.

The first step, as in the axiomatic proof, is to define the constant function c by the condition

$$c(x) = \text{the cycle leader of the cycle of } f \text{ to which } x \text{ belongs}$$

(For the definition of a cycle leader, see Section 5.5). We can then establish the partial correctness of P by proving

(1) $A(j, X) \subseteq \lambda x \, . \, (c(x) \geqslant j \rightarrow X(fx), X(x))$.

Since $c(x) \geqslant 1$ for $1 \leqslant x \leqslant n$, this result implies

$$L(X) = A(1, X) \subseteq \lambda x \, . \, X(fx),$$

which is just what is required.

In order to prove (1), let $r(j, X)$ denote the function $\lambda x \, . \, (c(x) \geqslant j \rightarrow X(fx), X(x))$. The basis for the fixed point induction on the definition of A is clear; for the induction step, we have to show

(2) $(j \leqslant n \rightarrow A(j + 1, F(j, X)), X) \subseteq r(j, X)$

under the assumption that (1) holds. (Here, as in subsequent proofs, we are deliberately stating the induction argument informally; it is left to the reader to give a precise statement of the appropriate induction hypothesis). If $j > n$, then

$$r(j, X) = X,$$

since $c(x) > n$ is known to be false. On the other hand, if $j \leqslant n$, then

$$A(j + 1, F(j, X)) \subseteq r(j + 1, F(j, X)),$$

so to complete the induction step we must show

(3) $r(j + 1, F(j, X)) \subseteq r(j, X)$.

This involves a second induction argument, based upon the definition of F. The basis of the induction is obvious, since

$$r(j + 1, \Omega) = \Omega \subseteq r(j, X),$$

where Ω is the everywhere undefined function. To complete the proof of (3) we must show

(4) if $j = B(j)$, then $r(j + 1, D(j, X)) \subseteq r(j, X)$

and

(5) if $j \neq B(j)$ then $r(j + 1, X) \subseteq r(j, X)$,

using the definition of F. Suppose we can establish the following two results:

(6) j is a cycle leader if and only if $j = B(j)$,

(7) if j is a cycle leader, then

$$D(j, X) \subseteq \lambda x \,.\, (c(x) = j \to X(fx), X(x)).$$

Using (6) and (7), we can prove (4) and (5) as follows:

Proof of (5): if $j \neq B(j)$, then j is not a cycle leader by (6), and so $c(x) \geqslant j + 1$ if and only if $c(x) \geqslant j$. Hence $r(j + 1, X) = r(j, X)$.

Proof of (4): if $j = B(j)$, then j is a cycle leader by (6). Using (7), we have

$$r(j + 1, D(j, X)) \subseteq \lambda x \,.\, (c(x) \geqslant j + 1 \to D(j, X)fx, D(j, X)x)$$
$$\subseteq \lambda x \,.\, (c(x) \geqslant j + 1 \to$$
$$(c(fx) = j \to X(ffx), X(fx)),$$
$$(c(x) = j \to X(fx), X(x))).$$

But since $c(x) = c(fx)$, the right hand side of this inequality simplifies to $r(j, X)$.

At this stage we are left with the proofs of (6) and (7). Once they have been established, the proof of partial correctness will be complete. To prove (6), suppose first that j is a cycle leader. This means that there exists a positive integer m such that $j = f^m j$ and $j < f^r j$ for $1 \leqslant r < m$. In this case we can show that

$$B(j) = C(j, fj) = C(j, f^m j) = f^m j = j.$$

Conversely, suppose j is not a cycle leader. In this case, there exists a positive integer r such that $j > f^r j$. Supposing r is the least integer with this property, we have

$$B(j) = C(j, fj) = C(j, f^r j) = f^r j \neq j.$$

This completes an informal proof of (6).

To prove (7), let us define the constant function s by the conditions

$$s(j, k) = \text{the least } s \geqslant 0 \text{ such that } f^{s+1} k = j,$$
$$= \omega, \text{ if no such } s \text{ exists.}$$

Suppose we can prove

(8) $E(j, k, y, X) \subseteq \lambda x \,.\, (\exists m \,.\, [0 \leqslant m < s(j, k) \land x = f^m k] \to X(fx),$
$$fx = j \to y, X(x)).$$

It then follows that

$$D(j, X) = E(j, j, Xj, X)$$
$$\subseteq \lambda x \,.\, (\exists m \,.\, [0 \leqslant m < s(j, j) \land x = f^m j] \to X(fx),$$
$$fx = j \to X(j), X(x)).$$

Furthermore, if j is a cycle leader, then

$$\exists m . [0 \leqslant m \leqslant s(j,j) \wedge x = f^m j]$$

just in the case that $c(x) = j$, and since $fx = j$ is equivalent to $x = f^{s(j,j)}j$, the proof of (7) is established.

The basis of the induction argument for proving (8) is obvious; for the induction step we distinguish two cases:

(a) $j = fk$; in this case $s(j, k) = 0$, and $fx = j$ if and only if $x = k$, Since we have

$$E(j, k, y, X) = G(k, y, X)$$
$$= \lambda x . (x = k \rightarrow y, X(x)),$$

the induction is established.

(b) $j \neq fk$; using (8) as the induction hypothesis we have

$$E(j, k, y, X) = E(j, fk, y, G(k, Xfk, X))$$
$$\subseteq \lambda x . (\exists m . [0 \leqslant m < s(j, fk) \wedge x = f^{m+1}k]$$
$$\rightarrow (fx = k \rightarrow X(fk), X(fx)),$$
$$fx = j \rightarrow y,$$
$$x = k \rightarrow X(fk), X(x)).$$

Now

$$\exists m . [0 \leqslant m < s(j, fk) \wedge x = f^{m+1}k]$$

if and only if

$$\exists m . [1 \leqslant m < s(j, k) \wedge x = f^m k],$$

since $s(j, fk) = 1 + s(j, k)$. Furthermore, supposing this condition holds, we can show that $fx \neq k$. Assume, to the contrary, that $fx = k$ and so $k = f^{m+1}k$. Since $j = f^{s+1}k$, where $s = s(j, k)$, we must have $s + 1 \leqslant m + 1$. This is impossible since we are supposing $m < s$. Thus

$$E(j, k, y, X) \subseteq \lambda x . (\exists m . [1 \leqslant m < s(j, k) \wedge x = f^m k] \rightarrow X(fx),$$
$$fx = j \rightarrow y,$$
$$x = k \rightarrow X(fk), X(x)).$$

Finally, since we are supposing $j \neq fk$, we know $fx = j$ implies $x \neq k$, and so we can rearrange the right hand side to read

$$\lambda x . (\exists m . [1 \leqslant m < s(j, k) \wedge x = f^m k] \rightarrow X(fx),$$
$$x = k \rightarrow X(fk), fx = j \rightarrow y, X(x)).$$

This completes the proof of (8), and so the partial correctness of the program is established.

Bibliographic Remarks

General

Further source books on the theory of computation include: Minsky (1967), Engeler (1973), and Manna (1974). For a survey of recent developments in the area, consult Aho (1973). Some of the ways in which fundamental results in computation theory influence the design and analysis of practical algorithms are explored in Aho, Hopcroft, and Ullman (1975).

Chapter 1

The approach of this chapter follows the suggestions of Scott (1967). For a definition of PASCAL see Wirth (1971). Knuth (1974) summarizes the current debate concerning the use of goto statements in programs. Procedure programs were first introduced by deBakker and Scott (1969), see also deBakker (1971). For a formal proof of the non-translatability of flowcharts into strongly equivalent while programs see Knuth and Floyd (1971), Ashcroft and Manna (1971), and Kosaraju (1974). For a discussion of other formal program models, see Constable and Gries (1972), Luckham, Park and Paterson (1970), and Ershov (1971).

Chapter 2

This chapter uses ideas from Korenjak and Hopcroft (1966) who deal with an analogous problem in formal language theory. A different algorithm for restricted procedure programs has been given by Ashcroft, Manna and Pnueli (1973). Garland and Luckham (1973) contains an equivalence algorithm for linear procedure programs (in which, roughly speaking, the defining expressions can contain only one procedure identifier). The equivalence problem for flowchart programs was first described by Ianov (1960), and is discussed further in Rutledge (1964) and Kaplan (1969). See also Paterson (1967), Milner (1970), and Valiant (1973).

Chapter 3

The machine NORMA is virtually the same as the URM of Shepherdson and Sturgis (1963). Theorem 2 is due to Minsky (1961); see also Minsky (1967). The problem of translating procedure programs into flowcharts is considered in

Strong (1971) and Walker and Strong (1973) among others. Turing machines were first defined in Turing (1936). They are discussed in detail in the books by Minsky (1967) and Hopcroft and Ullman (1969). For other historical approaches to the problem of characterizing algorithms see Church (1936), Kleene (1936) and Post (1936).

Chapter 4

A source book on undecidable problems is Davis (1965). For further results in the area consult Rogers (1967). An excellent discussion of Post Normal Systems can be found in Minsky (1967), from which our proof of the unsolvability of the PCP is drawn. For undecidable properties of register machine programs see Paterson (1967, 1968). The algorithm for the equivalence of two-register machine programs is given in Bird (1973).

Chapter 5

The method of inductive assertions was first explicitly suggested by Floyd (1967). Its formulation as an axiomatic method for **while** programs was given by Hoare (1969) with extensions in Hoare (1970) and Clint and Hoare (1972). The rules for proving termination follows that of Manna and Pnueli (1974). Hoare (1971) contains an excellent example of the proof of partial correctness of a program FIND. The program for *in situ* permutation was taken from Knuth (1971); a proof of a slightly different algorithm is given in Duivestijn (1972). Heuristic approaches to finding inductive assertions are considered in Katz and Manna (1973) and Wegbreit (1973). See also the books by Wirth (1973) and Dahl, Dijkstra and Hoare (1972). Three texts on Mathematical Logic are by Hilbert and Ackermann (1950), Mendelson (1964), and Kleene (1968). Nievergelt, Farrar and Reingold (1974) contains a discussion on the program **while** $x \neq 1$ **do if** $2/x$ **then** $x: = x \div 2$ **else** $x: = 3x + 1$.

Chapter 6

Much of the material of this chapter is drawn from McCarthy (1963); see also McCarthy (1962) and McCarthy (1960). Various evaluation rules are discussed in Manna and Cadiou (1972), Landin (1964), and Morris (1968). Church (1951) contains a full discussion of λ-notation.

Chapter 7

Although the fixed point theorem was discussed in Kleene (1952), most of original work on partial functions and fixed points in computation is due to Scott—see Scott (1970). Manna and Vuillemin (1972) discuss various applications, as does Milner (1972). Igarashi (1972) deals with the subject of admissible predicates in greater detail, and various other forms of the fixedpoint induction rule are contained in Manna, Ness and Vuillemin (1972); see also Manna (1974), Hitchcock and Park (1972), Morris (1971), Cadiou (1972), Burstall (1969), and Park (1969).

References

Aho, A. V. (Ed) (1973). *Currents in the Theory of Computing*, Prentice-Hall, Englewood Cliffs, N.J.

Aho, A. V., Hopcroft, J. E., Ullman, J. D. (1975). *The Design and Analysis of Computer Algorithms*, Addison-Wesley, Reading, Mass.

Ashcroft, E. and Manna, Z. (1971). The translation of GOTO programs into WHILE programs, *Proc. IFIP Congress*, North-Holland, Amsterdam, 250–255.

Ashcroft, E., Manna, Z. and Pnueli, A. (1973). Decidable properties of monadic functional schemas, *J. Assoc. Comp. Mach.* **20** (3), 489–499 (July).

Bird, M. (1973). The equivalence problem for deterministic two-tape automata, *J. Computer and System Sciences* **7** (2), 218–238.

Brown, S., Gries, D., and Szymanski, T. (1972). Program schemes with pushdown stores, *SIAM J. Computing* **1** (4), 242–268 (Dec).

Burstall, R. M. (1969). Proving properties of programs by structural induction, *Computer Journal* **12** (1), 41–48.

Cadiou, J. M. (1972). *Recursive Definitions of Partial Functions and their Computation*. Ph.D. Thesis, Computer Science Department, Stanford University, Stanford, California.

Chandra, A. K. (1973). *On the Properties and Applications of Program Schemas*. Ph.D. Thesis, Computer Science Department, Stanford University, Stanford, California.

Church, A. (1936). An unsolvable problem in elementary number theory, *Amer. J. of Mathematics* **58**, 345–363.

Church, A. (1951). *The Calculi of Lambda-Conversion*, Annals of Mathematics Studies No. 6, Princeton University Press. Princeton N.J.

Clint, M., and Hoare, C. A. R. (1972). Program proving: jumps and functions, *Acta Informatica* **1** (3), 214–224.

Constable, R. L., and Gries, D. (1972). On classes of program schemata, *SIAM J. of Computing* **1** (1), 66–118 (March).

Dahl, O.-J., Dijkstra, E. W., and Hoare, C. A. R., (1972). *Structured Programming*, Academic Press, New York.

Davis, M. (Ed) (1965). *The Undecidable*, Raven Press, Hewlett, New York.

DeBakker, J. W., and Scott, D. (1969). A theory of programs, IBM Seminar, Vienna (August), unpublished notes.

DeBakker, J. W. (1971). *Recursive Procedures*, Mathematical Centre, Amsterdam.

Duijvestijn, A. J. W. (1972). Correctness proof of an In-place permutation, *B.I.T.* **12** (3), 318–324.

Engeler, E. E. (1973). *Introduction to the Theory of Computation*, Academic Press, New York.

Ershov, A. P. (1971). Theory of program schemata, *Proc IFIP Congress*, North-Holland, Amsterdam, 28–45.

Floyd, R. W., (1967). Assigning meanings to programs, in J. T. Schwartz (Ed), *Proc Symp. Applied Maths*, Vol. 19, *Aspects of Computer Science*, American Mathematical Society, New York, 19–32.

Garland, S. J., and Luckham, D. C. (1973). Program schemes, recursion schemes, and formal languages, *J. Comp. and System Sciences* **7** (1), 119–160 (Jan).

Hilbert, D., and Ackermann, W. (1950). *Principles of Mathematical Logic*, Chelsea, New York.

Hitchcock, P., and Park, D. (1972). Induction rules and proofs of termination, IRIA Conf. Automata, Languages and Programming Theory, France (July).

Hoare, C. A. R. (1969). An axiomatic basis for computer programming, *Comm. Assoc. Comp. Mach.* **12** (10) 576–580 (Oct).

Hoare, C. A. R. (1970). Procedures and parameters: an axiomatic approach, in E. Engeler (Ed) *Lecture notes* in *Mathematics*, Vol. 188, Springer–Verlag Berlin, 102–116.

Hoare, C. A. R. (1971): Proof of a program: FIND, *Comm. Assoc. Comp. Mach.* **14** (1), 39–45 (Jan).

Hopcroft, J. E., and Ullman, J. D. (1969): *Formal Languages and their relation to Automata*, Addison-Wesley, Reading, Mass.

Ianov, Y. I. (1960): The logical schemes of algorithms, *Problems of Cybernetics* **1**, 82–140, Pergamon, New York (English translation).

Igarashi, S. (1972). Admissibility of fixed point induction in first order logic of typed theories, *Research Report STAN-CS-72-287*, Computer Science Department, Stanford University, Stanford, Calif.

Kaplan, D. M. (1969): Regular expressions and the equivalence of programs, *Journal of Computer and System Sciences* **3** (4), 361–385 (Nov.).

Katz, S. M., and Manna, Z. (1973). A heuristic approach to program verification Third Inter. Conf. on Artificial Intelligence, Stanford, Calif. 500–512 (August).

Kleene, S. C. (1936). General recursive functions of natural numbers, *Math. Annalen* **112**, 727–742.

Kleene, S. C. (1952). *Introduction to Metamathematics*, Van Nostrand, Princeton, N.J.

Kleene, S. C. (1968). *Mathematical Logic*, John Wiley and Sons, New York.

Knuth, D. E. (1971). Mathematical analysis of algorithms, *Proc.* IFIP *Congress*, North-Holland, Amsterdam, (also Stanford University Research Report STAN-CS-71-206).

Knuth, D. E. (1974). Structured programming with goto statements, *ACM Computing Surveys* **6** (4), 261–302 (Dec).

Knuth, D. E., and Floyd, R. W. (1971). Notes on avoiding GOTO statements, *Inf. Process. Letters* **1** (1), 23–31 (Jan).

Korenjak, A., and Hopcroft, J. (1966). Simple deterministic languages, *IEEE 7th Ann. Symp. on Switching and Automata Theory*, 36–46.

Kosaraju, S. Rao (1974). Analysis of structured programs, *J. Computer and System Sciences* **9** (3), 232–255 (Dec).

Landin, P. J. (1964). The mechanical evaluation of expressions, *Computer Journal* **6** (4), 308–320.

Luckham, D. C., Park, D. M. R., and Paterson, M. S. (1970). On formalized computer programs, *J. Computer and System Sciences* **4** (3), 220–249 (June).

McCarthy, J. (1960). Recursive functions of symbolic expressions and their computation by machine, Part I, *Comm. Assoc. Comp. Mach.* **3** 184–195 (April).

McCarthy, J. (1962). Towards a mathematical science of computation, in C. M. Popplewell (Ed.) *Proc. IFIP Congress*, 1962, North-Holland, Amsterdam, 21–28.

McCarthy, J. (1963). A basis for a mathematical theory of computation, in Braffort, E. and Hirschberg, D. (Eds): *Computer Programming and Formal Systems*, North-Holland, Amsterdam, 33–70.

Manna, Z., and Cadiou, J. M. (1972). Recursive definitions of partial functions and their computations, *Proc. ACM Conf. on Proving Assertions about Programs*, Las Cruces, N. Mexico 58–65.

Manna, Z., and Vuillemin, J. (1972). Fixpoint approach to the theory of computation, *Comm. Assoc. Comp. Mach.* **15** (7), 528–536 (July).

Manna, Z., Ness, S., and Vuillemin, J. (1973): Inductive methods for proving properties of programs, *Comm. Assoc. Comp. Mach.* **16** (8) 491–502 (August).

Manna, Z. (1974). *Mathematical Theory of Computation*, McGraw-Hill, New York.

Manna, Z., and Pnueli, A. (1974). Axiomatic approach to total correctness of programs, *Acta Informatica* **3** (3), 243–264.

Mendelson, E. (1964). *Introduction to Mathematical Logic*, Van Nostrand, Princeton, N.J.

Milner, R. (1970). Equivalences on program schemes, *Journal of Computer and Systems Sciences* **4** (3), 205–219 (June).

Milner, R. (1972). Implementation and applications of Scott's logic for computable functions *Proc. ACM Conf. on Proving Assertions about Programs*, Las Cruces, N. Mexico.

Minsky, M. L. (1961). Recursive unsolvability of Post's problem of 'Tag' and other topics in the theory of Turing machines, *Ann. Math.* **74** (3), 437–454.

Minsky, M. L. (1967). *Computation: Finite and Infinite Machines*, Prentice-Hall, Englewood Cliffs, N.J.

Morris, J. H. (1968). *Lambda-calculus Models of Programming Languages*, Ph.D. Thesis, Project MAC, MAC-TR-57 M.I.T., Cambridge, Mass.

Morris, J. H., (1971). Another recursion induction principle, *Comm. Assoc. Comp. Mach.* **14** (5), 351–354 (May).

Nievergelt, J., Farrar, J. C., and Reingold, E. M. (1974). *Computer Approaches to Mathematical Problems*, Prentice-Hall, N.J.

Park, D. (1969). Fixpoint induction and proofs of program properties, in Meltzer, B. and Michie, D. (Eds), *Machine Intelligence 5*, Edinburgh University Press, Edinburgh, pp. 59–78.

Paterson, M. S. (1967). *Equivalence Problems in a Model of Computation* Ph.D. Thesis, University of Cambridge, Cambridge, England. [Reprinted: A.I. Memo – 1, M.I.T. Cambridge, Mass (1970)].

Paterson, M. S. (1968). Program Schemata in D. Michie (Ed), *Machine Intelligence 3*, Edinburgh University Press, Edinburgh, 19–31.

Post, E. L. (1936). Finite combinatory processes—formulation 1, *Journal of Symbolic Logic* **1**, 103–105.

Post, E. L. (1946). A variant of a recursively unsolvable problem, *Bull. Amer. Math. Soc.* **52** (4), 264–268.

Rogers, H. (1967). *Theory of Recursive Functions and Effective Computability*, McGraw-Hill, New York.

Rutledge, J. D. (1964). On Ianov's program schemata, *J. Assoc. Comp. Mach.* **11** (1), 1–9 (Jan).

Scott, D. (1967). Some definitional suggestions for automata theory, *J. Computer and System Sciences* **1** (2), 187–212.

Scott, D. (1970). Outline of a mathematical theory of computation, *4th Ann. Princeton Conf. on Information Sciences and Systems*, 169–176, (also *Tech. Monograph PRG-2*, Oxford University Computing Laboratory, Oxford, England).

Shepherdson, J. C., and Sturgis, H. E. (1963). Computability of recursive functions, *J. Assoc. Comp. Mach.* **10**, 217–255.

Strong, H. R. (1971). Translating recursion equations into flowcharts, *J. Computer and System Sciences* **5** (3), 254–285 (June).

Turing, A. M. (1936). On computable numbers with an application to the Entscheidungs-problem, *Proc. Lond. Math. Soc. Ser* **2**, 42, 230–265, correction, *ibid* 43, 544–546 (1937).

Walker, S. A., and Strong, H. R. (1973). Characterizations of flowchartable recursions, *Journal of Computer and System Sciences* 7, 404–447.

Wegbreit, B. (1973). Heuristic methods for mechanically deriving inductive assertions, *Third. Inter. Conf. on Artificial Intelligence*, Stanford, Calif. 524–536 (August).

Wirth, N. (1971). The programming language PASCAL, *Acta Informatica* 1, 35–63.

Wirth, N. (1973). *Systematic Programming: An Introduction*, Prentice-Hall, New Jersey.

Valiant, L. (1973). *Decision Procedures for Families of Deterministic Pushdown Automata*, Ph.D. Thesis, Department of Computer Science, University of Warwick, Coventry, England.

Index